Data Mining

FOR DUMMIES®

A Wiley Brand

by Meta S. Brown

Data Mining For Dummies®

Published by: **John Wiley & Sons, Inc.,** 111 River Street, Hoboken, NJ 07030-5774, www.wiley.com

Copyright © 2014 by John Wiley & Sons, Inc., Hoboken, New Jersey

Media and software compilation copyright © 2014 by John Wiley & Sons, Inc. All rights reserved.

Published simultaneously in Canada

No part of this publication may be reproduced, stored in a retrieval system or transmitted in any form or by any means, electronic, mechanical, photocopying, recording, scanning or otherwise, except as permitted under Sections 107 or 108 of the 1976 United States Copyright Act, without the prior written permission of the Publisher. Requests to the Publisher for permission should be addressed to the Permissions Department, John Wiley & Sons, Inc., 111 River Street, Hoboken, NJ 07030, (201) 748-6011, fax (201) 748-6008, or online at www.wiley.com/go/permissions.

Trademarks: Wiley, For Dummies, the Dummies Man logo, Dummies.com, Making Everything Easier, and related trade dress are trademarks or registered trademarks of John Wiley & Sons, Inc. and may not be used without written permission. Samsung and Galaxy S are registered trademarks of Samsung Electronics Co. Ltd. All other trademarks are the property of their respective owners. John Wiley & Sons, Inc. is not associated with any product or vendor mentioned in this book.

For general information on our other products and services, please contact our Customer Care Department within the U.S. at 877-762-2974, outside the U.S. at 317-572-3993, or fax 317-572-4002. For technical support, please visit www.wiley.com/techsupport.

Wiley publishes in a variety of print and electronic formats and by print-on-demand. Some material included with standard print versions of this book may not be included in e-books or in print-on-demand. If this book refers to media such as a CD or DVD that is not included in the version you purchased, you may download this material at http://booksupport.wiley.com. For more information about Wiley products, visit www.wiley.com.

Library of Congress Control Number: 2014935519

ISBN 978-1-118-89317-3 (pbk); ISBN 978-1-118-89316-6 (ebk); ISBN 978-1-118-89319-7 (ebk)

Manufactured in the United States of America

10 9 8 7 6 5 4 3 2 1

Contents at a Glance

Table of Contents

Introduction

. . . .

Data mining is the way that businesspeople can explore data independently, make informative discoveries, and put that information to work in everyday business. You don't need to be an expert in statistics, a scientist, or a computer programmer to be a data miner. You don't need mountains of data or special computers to do data mining.

This book is written for people who know much more about their own business than about math. It's for people who have ordinary computers, the same ones they use every day for word processing and spreadsheet juggling. The most important thing is that this book is for people who have real business problems to solve, and are motivated to use data to help solve those problems.

About This Book

This is a guidebook for people who have heard a little about data mining and want to give it a try. It contains all the information you need to get started as a hands-on data miner. If you don't want to become a data miner yourself, but do want to know what data mining is all about, this book will work for you, too. And although the book was aimed for beginners, data miners with some experience may flip through and find a few fresh pointers, too.

If you try out all (okay, most) of the methods in this book, use them to investigate your own data, and solve a business problem of your own, you'll become a data miner.

Read on, and you will discover the following:

- How data miners work, and the principles and processes of data mining
- Why teaming with other roles is essential to successful data mining
- Why your data is valuable
- How and where to get additional data
- Why choosing tools shouldn't be your first concern

✔ What data-mining techniques are basics for data mining

✔ How you can extend your bag of tricks with new techniques

✔ Where to go to keep on learning

Foolish Assumptions

If you think it's foolish to make assumptions, try going a week without making one. Assumptions give us a starting point for everything we do. The trick is not to make too many assumptions or unreasonable ones.

This book assumes a few things. It assumes that you are comfortable with everyday business computing like using office applications. It assumes that you are fairly comfortable with numbers and interpreting tables and graphs. And it assumes that you have a real-life job to do and you want to do it better with the help of data mining. It would not hurt if you've had some exposure to statistical analysis, but that won't be assumed.

One more thing: It assumes that you're new to data mining. If you're a little more experienced, you may want to skip over sections on familiar topics and get right into the stuff that's new to you.

Icons Used in This Book

As you read this book, you'll see icons in the margins that indicate special kinds of material. This section briefly describes each icon in this book.

Tips are the handy hints that help you do things a little more easily, quickly, or thoroughly than you might do otherwise. These are the little tricks that experienced data miners wish they had known from the start.

Warnings are there to help you avoid pitfalls. Sometimes, they are also code for "Don't do the same stupid thing that I did that one time. Or maybe twice. Okay, 12 times."

You won't see many of these in this book. They are geeky bits put in to satisfy the nagging curiosity of people who are a little more familiar with statistics than the typical novice data miner. It's usually okay to skip these paragraphs.

When it says "Remember," read that part a couple of times, because it's so easy to forget stuff, and you'll be better off if you remember this material.

Beyond the Book

You'll find more about data mining at www.dummies.com. Go online to find these resources:

✔ **Online articles covering additional topics can be found at**

www.dummies.com/extras/datamining

Here you'll find out how to start a search for data on the federal government's data portal, what common data-mining mistakes you can avoid, and more.

✔ **The Cheat Sheet for this book can be found at**

www.dummies.com/cheatsheet/datamining

This is a handy quick reminder sheet of information drawn from this book.

✔ **Updates to this book may be found at**

www.dummies.com/extras/datamining

Where to Go from Here

Your journey to become a data miner begins now.

This book was written with beginners in mind, so if you are new to data mining, begin with Chapter 1 to get an overview, or Chapter 2, which shows the work you might do in a typical day as a data miner working with data to address a real application, and see which topics interest you the most. Then go directly to the chapters that cover those topics, or, alternatively, work your way through the rest of the chapters in order.

Part I, Getting Started with Data Mining, lets you know what data mining really is, and what it's like to be a data miner.

Part II, Exploring Data Mining Mantras and Methods, takes you deeper to understand how data miners work. You'll find out about data-mining principles, processes, planning, and tools.

And in Part III, Gathering the Raw Materials, you'll get into the heart of data mining: data itself. You'll discover what's great about your own data, how to obtain new data to fill gaps in what you have, and how and where to look for data from public and commercial sources.

If you have no patience for any of that, and want to try some new computing tricks right away, skip to Part IV, A Data Miner's Survival Kit, where you'll find out about getting data into your data-mining tool, making it do your bidding, exploring it with graphs, and getting started in predictive modeling.

For those who have plowed through the survival kit and still yearn for more, continue to Part V, More Data-Mining Methods. The fancy stuff is in there. If you already have data-mining experience and you're looking for new tricks, you can skip to this part.

Finally, you reach Part VI, The Part of Tens. This is the book's goody bag, where you'll find leads on more resources for data miners, like what to read and where to network with other data miners, and discover a bunch of complementary data analysis techniques that aren't data mining, but may come in very handy one day.

Part I
Getting Started with Data Mining

In this part . . .

- ✔ Understanding how data miners work
- ✔ Looking over a data miner's shoulder
- ✔ Working constructively with your counterparts in complementary professions
- ✔ Keeping it legal with good data privacy protection
- ✔ Communicating with executives

Chapter 1

Catching the Data-Mining Train

. . . .

You've picked an exciting moment to become a data miner.

By some estimates, more than 15 exabytes of new data are now produced each year. How much is that? It's really, ridiculously big — that's how much! Why is this important? Most organizations have access to only a teeny, tiny fraction of that data, and they aren't getting much value from what they have.

Data can be a valuable resource for business, government, and nonprofit organizations, but quantity isn't what's important about it. A greater quantity of data does not guarantee better understanding or competitive advantage. In fact, used well, a little bit of relevant data provides more value than any poorly used gargantuan database. As a data miner, it's your mission to make the most of the data you have.

This chapter goes over the basics of data mining. Here I explain what data miners do and the tools and methods they use to do it.

Getting Real about Data Mining

Maybe you've heard news reports or ads hinting that all you need to make valuable information pop out like magic is a big database and the latest software. That's nonsense. Data miners have to work and think to make valuable discoveries.

Maybe you've heard that to get results out of your database, you must first hire one of a special breed of people who have nearly super-human knowledge of data, people known to be very expensive, nearly impossible to find, and absolutely necessary to your success. That's nonsense, too. Data miners are ordinary, motivated people who complement their business knowledge with the fundamentals of data analysis.

Data mining is not magic and not art. It's a craft, one that mere mortals learn every day. You can find out about it, too.

Not your professor's statistics

Perhaps you took a class in statistics a long time ago and felt overwhelmed by the professor's insistence on rigorous methods. Relax. You're out to find information to support everyday business decisions, and many everyday business problems can be solved using less formal analysis methods than the ones you learned at school. Give yourself some slack.

How do you give yourself slack? By data mining, that's how.

Data mining is the way that ordinary businesspeople use a range of data analysis techniques to uncover useful information from data and put that information into practical use. Data miners use tools designed to help the work go quickly. They don't fuss over theory and assumptions. They validate their discoveries by testing. And they understand that things change, so when the discovery that worked like a charm yesterday doesn't hold up today, they adapt.

The value of data mining

Business managers already have desks piled high with reports. Some have access to computer dashboards that let them see their data in myriad segments and summaries. Can data mining really add value? It can.

Typical business reports provide summaries of what has happened in the past. They don't offer much, if anything, to help you understand why those things happened, or how you might influence what will happen next.

Data mining is different.

Here are examples of information that has been uncovered through data mining:

- A retailer discovered that loyalty program sign-ups could be used to identify which customers were most likely to spend a lot and which would spend a little over time, based on just the information gathered on the customer's first visit. This information enabled the retailer to focus marketing investment on the high spenders to maximize revenue and reduce marketing costs.

- A manufacturer discovered a sequence of events that preceded accidental releases of toxic materials. This information enabled the manufacturer to keep the facility operating while preventing dangerous accidents (protecting people and the environment) and avoiding fines and other costs.

> ✔ An insurance company discovered that one of its offices was able to process certain common claim types more quickly than others of comparable size. This information enabled the insurance company to identify the right place to look for best practices that could be adopted across the organization to reduce costs and improve customer service.

Data mining helps you understand how the elements of your business relate to one another. It provides clues about actions that you can take to make your business run more smoothly and generate more revenue. It can help you identify where you can cut costs without damaging the organization, and where spending brings the best returns.

Data mining provides value by helping you to better understand how your business works.

Working for it

A lot of people have unrealistic expectations about data mining. That's understandable, because most people get their information about data mining from people who have never done it.

Trust data or trust your gut?

Can intuition tell you what motivates people to buy, donate, or take action? Many people believe that no data analysis can outdo their own gut feel for guiding decisions.

I challenged business managers to put their intuition to the test. They came from a variety of industries, businesses small and large, and included both young and experienced managers. Each viewed ten pairs of ads like these:

✔ Two nearly identical ads, differing only in that one showed a female face and the other a male. Which generated more leads?

✔ An ad with many images was contrasted with one that had just a few. Which one resulted in more purchases?

✔ Two ads had the same copy (text) but different layouts. Which would draw more donations for a charity?

Small variations in images, layout, or copy can make dramatic differences in an ad's effectiveness. Tests of the samples in this guessing game demonstrated that the right choice could lift *conversions* (actions on the part of the customer, such as buying, donating, or requesting information) by 10 percent, 30 percent, and sometimes more. In one case, the superior ad resulted in 100 percent more conversion than the alternative.

Could anyone tell, just by looking, which alternatives would perform best? No. None of the managers were effective at picking the best ads. Flipping a coin worked just as well.

If you want to make good business decisions, you need data. Use your brain, not your gut!

Some people expect data mining to be so easy that they will only need to feed data into the right software and a tidy summary of valuable information will automatically pop out. On the other hand, some expect data mining to be so difficult that only someone with expert programming skills and a Ph.D. in physics can tackle it. Some expect data mining to produce great results even if the data miner doesn't know what anything in the data means. These are all unrealistic expectations, but they're understandable. News reports, sales pitches, and misinformed people often circulate ideas about data mining that are just plain wrong. How is anyone to know what's reasonable and what's hype?

Here's what's realistic: Many novice data miners find that a few days of training and a month of practicing what they have learned (part-time, while still performing everyday duties) are enough to get them ready to begin producing usable, valuable results. You don't need to have a mind like Einstein's, a Ph.D., or even programming skills. You do need to have some basic computer skills and a feel for numbers. You must also have patience and the ability to work in a methodical way.

Data mining is hard work. It's not hard like mining coal or performing brain surgery, but it's hard. It takes patience, organization, and effort.

Doing What Data Miners Do

If you think of data as raw material, and the information you can get from data as something valuable and relatively refined, the process of extracting information can be compared to extracting metal from ore or gems from dirt. That's how the term *data mining* originated.

Do the words *data miner* conjure up a mental image of a gritty worker in coveralls? That's not so far off the mark. Of course, nothing is physically dirty about data mining, but data miners do get down and dirty with data. And data mining is all about power to the people, giving data analysis power to ordinary businesspeople.

Focusing on the business

Data miners don't just ponder data aimlessly, hoping to find something interesting. Every data-mining project begins with a specific business problem and a goal to match.

As a data miner, you probably won't have the authority to make final business decisions, so it's important that you align your work with the needs of decision makers. You must understand their problems, needs, and preferences, and focus your efforts on providing information that supports good business decisions.

Your own business knowledge is very important. Executives are not going to sit next to you while you work, providing feedback on the relevance of your discoveries to their concerns. You must use your own experience and acumen to judge that for yourself as you work. You may even be familiar with aspects of the business that the executive is not, and be able to offer fresh perspectives on the business problem and possible causes and remedies.

Understanding how data miners spend their time

It would be great if data miners could spend all day making life-changing discoveries, building valuable models, and integrating them into everyday business. But that's like saying it would be great if athletes could spend all day winning tournaments. It takes a lot of preparation to build up to those moments of triumph. So, like athletes, data miners spend a lot of time on preparation. (In fact, that's one of the 9 Laws of Data Mining. Read more about them in Chapter 4.)

In Chapter 2, you'll see how you might spend your time on a typical day in your new profession. The biggest chunk goes to data preparation.

Getting to know the data-mining process

A good work process helps you make the most of your time, your data, and all your other resources. In this book, you'll discover the most popular data-mining process, CRISP-DM. It's a six-phase cycle of discovery and action created by a consortium of data miners from many industries, and an open standard that anyone may use.

The phases of the CRISP-DM process are

1. Business Understanding
2. Data Understanding
3. Data Preparation
4. Modeling
5. Evaluation
6. Deployment (using models in everyday business)

Each phase carries equal weight in importance to the quality of the results and value to the business. But in terms of the time required, data preparation dominates. Data preparation routinely takes more time than all other phases of the data-mining process combined.

CRISP-DM, and the details of the work done in each phase, are described in detail in Chapter 5.

Making models

When the goals are understood, and the data is cleaned up and ready to use, you can turn your attention to building predictive models. Models do what reports cannot; they give you information that supports action.

A report can tell you that sales are down. It can break sales down by region, product, and channel so that you know where sales declined and whether these declines were widespread or affected only certain areas. But they don't give you any clues about *why* sales declined or what actions might help to revive the business.

Models help you understand the factors that impact sales, the actions that tend to increase or decrease sales, and the strategies and tactics that keep your business running smoothly. That's exciting, isn't it? Maybe that's why most data miners consider modeling to be the fun part of the job. (You find out a lot about the fun part of the job in Chapter 15.)

Understanding mathematical models

Mathematical models are central to data mining, but what are they? What do they do, how do they work, and how are they are created?

A mathematical model is, plain and simple, an equation, or set of equations, that describe a relationship between two or more things. Such equations are shorthand for theories about the workings of nature and society. The theory may be supported by a substantial body of evidence or it may be just a wild guess. The language of mathematics is the same in either case.

Terms such as *predictive model, statistical model,* or *linear model* refer to specific types of mathematical models, the names reflecting the intended use, the form, or the method of deriving a particular model. These three examples are just a few of many such terms.

When a model is mentioned in a business setting, it's most likely a model used to make predictions. Models are used to predict stock prices, product sales, and unemployment rates, among many other things. These predictions may or may not be accurate, but for any given set of values (known factors like these are called *independent variables* or *inputs*) included in the model, you will find a well-defined prediction (also called a *dependent variable, output,* or *result*). Mathematical models are used for other purposes in business, as well, such as to describe the working mechanisms that drive a particular process.

In data mining, we create models by finding patterns in data using machine learning or statistical methods. Data miners don't follow the same rigorous approach that classical statisticians do, but all our models are derived from actual data and consistent mathematical modeling techniques. All data-mining models are supported by a body of evidence.

Why use mathematical models? Couldn't the same relationships be described using words? That's possible, yet you find certain advantages to the use of equations. These include

- ✔ **Convenience:** Compared with equivalent descriptions written out in sentences, equations are brief. Mathematical symbolism has evolved specifically for the purpose of representing mathematical relationships; languages such as English have not.

- ✔ **Clarity:** Equations convey ideas succinctly and are unambiguous. They're not subject to differing interpretations based on culture, and the symbolism of mathematics is a sort of common language used widely across the globe.

- ✔ **Consistency:** Because mathematical representations are unambiguous, the implications of any particular situation are clearly defined by a mathematical model.

Putting information into action

A model only delivers value when you use it in the business. A model's predictions might support decision making in a variety of ways. You might

- ✔ Incorporate predictions into a report or presentation to be used in making a specific decision.

- ✔ Integrate the model into an operational system (such as a customer service system) to provide real-time predictions for everyday use. (For example, you might flag insurance claims for immediate payment, immediate denial, or further investigation.)

- ✔ Use the model for batch predictions. (For example, you could score the in-house customer list to decide which customers should receive a particular offer.)

Discovering Tools and Methods

Data miners work fast. To get speed, you'll need to use appropriate tools and discover the tricks of the trade.

Visual programming

Your best data-mining tool is your brain, with a bit of know-how. The second-best tool is a data-mining application with a visual programming interface, like the one shown in Figure 1-1.

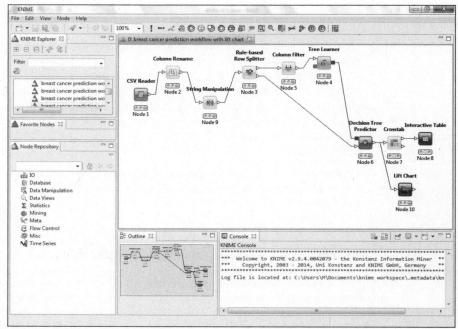

Figure 1-1: A data-mining application with a visual programming interface.

With visual programming, the steps in your work process are represented by small images that you organize on the screen to create a picture of the flow and logic of your work. Visual programming makes it easier to see what you're doing across several steps than it would be with commands (programming) or conventional menus.

In this example, you can see the work process in the main area of the data-mining application. Around it are menus of recent projects, tools for data-mining functions, a viewer to help you navigate complex processes, and a log. These details vary a little from one product to another.

Look more closely at the process. (See Figure 1-2.) Although you are just setting out in your quest to be a data miner, you can probably understand a lot of what's going on just by looking at this diagram, including the following:

✔ You can see the CSV Reader. If you're aware of the .csv (comma-separated values) data format, you probably already know that this is data import. (And it's the first step; you need data to do anything else.)

✔ Then you see tools clearly labeled by functions like *Column Rename* and *String Manipulation*. These are data preparation steps.

✔ Tree Learner might be mysterious if you're new to modeling, but this tool creates a *decision tree* model from a subset of the data.

✔ The final steps apply the model to data that was kept separate for testing, and perform some evaluation techniques.

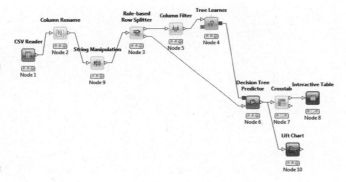

Figure 1-2:
Work process from a visual programming interface.

Working quick and dirty

Visual programming helps data miners to work fast. It's much easier and faster to lay out a work process using these small images than by programming from scratch. And it's easy to see what you're doing when you see something like a map of many steps at once, so visual programming is also faster than using conventional menu-driven software.

Data miners have another important way to work fast. Data miners don't always fuss over every detail of mathematical theory and assumptions. The good news is, lack of fuss lets you build models faster. The bad news is, if you don't fuss over theory and assumptions, your model might not be any good.

Data miners break rules of statistics, because data miners choose models by experiment, rather than based on statistical theory and assumptions. But data miners also break their own rules, because some data miners have statistical knowledge, and they do make a point of considering assumptions. (It's a little-known fact that the CRISP-DM standard process for data mining includes a step for reporting assumptions.)

Testing, testing, and testing some more

As a data miner, you won't be able to defend the models that you create based on statistical theory because

- ✔ Your work methods won't take theory into account
- ✔ You use the data you can get, and it's certain to have some issues that aren't consistent with the theory behind the model you're using
- ✔ You may not have sufficient statistical knowledge to make theoretical arguments

But that's okay. Data miners evaluate their models primarily by testing, testing, and testing some more. Many modeling tools do some testing internally as they build models. You'll set data aside to test the model after you build it. You'll field test whenever possible. And you'll monitor your model's performance after deployment. When you're a data miner, the testing never ends!

Chapter 2

A Day in Your Life as a Data Miner

• •

• •

Good morning! Welcome to an ordinary day in your data-mining career.

Today, you will meet with other members of the data-mining team to discuss a project that is already under way. A subject matter expert will help you understand the project's business goals, and explain why they are important to your organization, to make sure that everyone is working toward the same end. Another member of the team has already begun gathering data and preparing it for exploration and modeling. (You're lucky to have a strong team!)

After the meeting, you'll begin working with the data hands-on. You'll get familiar with the data. Although some of the data preparation work has been done, you will still have more data preparation to do before you can start building predictive models. Data miners spend a lot of time on data preparation!

Later today, you'll begin exploring the data. Perhaps you'll begin to build a model that you'll continue to refine and improve in the days to come. And of course, you'll document all your work as you go.

It's just another day in the life of a data miner. This chapter shows you how it's done.

Starting Your Day Off Right

You've had a good night's sleep, and now you wake up early for a little exercise and a good breakfast. This has little to do with data mining, but it is a nice way to start your day.

On your way to work, ponder this: Successful data mining is a team effort. No one person possesses all the knowledge, all the resources, or all the authority required to carry out a typical data-mining project and put the results into action. You need the whole team to get things done. Your coworkers may be charming people with the best of skills and the purest of motivations, or they may have challenging personalities and hidden agendas, but you vow to start your data-mining day right by setting out to treat each person with patience, to listen to everyone with respect, and to explain yourself plainly in terms that other team members can understand.

Meeting the team

Today you'll be meeting with your team: Virginia, your resource for business expertise, and Matt, your data sourcing and programming expert. They are charming people with the best of skills and the purest of motivations.

Virginia will act as the client liaison and explain your organization's business goals. She'll explain the business problem and its impact on the organization. She can point out factors that are likely to be important. And she can answer most of your questions about the workings of the business, or help you reach someone who can.

Matt is very familiar with the data that you'll be using. He has prepared datasets for you to use, derived from public sources and further developed with a few calculations of his own. This simplifies your work and saves you a lot of time. He'll be the person you rely on for information about data sources, documentation, and the details of how and why he has restructured the data.

Virginia and Matt rely on you, too. Matt needs your input to understand what data is most useful for data mining and how to organize data for your use. He needs you to point out any errors (or suspected errors) in the data so that he can investigate and address any problems. Others are depending on the information he provides — not just you — so don't let errors linger! Virginia needs your input about what kinds of analysis you can provide, clear information about your results, and good documentation of your work.

Exploring with aim

Saying that data miners explore data in search of valuable patterns may create a mental image that's a bit magical or mysterious. You're about to replace that image with one that is far more down to earth and approachable. Data mining isn't magical, and its purpose is to eliminate mystery, a little bit at a time, from your business.

You might explore a shopping mall or a quaint little town just for the experience of looking around, but when you're data mining, you're exploring with a specific purpose. The very first thing you'll do in any data-mining project will be to get a clear understanding of that purpose. As you work with data, you will frequently revisit your goals and give thought to whether and how the information you find within the data supports them.

You'll be faced with temptation now and then, temptation to spend time examining some pattern in the data that is not immediately relevant to the goals at hand. As with other temptations, you may be free to indulge a little bit, if you have some time and resources to spare, but your first priority must always be to address the business goals established at the start of the project.

Introducing the real people on your project team

The project described in this chapter is real in every way. It addresses a real business issue that impacts people and businesses in a real community. The data is real. And the people on your team, Virginia and Matt, are also real.

Virginia Carlson is a data strategist. She is principal researcher for data integration at Impact Planning Council (www.impactinc.org/impact-planning-council), a Milwaukee, Wisconsin, based organization devoted to improving lives of community members, and associate professor at University of Wisconsin, Milwaukee. She's an expert in the collection and use of data to support social sector initiatives. She's led significant economic research organizations and projects, and she's the coauthor of *Civic Apps Competition Handbook, A Guide to Planning, Organizing, and Troubleshooting* (published by O'Reilly Media) (http://shop.oreilly.com/product/0636920024484.do).

Matt Schumwinger is an independent data analyst. He's the owner of Big Lake Data (http://biglakedata.com), a services firm that helps its clients to visualize, analyze, and present quantitative information. Matt studied labor economics and labor relations at Cornell University, and has devoted much of his career to improving the well-being of Americans by organizing low-wage workers across the United States.

Virginia and Matt share common interests in improving the lives of public citizens and using data to support communities. In that context, they have worked together as a team, bringing together their complementary talents and experiences to work toward common goals.

Your project is an extension of Virginia's and Matt's real work. The example builds on projects that they have done in the past to create something entirely new. As members of your team, they provide expertise in community development and data management. Each of them is capable of data mining, but they have their own jobs to do! Besides, you know things they don't know and have skills they don't have. They need you to bring your own special mix of knowledge and experience to the team, and enrich everyone's knowledge. Together with Virginia and Matt, you can make discoveries that will help build stronger communities.

Structuring time with the right process

Many a would-be data miner has downloaded and installed software, started it up, and wondered, "Now what?" That won't happen to you today.

You'll know how to use your time, because you will take advantage of groundwork that data miners from hundreds of organizations have done for you when they developed and published a model process for data mining. The *Cross-Industry Standard Process for Data Mining (CRISP-DM),* an open standard, provides you with guidelines for organizing and documenting your work. It's a six-phase process that begins with defining business goals and ends with integrating your results into routine business and reviewing your work for next steps and opportunities for improvement.

Chapter 5 explains the CRISP-DM process in detail. There you will see that each of the six phases calls for several defined tasks, and that each task has one or more deliverables, which may be reports, presentations, data, or models. In this chapter, you won't see every one of those details, but you will touch on each of the six major phases in the CRISP-DM process.

Understanding Your Business Goals

Virginia explains the data-mining team's latest project: helping a local planning council. Its mission is to promote economic well-being by encouraging land use that makes the community attractive to businesses and residents. A key part of its work is retaining and attracting businesses that employ local residents and offer good compensation.

Your team's role is to provide new and relevant information, grounded in data and analysis, that the planning council can use to decide where to focus efforts to make the most of its resources. Virginia and Matt have already been involved in projects supporting these aims. In earlier projects, they've produced analyses of factors that impact land use and shared information through consultations and presentations, written reports, and interactive maps.

The council understands that the best opportunity to influence the use of a particular parcel of land comes when the land is about to change ownership. But land owners aren't going to just drop in and announce their intentions to sell. Many significant real estate transactions are arranged quietly, so the council might not know a thing about the opportunity until after the property has been sold.

So, the council's business goal is to identify parcels of land that are about to change ownership, and to do so early enough to influence the use of the land.

How will the council decide whether it is successful in meeting that goal? At this stage, the council has only informal (and not entirely consistent) ways of predicting which parcels of land are about to change hands. The stated success criteria simply call for establishing a process to make change-of-ownership predictions in a consistent way. (Future projects will build on this goal and have quantitative success criteria.)

When you're presented with a goal, always discuss and document success criteria from the start. Although you may only be responsible for a narrow part of the work needed to achieve the business goal, understanding how the ultimate results will be evaluated helps you to understand the best ways to contribute to the project's success.

These success criteria may sound simple, but you have doubts. You ask questions like these:

- ✓ **Does the council expect that just one model will work for all types of property?** Industrial, commercial, single-family, multifamily, and so on — it's not realistic to think that you'll find one big equation to address them all.

- ✓ **How many property types exist?** You could have dozens.

- ✓ **Is the council equally interested in all properties?** You'd think large, industrial parcels would be the most important.

- ✓ **Which property types are most important to the council?** You may want to push for modeling just one or two important categories on the first round.

Always ask about recent mishaps. Unspoken goals often include not repeating something that just went wrong.

Asking questions helps you to get more information, of course, but your questions do more than that. They help others on the team (including executives, if you have the opportunity to meet with them) become aware of what's missing, what's going to be challenging, and what's a lot more complicated than they thought it would be! By asking probing questions in the business-understanding phase, you help everyone to clarify thinking, define reasonable goals, and set realistic expectations.

After some discussion, it's agreed (and documented!) that the business goal for this project will be to demonstrate the feasibility of modeling to predict land ownership change — a narrower and less grand goal than the one initially suggested. You're not expected to create a megamodel (no, that's not a technical term) that covers all types of property. If the council finds that even one factor has predictive value for property transfers, that will be satisfactory for the first round. No quantitative criteria will be stated for model performance on this first investigation. The object is just to demonstrate that potential exists to develop a useful model to predict property ownership changes using the available data.

Business goals are determined by the client (external or internal), not the data miner. If you and your team have doubts about a particular goal, don't change it on your own. Clients won't accept that! Instead, enter into a discussion with the client, explain your concerns, and come to an agreement about reasonable business goals for the project.

Based on the business goals, you define data-mining goals. Because the business goal is to demonstrate the feasibility of modeling to predict land ownership change, you will set a data-mining goal of creating a rudimentary predictive model for change of property ownership. Because you have no specific numbers about the performance of the current, informal approach to predicting ownership changes, you'll simply aim to demonstrate that at least one variable has measurable value for prediction. (As with the business goals, future projects will build on this, and you'll set more specific quantitative success criteria at that stage.)

You'll complete this phase of the data-mining process by outlining your step-by-step action plan for completing the work (including a schedule and details of resources required for each step) and your initial assessment of the appropriate tools and techniques for the project.

Understanding Your Data

In the data-understanding phase, you will first gather and broadly describe your data. You won't have to start from scratch to gather data, because Matt has already assembled several datasets for you to use. He's drawn from data used in earlier projects and derived some additional fields that you will need. Then you'll examine the data in a little more depth, exploring the data one variable (field) at a time, checking for consistency with expectations and any obvious signs of data quality problems.

You begin to review the data, making notes for your report as you work.

Describing data

The data is in several text files, each in comma-separated value (.csv) format. The files are somewhat large, 50–100MB, but not too large to handle with the computer and software that you have available. You note the name and size of each file.

Your first concern is to identify the variables in each file and confirm that you have adequate documentation for each of them. Several of the files contain historic public property records; a lengthy document defines those variables. You've also been given notes explaining how derived variables were created. You review each variable in the data, comparing the variable names to the information in the documentation.

You note findings about the data and the documentation, including the following:

- ✔ Most of the fields appear consistent with the documentation that you have.
- ✔ Some of the fields in the property record data files are not explained in the documentation.
- ✔ Some of the fields described in the property record documentation don't appear in the data.
- ✔ One of the property record data files contains many more fields than the others, and those fields are not explained in the documentation.

You write detailed notes about each file and each variable. Using your notes as a reference, you look for information to address the discrepancies. You find that

- ✔ A few of the fields in the data from public sources simply don't match the documentation provided (public data isn't always perfect data).
- ✔ Additional notes are available to explain how some of the derived fields were created.
- ✔ Some of the undocumented data was obtained by *web scraping* (using specialized software to automatically extract information from websites), and you can't find any dependable documentation for it.

You update your notes about the data, revising them with additional documentation. You note which variables are still undocumented. Although some of those fields seem likely to have predictive value for modeling property ownership changes (such as foreclosures), a number of disadvantages exist to using them for predictive modeling, including the following:

- ✔ Some of the data was collected by web scraping. You're not confident that you'll be able to get that data in the future.
- ✔ You don't have details on the scraping process, so you can't be sure that scraped data was defined consistently.
- ✔ You'll have a heck of a time explaining the meaning of data without documentation.

So you decide that on the first attempt to develop a predictive model for property ownership change, you'll use only those fields that have been adequately documented. In a future project, you may seek out alternative sources for some of the other fields.

Exploring data

Now it's time to briefly examine the data for each variable in each file. You must check basics, such as whether the data is string or numeric, that the range of values is appropriate, and that the distribution of values looks reasonable. You'll note any discrepancies from the documentation and your own reasonable expectations.

The procedures you'll use to generate diagnostic information about your data vary with the kind of data that you have, the tools available, and the way that you like to work. Your may use highly automated functions or you may work with variables in small groups or one at a time. You'll almost always have a choice of ways to go about it.

For each field, you prepare a brief summary, with a name and description, number of missing cases, and the range of values (low and high). You may also include additional information such as a distribution graph, the average (mean), and most frequently occurring (mode) value of the variable. At this point, you won't try to relate one variable to another.

You start by using software that produces a basic report for each variable in the data, including information such as the range of values, the average for continuous variables, the most common value for categorical variables, and so on (shown in Figure 2-1). This report is a starting point for understanding your data. You use it to identify what data you have and whether the data is consistent with what you were led to expect by the documentation and your colleagues. You add to it by using graphs or other simple methods for adding detail to your understanding of each variable.

Name	Type	Miss.	S...	Filter (76 / 76 attributes): Filter ▼		
TAXKEY	Integer	30			Min	9999000
BI_VIOL	Binominal	0	Least XXXX (162403)		Most XXXX (162403)	
DIV_ORG	Integer	0	Min 0	Max 999	Average 43.951	
YR_ASSMT	Integer	0	Min 2010	Max 2010	Average 2010	
SUB_ACCT	Integer	0	Min 0	Max 0	Average 0	
P_A_LAND	Integer	0	Min 0	Max 19029000	Average 25320.01	
NR_UNITS	Integer	0	Min 0	Max 718	Average 1.610	
C_A_LAND	Integer	0	Min 0	Max 19029000	Average 25478.03	
DIV_DROP	Integer	0	Min 0	Max 0	Average 0	
			Min	Max	Average	

Showing attributes: 1 - 76   Examples: 162,...   Special Attributes: 0   Regular Attributes: 76

Figure 2-1: Variable summaries.

As you review each variable, you describe it and make note of any concerns and what should be done to address them. In your summaries, you state whether the variable appears ready for use in modeling, needs further preparation, or is in such poor condition that it cannot be used.

Your individual variable summaries read like the examples shown in Table 2-1.

Table 2-1	Dataset: 2010 Property Data
Variable Name	**Description**
BI_VIOL	**Description:** Unknown (No documentation available for this variable) **Variable type:** String **Range:** XXXX to XXXX **Number of missing cases:** 0 **Assessment:** Not acceptable for modeling. All cases have the same value. Reason unknown. **Next steps:** Will not use in this project.
TAXKEY	**Description:** Ten-digit property ID code number **Variable type:** Identifier (string) **Range:** 9999000–7369999110 **Number of missing cases:** 30 **Assessment:** A small number of cases are missing. Some cases have fewer than ten digits, possibly due to trimming of leading zeros because the variable format was read as integer, rather than string. **Next steps:** Must clean this variable as well as possible, as it is the unique ID for each property. Change variable type from integer to string. Reassess.
C_A_ CLASS	**Description:** Assessment class code — defines property use. Detailed explanations of codes in Appendix A. **Variable type:** Nominal **Range:** 1–9 **Number of missing cases:** 0 **Assessment:** Distribution (Figure 2-2) looks appropriate with Class 1 (residential) the most frequently occurring category. No obvious signs of quality issues. **Next steps:** This field appears ready for modeling use.
DIV_ ORG	**Description:** A control number used by the assessor's office **Variable type:** String **Range:** 0–999 **Number of missing cases:** 0 **Assessment:** This is used for administration within the assessor's office and does not appear to have any value for modeling purposes. **Next steps:** None.

Some of these variables won't be useful for modeling. For example, BI_VIOL sounds like it might represent the number or kind of building inspection violations reported for a property. Maybe it was used for that purpose at some time, but in this dataset, every case has the same value, "XXXX." The field is not mentioned in any of the documentation that you have. Building violations could be valuable information for predicting property transfers, but you may have to wait for a future project when you have time to track down another source for that information.

Fortunately, some fields are in much better condition. For example, C_A_CLASS, the assessment class code, identifies the use of the property in major classes such as residential, manufacturing, and commercial. This could be very important for modeling, because you expect different behavior patterns for different property uses. No cases are missing for C_A_CLASS, the range of values is consistent with the documentation, and a bar chart (see Figure 2-2) shows that the distribution of property uses appears reasonable, with the residential class occurring far more often than any other use.

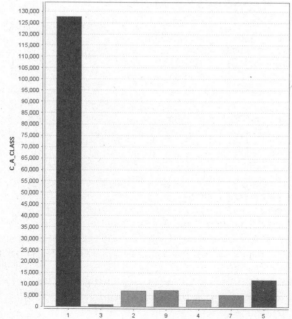

Figure 2-2:
Bar chart for
C_A_CLASS.

You notice that many of the fields that might at first appear valuable for modeling are not in a good state. Many are undocumented, some are not being maintained by the public source (and the documentation says so), and others don't vary or don't seem consistent with your expectations. You have doubts that the remaining data will be sufficient to build a useful model.

Cleaning data

You've explored the data and found that some of the fields that seem to have value for modeling exhibit minor errors or other issues that you want to correct first.

The TAXKEY field is a good example. It's the code number that identifies each individual parcel of property. Strictly speaking, an identifier is not a modeling variable, but your model won't have any value unless you can match your predictions to specific properties. You've noticed two issues in the data:

- A few cases (a fraction of a percent of the total) are missing identifier codes.

- Many cases have fewer than the ten digits that the documentation says they should.

You take a moment to ponder the missing cases (30 out of more than 160,000 total). In theory, the public agency that shared the data can fill in those blanks. But you imagine phoning the property assessor's office and explaining the problem, perhaps many times over, looking for someone who understands it and is willing to help. When you reach that person, you have no assurance that willingness to help will translate into success in correcting the flaws in the data. You think that you can do more productive things with that time and decide to live without those 30 cases.

Then some cases have fewer than ten digits in their property codes. This problem occurs frequently, but you suspect that you can find an easy fix for it. Because the code is numeric, your software has interpreted it as an integer, but a string would be more appropriate. Changing the field type to a string would prevent the software from trimming any leading zeros in the property codes. So you import the data into the software again, this time making sure to identify the field as nominal (like a name). Still, you find many cases where the values have fewer than ten digits. Your easy fix did not fix anything.

You peek at the data in a text editor (because this data is in a text format, you could use a word processor or perhaps a spreadsheet to view it) and confirm that the problem has nothing to do with trimming leading zeros. Some of the values are simply shorter than the ten digits that the documentation led you to expect. You make a note of this for your report and decide (for today) to put your faith in the data rather than the documentation.

You go through a similar process for each of the fields that you've found to be potentially useful, but not in perfect condition. As you work, you document your observations and any changes that you make. For each field, you judge whether it is good enough to use in modeling. (You're not deciding whether the variable will be in the final model or work well as a predictor, just whether it is of sufficient quality to test.) Finally, you combine your notes on these observations and actions into a data quality report.

How data miners spend their time

Cooks who serve delicious dinners spend a lot of time chopping vegetables. Runners who win races spend a lot of time stretching and training. Data miners who develop valuable predictive models spend a lot of time preparing data.

People who haven't tried data mining sometimes think that it is a nonstop thrill ride of discovering great insights and developing powerful models. It isn't. Most of your time goes to doing all the things that must be done right before you can start building models.

Data preparation isn't the most glamorous aspect of the job. It's painstaking work, and you have a lot to do, so much that data miners spend more time preparing data than doing anything else. Yet data preparation is worth the effort, because it makes meaningful discovery possible.

Preparing Your Data

Now that you've gathered data and reviewed the fields one by one to familiarize yourself with the data and check for quality problems, you move forward and prepare the data for modeling. In this phase of your work, you do the necessary tasks to transform the data from its original form into the form you require for modeling, such as

- ✓ Joining datasets
- ✓ Specifying the roles of the fields
- ✓ Sampling the data
- ✓ Splitting your sample into subsets for building and testing models

Many projects call for deriving new fields based on the ones that are already in the data. For example, the indicator variable that you will need to identify properties that changed ownership does not exist in the public data. That must be calculated from other fields. Lucky for you, your colleague Matt has already created that variable and saved you a step on this project. But you will have to derive some other new fields for yourself.

Taking first steps with the property data

In the data-understanding phase, you identified a number of fields that you won't use for modeling. You have ruled each of them out for one of these reasons:

✔ **Does not make sense as a predictor:** Includes unique fields such as an address or names, or something that you believe to have no relationship to ownership change

✔ **Data quality is poor:** Many missing cases or incorrect values

✔ **Does not vary:** All cases have the same value (not necessarily a data quality problem)

You work with specialized data-mining software. Although you can do any of the same operations with other kinds of tools, your data-mining software is designed to help you view the steps of your process easily, and work quickly, by stringing together a sequence of operations represented by small icons. Each icon is a tool with a specific function and its own options and settings. This is called a *visual programming* interface.

The property data file is fairly large, so to begin, you will import the property data file, remove the variables you cannot use, and save the rest in a new (somewhat smaller) file. First, you choose a tool to read the data and place the tool on the main work area of your data-mining software, as shown in Figure 2-3. A *wizard* (a special user interface that simplifies complex tasks) helps you import the data correctly. One step from the wizard is shown in Figure 2-4. After the data has been imported, you can view it and verify that it looks right to you (see Figure 2-5).

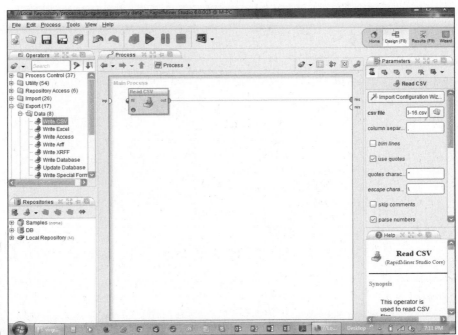

Figure 2-3:
Working with data-mining software.

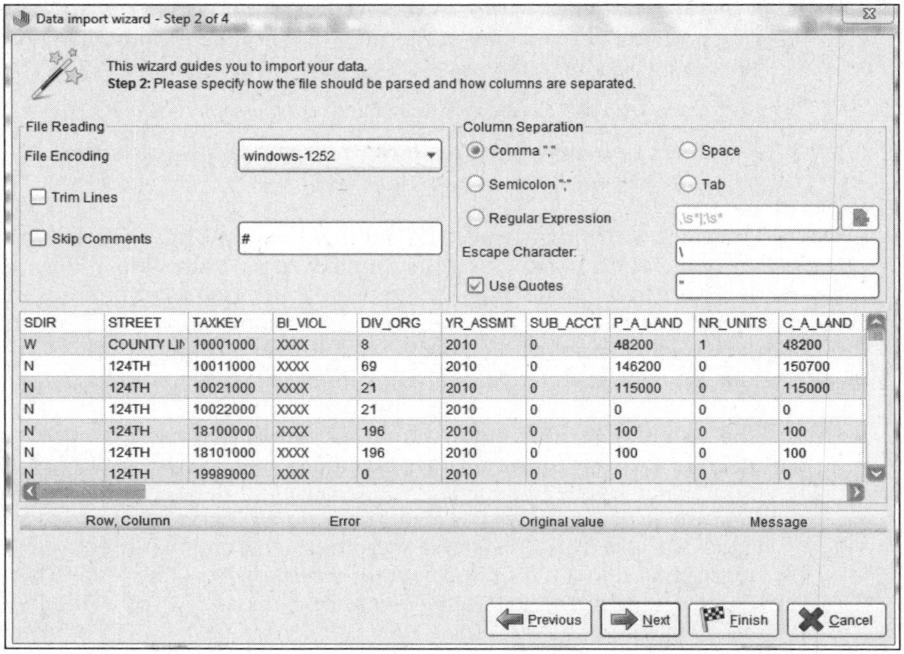

Figure 2-4: A wizard makes complex tasks easier.

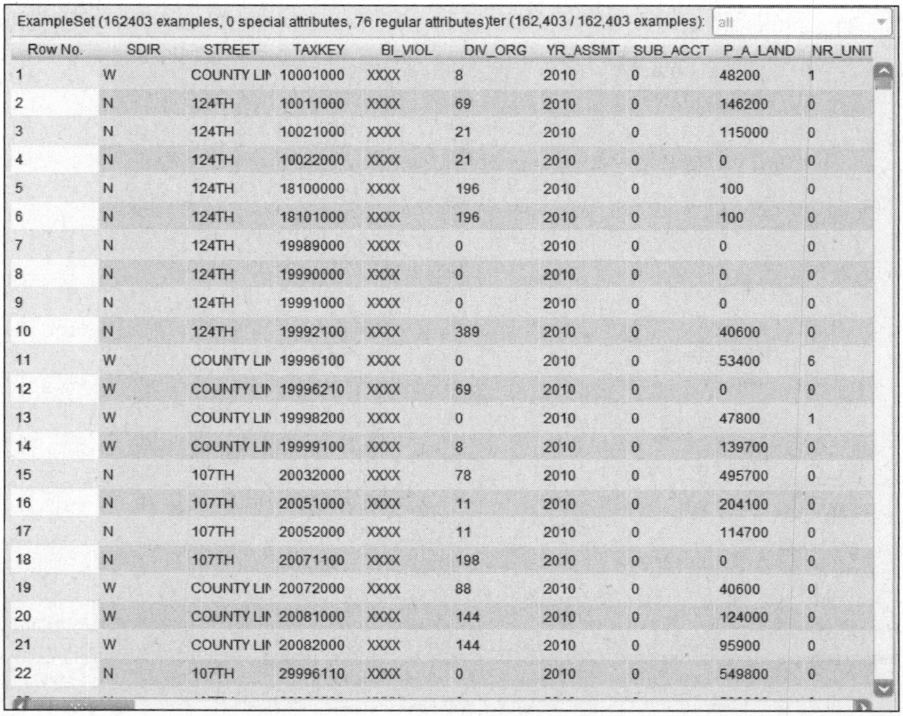

Row No.	SDIR	STREET	TAXKEY	BI_VIOL	DIV_ORG	YR_ASSMT	SUB_ACCT	P_A_LAND	NR_UNIT
1	W	COUNTY LIN	10001000	XXXX	8	2010	0	48200	1
2	N	124TH	10011000	XXXX	69	2010	0	146200	0
3	N	124TH	10021000	XXXX	21	2010	0	115000	0
4	N	124TH	10022000	XXXX	21	2010	0	0	0
5	N	124TH	18100000	XXXX	196	2010	0	100	0
6	N	124TH	18101000	XXXX	196	2010	0	100	0
7	N	124TH	19989000	XXXX	0	2010	0	0	0
8	N	124TH	19990000	XXXX	0	2010	0	0	0
9	N	124TH	19991000	XXXX	0	2010	0	0	0
10	N	124TH	19992100	XXXX	389	2010	0	40600	0
11	W	COUNTY LIN	19996100	XXXX	0	2010	0	53400	6
12	W	COUNTY LIN	19996210	XXXX	69	2010	0	0	0
13	W	COUNTY LIN	19998200	XXXX	0	2010	0	47800	1
14	W	COUNTY LIN	19999100	XXXX	8	2010	0	139700	0
15	N	107TH	20032000	XXXX	78	2010	0	495700	0
16	N	107TH	20051000	XXXX	11	2010	0	204100	0
17	N	107TH	20052000	XXXX	11	2010	0	114700	0
18	N	107TH	20071100	XXXX	198	2010	0	0	0
19	W	COUNTY LIN	20072000	XXXX	88	2010	0	40600	0
20	W	COUNTY LIN	20081000	XXXX	144	2010	0	124000	0
21	W	COUNTY LIN	20082000	XXXX	144	2010	0	95900	0
22	N	107TH	29996110	XXXX	0	2010	0	549800	0

Figure 2-5: Viewing data after importing.

You add another tool to the work area, shown in Figure 2-6, to select variables to keep in the data. This is not complicated to set up. The tool displays a list of variables in the data, and you select the ones that you want to keep. Figure 2-7 shows the setup. The list on the right includes all variables selected to keep.

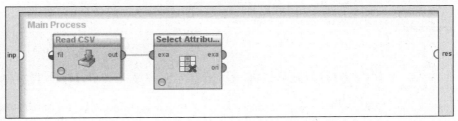

Figure 2-6:
Adding a
tool to select
variables.

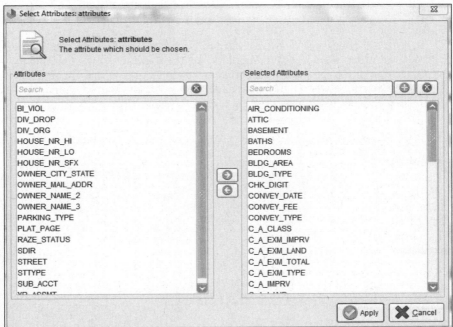

Figure 2-7:
Setting up
variable
selection.

One more tool (see Figure 2-8) lets you save the variables that you have selected in a new file.

The data-mining software used in this example has many of these specialized tools. For example, it has a different tool for each of the file types that it can read and each type that it can save. Not every product takes this approach; others might have a single tool that could save your choice of several types of files.

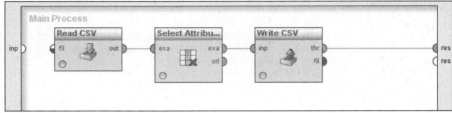

Figure 2-8:
Saving
selected
data in a
new file.

Preparing the ownership change indicator

Matt made your job easier by deriving a variable that indicates which properties have and have not changed ownership. This will be your dependent, or *target,* variable for modeling. You'll still need to do some preparation with this part of the data, particularly selecting the right settings for your data-mining software to identify the target variable.

You create a sequence similar to the one that you used in the previous section for the property data. You'll import the data, select the variable to keep, and write it to a new file. But you can see in Figure 2-9 that this time, another tool exists between data import and data selection. With it, you indicate which variable is the target by setting the tool's properties, as shown in Figure 2-10.

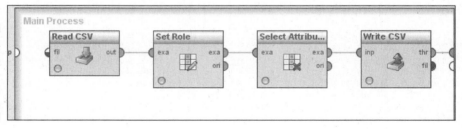

Figure 2-9:
Preparing
the owner-
ship change
data.

Merging the datasets

You have property data in one file and data about which properties changed ownership in another. You need to merge the two.

The process is shown in Figure 2-11. You read in each of the files that you have created earlier. For each, you indicate the name of the property identification variable by setting the properties of the appropriate tool (see Figure 2-12). The identification variable guides the merging of the two files, matching the general data for each property with the results: Did the property change ownership?

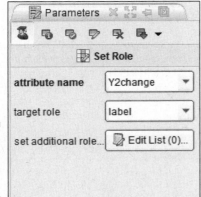

Figure 2-10:
Setting a
variable's
role.

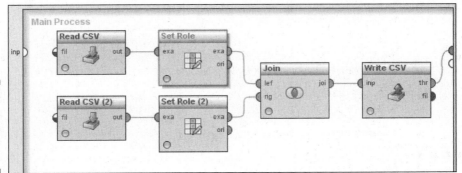

Figure 2-11:
Process
for merging
data
sources.

Figure 2-12:
Selecting
the iden-
tification
variable.

Deriving new variables

Data-mining software does a lot of work for you, but you have no substitute for your business knowledge. You understand that one variable represents the price paid for a property, another the investments to improve the property, and a third, the assessed value — but the software doesn't. The software only sees numbers and categories and text, not meaning. You understand that you have something of special interest about the relationships among those three variables, apart from any others. The software doesn't. You integrate this kind of business knowledge into your analysis by using it to derive appropriate new variables for modeling.

Choosing a starting point

Virginia and Matt have told you about a number of factors that may be good indicators of imminent changes of property ownership. These suggestions are a result of investigations and interviews that they performed in earlier projects. Some of these factors are

- The owners do not live in the area.
- The owner is the local government.
- Taxes are unpaid.
- The property is vacant.
- Zoning and actual use are not matched.
- The value is not consistent with the assessment.
- Improvements are low relative to the value of the property.
- Building code violations are open.
- Many building code violations have been closed.
- Many calls for service have been closed.
- The property is marketed for lease or sale.
- The property is in foreclosure.

Although you have good reasons to believe that each of these factors is important, no one has yet confirmed their value by building and testing a predictive model. You'd like to investigate each of them — and others as well. But you don't have adequate data for some, and the others will all require effort for data preparation.

Your goal for this project is not to develop the greatest possible model, but to use the data to demonstrate that at least one variable has value for predicting changes in property ownership. The idea is to quickly provide concrete evidence that predictive modeling is feasible. In the interest of speed, you choose a couple of items from this list to try first. (If they don't work, you can come back and try others.)

You choose to look at properties with owners who do not live in the area and properties with unpaid taxes first. Your reasons are simple: You have adequate data for those variables, and the preparation required is reasonably straightforward.

Performing calculations

This part of the process (see Figure 2-13) is more elaborate than the steps you have taken so far. You'll create two new variables, select a subset of cases to use for modeling, and remove any cases that don't have adequate data to use in the modeling process.

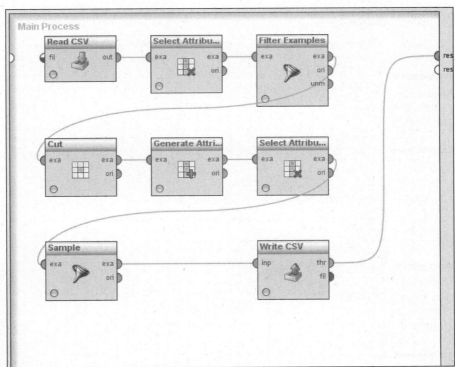

Figure 2-13:
Process for deriving new variables.

Before creating any new variables, you do a little housekeeping. Although you find many variables in the data, you've decided to use just a handful for your first model, so you select just those from the data (see Figure 2-14). Modeling tools, and even some data preparation tools, don't perform well, and may not function at all, if you have missing values in the data, so you filter out cases with missing values. The relevant setup for the filtering tool is shown in Figure 2-15.

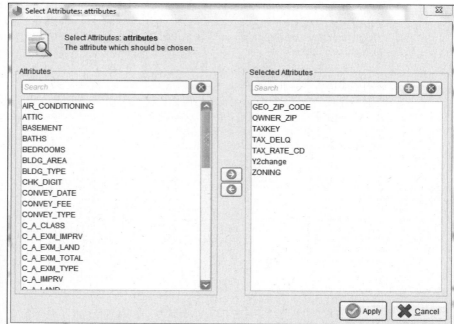

Figure 2-14:
Selecting variables to use.

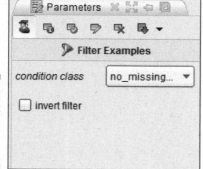

Figure 2-15:
Filtering out cases with incomplete data.

To identify property owners who don't live in, or very close to, their properties, you want to compare the owner's home zip code to the zip code of the property. You have data for each of those, but some challenges exist for comparing the two. Some of the zip codes are recorded as five digits; others are in longer formats. So you'll need to get all the zip codes into a consistent format before you can create an indicator variable for properties whose owners are not local. You set the variable cut to keep the first five characters (see Figure 2-16) of the two zip code variables (see Figure 2-17).

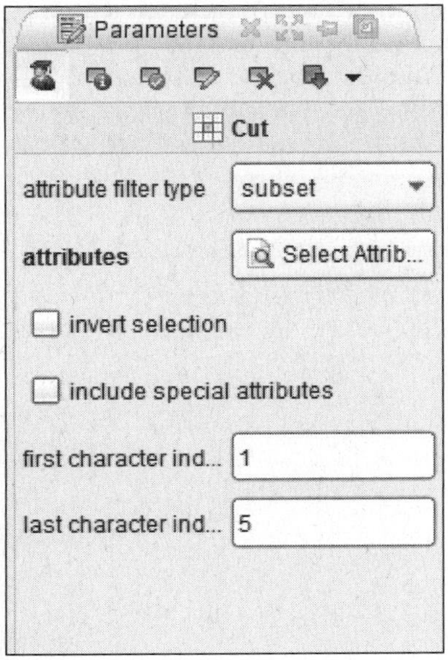

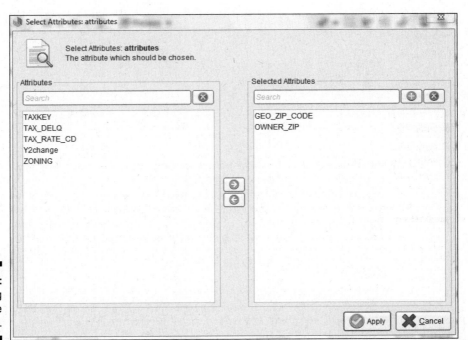

Figure 2-16:
Cutting
variables
down to five
characters.

Figure 2-17:
Identifying
the zip code
variables.

A variable already exists in the property data to indicate which properties have unpaid taxes, but it's not in good form to use for modeling. That variable has a value of 1 if taxes are unpaid, but "NA" otherwise. Modeling tools don't like that! So, you'll create a nice, new variable, with a value of 1 if taxes are unpaid and 0 otherwise. The setup for creating both of the new indicator variables is shown in Figure 2-18.

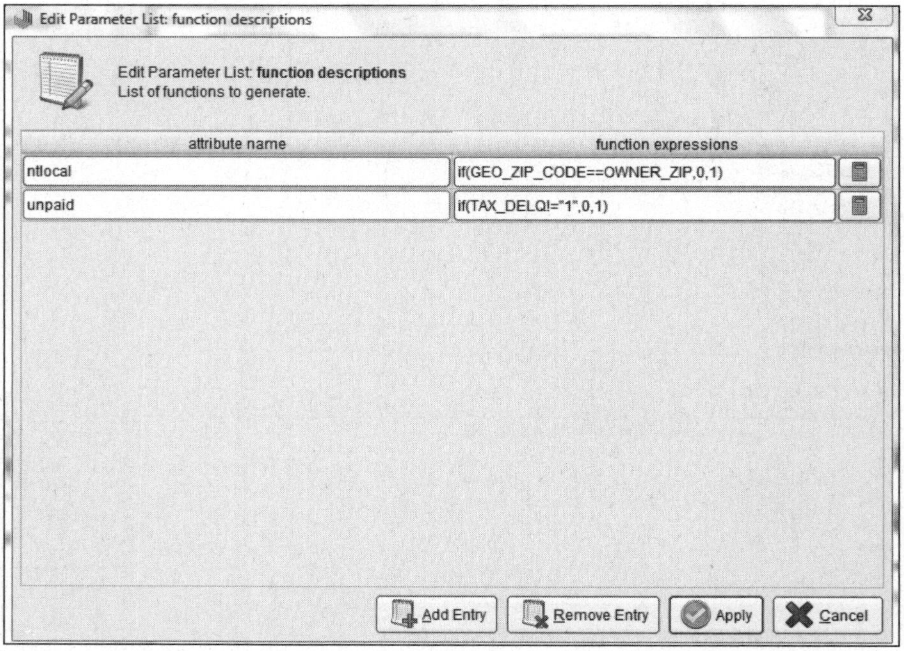

Figure 2-18: Functions for generating new variables.

You have a few more steps before moving on to the modeling phase. Now that you've derived new variables, you won't need the old ones, so you use the variable selection tool (see Figure 2-19) to keep just what you need. And you'll use a data-sampling tool to *balance* the data and select a sample with roughly equal proportions of properties that did and did not change ownership. Figure 2-20 shows the setup for balancing the dataset. You request about 4,000 cases in each group, but you understand that the actual sample sizes may be a little different.

Wow, what a lot of steps! And the data preparation for this example is simpler than most. That's why the 3rd Law of Data Mining states that data preparation is more than half of every data-mining process (see Chapter 4 to read about the 9 Laws of Data Mining).

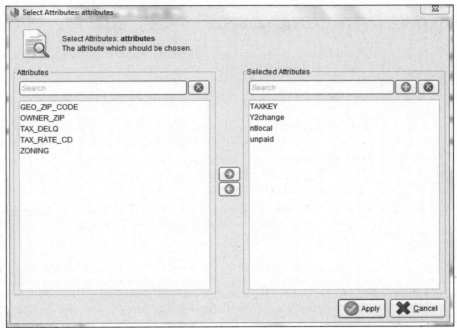

Figure 2-19:
Discarding
variables
that are
no longer
needed.

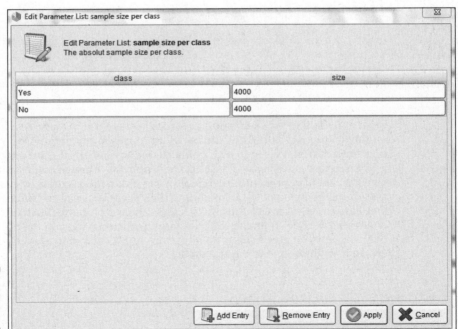

Figure 2-20:
Balancing
the data.

Modeling Your Data

Predictive models are nothing more than equations that help you make educated guesses in methodical, consistent ways, based on data.

People make predictions informally all the time, at home and at work:

- **Buying groceries:** Estimating consumption based on recent experience and anticipated changes, such as guests in the house or upcoming travel

- **Budgeting:** Planning for financial needs using information such as past spending, known upcoming events, and estimated requirements for emergency funds

- **Sales forecasting:** Anticipating future sales based on historical performance, envisioned deals, attitudes about the economy, and perhaps just a bit of wishful thinking

Because these informal predictions are made in an inconsistent, undocumented, and subjective way, it's hard to improve them. As a data miner, you create dependable fact-based predictive models, and you document the process so that you can update and improve your models in the future.

Using balanced data

In the data preparation phase, you took a special type of sample from the property data. The sample was balanced, that is, it included roughly equal numbers of cases for properties that changed ownership within a specific time frame, and properties that did not. Now that you are established as a data miner, you do this as a matter of habit.

Balancing data often seems odd or wrong to data-mining novices. It's not obvious why data miners would use data representing equal proportions of events that don't occur with equal frequency in real life. For example, in any given year, only a small fraction of properties change ownership. Why give this event representation equal to the much more common case where a property remains in the same hands? It's done because the purpose of the model is to differentiate these two events, based on patterns in the data. To construct a model that can differentiate these patterns, you need examples of each, and you give each type of pattern equal importance in modeling by giving it equal frequency in the data.

Splitting data

Some of the machine learning techniques that are widely used in data mining, such as decision trees and neural networks, call for one last bit of data preparation before constructing a model. (Data preparation goes on and on and on, doesn't it?)

Data miners can't always use theory to find one best model from data, as classical statisticians do. So data miners evaluate models by testing, testing, and testing. Some of the testing is hidden within the model-fitting process, automatic and (almost) unnoticed as you work. Some testing is done in the field through small-scale or full-scale deployment. And some of it is done by splitting off a portion of the data (called *test* or *holdout* data) before modeling and using your model to predict results for that data so that you can compare those predictions with what actually happened.

Your work process for splitting the data, building a model, and beginning the evaluation is shown in Figure 2-21. To split the data, you use a special sampling tool and specify two things: the sampling method (see Figure 2-22) and the proportions of data to use for training and testing the model (see Figure 2-23). You specify *stratified sampling,* which maintains the balance of proportions of properties that did or did not change hands in the training and testing samples. And you choose to use 70 percent of the data for training and 30 percent for testing.

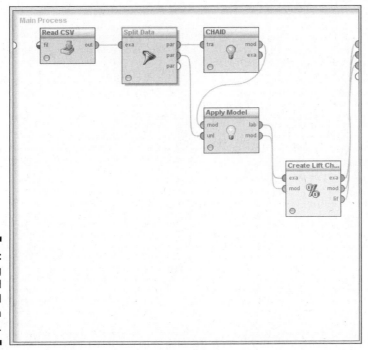

Figure 2-21:
Splitting
data, and
building and
evaluating a
model.

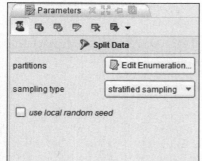

Figure 2-22:
Selecting
the sampling
method.

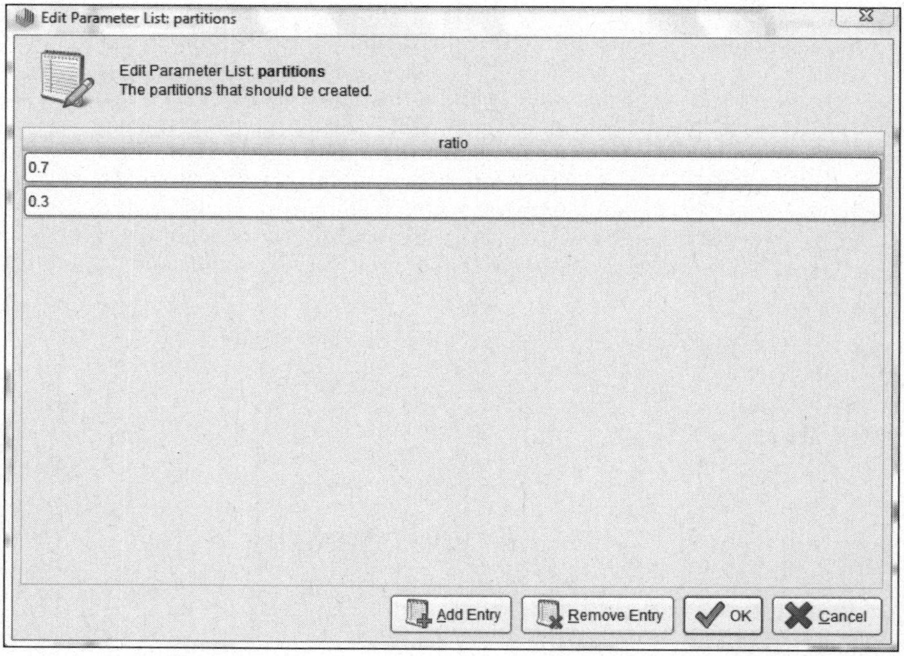

Figure 2-23:
Splitting
data into
training
and testing
subsets.

Building a model

Compared to all the work that you've invested to prepare data, creating your first model for this data takes little effort.

You have only two *predictor* variables ready to try in a model so far. One indicates whether the property owner is local (the owner address has the same zip code as the property) or not. The other indicates whether unpaid taxes exist for the property. Both are categorical variables, which narrows your choice of modeling techniques.

You choose the Chi-squared Automatic Interaction Detector (CHAID) model, a type of decision-tree model, for your first try, because it is a good fit for working with categorical variables. It's easy to use. You just add the tool (see Figure 2-24) to your process and run data through to build a model without even changing any parameters. Later, you may choose to tweak settings, but it's not necessary for your first try.

Figure 2-24: CHAID modeling tool.

Before you run the model, you connect two tools to the data that you split earlier. The CHAID tool will use the 70 percent of the data that you've put in the training partition, and the 30 percent of the data that you set aside for testing connects to another tool. This tool will apply the CHAID model to the testing data.

Finally, you add one last element to your process. A chart will help you visualize the results of the model test. The chart tool requires a little bit of setup (see Figure 2-25). You specify the category that you're most interested in predicting. In this case, it's the "Yes" category.

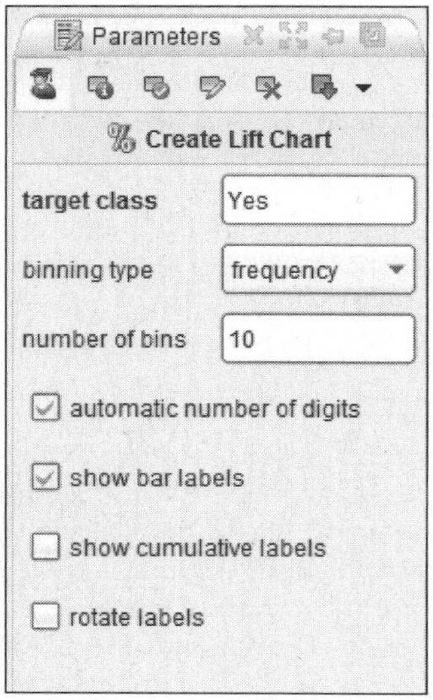

Figure 2-25:
Setting up a
diagnostic
chart.

Evaluating Your Results

Now that you've created a model, it's time to look the model over, see how it performs, and choose your next steps.

Examining the decision tree

You've tried only two predictor variables on your first modeling attempt, so you're not expecting an elaborate result. The big question is whether you will find that even one of those variables has predictive value.

Your data-mining software displays the CHAID model as a decision-tree diagram in an interactive results viewer (see Figure 2-26). At first, only the first branch is displayed. Tools on the left side of the viewer enable you to expand the tree, to zoom in on areas of interest, and to make other changes to the way that the tree is displayed. You also have the alternative of viewing the model another way: written in simple text (see Figure 2-28).

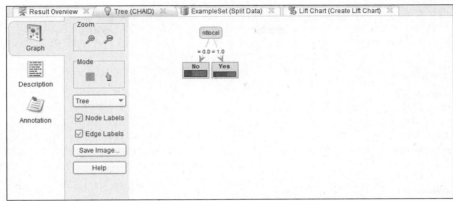

Figure 2-26:
Tree model
viewer.

The tree (see Figure 2-27) shows that the local owner variable is the most important predictor. The data branches into two groups. Local owners (ntlocal=0) are indicators for the "No" category; most kept their property. Nonlocal owners (ntlocal=1) are indicators for the "Yes" category; they were more likely to sell. In this example, most of the properties with nonlocal owners changed hands; you can see that from the tiny bar chart on the tree branch. (But differences don't have to be that dramatic to form a branch in the decision tree. Much more subtle differences can be detected if a strong-enough pattern exists in the data.)

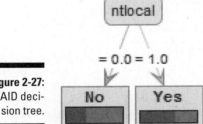

Figure 2-27:
CHAID deci-
sion tree.

You use the pointer tool and click on the tree branches. They don't expand. The local owner variable is the only one in the tree. A look at the model description (see Figure 2-28) shows the same thing in a different way.

Result Overview ✕   Tree (CHAID) ✕   ExampleSet (Split Data) ✕   Lift Chart (Create Lift Chart) ✕

Graph

Description

Annotation

Tree

```
ntlocal = 0.0: No {Yes=1192, No=2001}
ntlocal = 1.0: Yes {Yes=1332, No=799}
```

Figure 2-28:
CHAID
model
description.

Why didn't the second predictor, the unpaid tax variable, show up in the model? Perhaps it really isn't a good indicator of change in property ownership. Perhaps it has some value, but the type of model you've chosen, or the settings you used (you left them all at the default values), were not appropriate for detecting the relationship between unpaid taxes and changes in property ownership. That's all you know for now.

Using a diagnostic chart

Diagnostic charts help you understand how effectively your model makes accurate predictions from the data available. (This is not unique to data mining; classical statisticians also use diagnostic charts.) A variety of diagnostic charts exist. You choose them based on what's available in your data-mining software and your own preferences.

You use a *lift chart* (see Figure 2-29), which compares your model's predictions to random selection. The chart is based on model predictions for the 30 percent of your data that you set aside for testing purposes before building the model. The bar on the left shows the group that the model gives the greatest confidence for a "Yes," a change in ownership. From your examination of the decision tree, you know that this group is the nonlocal property owners. The model predicts that each member of the group will be a "Yes," a change in ownership. For that group, the predictions are correct in 62.5 percent of the cases. (The confidence level noted at the base of each bar is the same as the proportion of correct predictions.)

In this model, you only see two bars in the chart, but lift charts for more complex models often have many bars. The greatest-confidence group is always the first bar on the left, and each subsequent bar has the next-greatest confidence.

By using the model, you can select 909 of the 2,282 cases (909 nonlocal + 1,373 local owners) in your test dataset to predict in the "Yes" category, and 62.5 percent of them, 549 cases, will be true changes in property ownership. The line through the bars shows that choosing 909 cases at random would only turn up about 280 true property changes. So the model is nearly doubling your effectiveness at predicting true property changes.

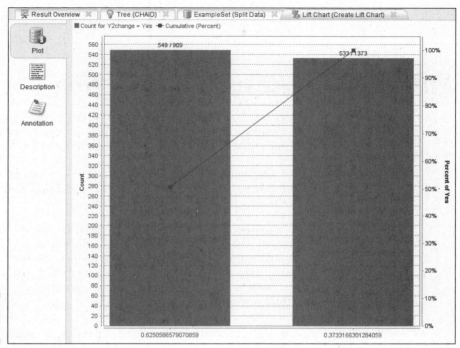

Figure 2-29:
Lift chart.

You'll find several types of lift charts. They all represent the advantages of using a model rather than random selection, but may vary in organization and appearance.

Assessing the status of the model

Your data-mining goal was to demonstrate the feasibility of using predictive modeling for property change ownership by showing that at least one variable has measurable predictive value for that purpose. Strictly speaking, you've met the goal. but if you still have time available before your deadline, you should use that time to improve on what you've done.

You have accomplished the minimum that you set out to provide. But you don't want to do just the minimum, so you keep working. You can try these things:

✔ Go back and do the data preparation needed for some more of the factors that Virginia and Matt suggested. (The list is in the "Choosing a starting point" section, earlier in this chapter.)

✔ Experiment with alternative model types.

✔ Refine the model settings.

You document what you've accomplished so far, and then return to the work to build the best model that you can before the project due date.

Putting Your Results into Action

In one day, you have not built a model that's ready to use in everyday business. That's fine; it was never your goal to do that. But you've already shown that predictive modeling is feasible, and that's pretty darned good for one day.

Because you've shown that modeling is a realistic option, chances are that the client will want you to go on and build the best model you can. When it's ready, you will put it into action making predictions.

You'll start by making lists of properties that are likely to change ownership. In fact, you've made one of these already. It's in the output from the chart tool (see Figure 2-30). A prediction exists for each property listed in the data. In the future, you can take advantage of other options to make predictions like these outside the data-mining software, and even integrate prediction capabilities into ordinary business applications.

Row No.	Y2change	prediction(Y2change)	confidence(Yes)	confidence(No)	TAXKEY	ntlocal	
1	No	Yes	0.625	0.375	20032000	1.0	0.0
2	No	No	0.373	0.627	30142000	0.0	0.0
3	No	No	0.373	0.627	40061000	0.0	0.0
4	No	Yes	0.625	0.375	50100000	1.0	0.0
5	Yes	Yes	0.625	0.375	50122000	1.0	0.0
6	Yes	Yes	0.625	0.375	310311000	1.0	0.0
7	Yes	Yes	0.625	0.375	320083000	1.0	0.0
8	Yes	Yes	0.625	0.375	340589000	1.0	0.0
9	Yes	Yes	0.625	0.375	340615000	1.0	0.0
10	No	Yes	0.625	0.375	340920000	1.0	0.0
11	Yes	Yes	0.625	0.375	340388000	1.0	1.0
12	No	Yes	0.625	0.375	330412000	1.0	0.0
13	No	Yes	0.625	0.375	330252000	1.0	0.0
14	Yes	Yes	0.625	0.375	340314000	1.0	0.0
15	No	No	0.373	0.627	330110000	0.0	0.0
16	Yes	Yes	0.625	0.375	340403000	1.0	0.0
17	Yes	No	0.373	0.627	330300000	0.0	0.0
18	Yes	Yes	0.625	0.375	420152000	1.0	0.0
19	No	Yes	0.625	0.375	409973100	1.0	0.0
20	Yes	Yes	0.625	0.375	409975110	1.0	0.0
21	No	Yes	0.625	0.375	400181000	1.0	0.0
22	No	Yes	0.625	0.375	390361000	1.0	0.0

Figure 2-30: A list of predictions.

Chapter 3

Teaming Up to Reach Your Goals

As a data miner, you'll make the most of your own business knowledge. Your understanding of the data's origins and implications is an invaluable asset. However, that doesn't mean you should work alone.

You're only one person. You can't do everything, and you can't know everything. By pairing your own knowledge and skills with the talents of your peers in complementary roles, you can get a deeper understanding of the challenges you face and a more realistic picture of what solutions might (or might not) be feasible. And the right team can prevent you from slipping into pitfalls with business processes, ethics, and even the law.

This chapter shows you the benefits of working with others.

Nothing Could Be Finer Than to Be a Data Miner

If you've read a few news reports about data mining, you may have gotten the impression that it's more complex than brain surgery. It isn't. You may have heard that data miners can learn things about you that you don't even know yourself. That's unlikely. You may have heard that you need a Ph.D. and reams of data to get started in data mining, and that's ridiculous.

You can be a data miner

Data mining is something that people in many professions have integrated into their work to get better information for making everyday business decisions. Data mining can be applied to any field, and many real-life data miners have produced positive returns on their first projects.

So, who can be a data miner? You can.

Data mining isn't the exclusive realm of people with advanced degrees. You don't need to be an expert in statistics or have a huge quantity of data at your fingertips. Data mining is for people who have a good understanding of their own business and its challenges, who are comfortable with ordinary computing (such as using office applications and other business software), and who have a decent grasp of numbers (such as the ability to properly interpret graphs and tables).

A data miner also needs patience and time to devote to the process. Data mining is fast compared to the alternatives, but it isn't instant.

Get some inspiration from these real-life data-mining successes:

- ✔ **Public safety:** The New York Fire Department uses data mining to identify factors that put buildings at risk for fire. Data miners have identified dozens of these risk factors, and developed a model to produce a fire risk score for more than 300,000 New York City buildings. Inspectors use these scores to decide which buildings to inspect first. Their aim is to reduce the number of fires and protect the lives of New Yorkers.

- ✔ **Retail:** Amazon.com uses data mining with its extensive data resources to provide individualized product recommendations to each of its customers. This retail giant doesn't just use data to decide what products to offer. It also tests every functional and cosmetic aspect of its website and email to discover details that increase sales.

- ✔ **Medical and survey research:** Smoking threatens the life and health of millions of Americans. A partnership of the Centers for Disease Control academic and commercial interests used data mining in combination with survey research to identify messaging that could effectively discourage youth from smoking, and used that information as the basis for an anti-smoking advertising campaign.

Using the knowledge you have

To become a data miner, you will discover new things. You'll find new data analysis methods, the data-mining process, and ways of evaluating and testing your discoveries. You'll try out new tools. You'll broaden your resources for obtaining data, whether you create it new or get it from a government or commercial source.

But you already have the most valuable resource for data mining: your own knowledge of your business. You know who does what and how. You know how your data is obtained. You know a lot about what solutions for your problems may be possible. No kind of mathematics, computer, or software substitutes for that information.

You also know something about who's who in your organization. And that means that you can tap into an even more extensive repository of relevant business knowledge, the knowledge held in the minds of your coworkers and other colleagues. This is the most valuable resource available for data mining, and it's yours already.

Data Miners Play Nicely with Others

Effective data mining calls for working with counterparts from all over your organization. You're going to need information and resources from many other people, and they will be depending on you, too. It's part of what makes data mining such interesting work, and what makes it vital to the success and impact of your projects.

Cooperation is a necessity

You can work alone and do everything entirely your own way if you

- ✔ Don't expect to be paid for your work
- ✔ Won't need any resources you don't already possess
- ✔ Aren't expecting anyone to take your results seriously

But no real data miner has ever been in that situation.

The world of a data miner is cross-disciplinary. It's not just that you'll be integrating your own business knowledge with computing and analytics. You're going to be supporting and depending on others throughout your organization to a degree that you may never have experienced before.

You'll need data. You'll need computing resources. You'll need to know how other business units work and why. Most importantly, you'll need the attention and respect of decision makers to put your discoveries to work. And that means you'll need to earn the help, respect, and trust of others. Data mining is not for loners; it's a team endeavor.

A diverse team helps you succeed

An insurance company invited me to make a presentation on the value of data mining, and demonstrate what I could do with their data. The company provided sample data and not much else. I had no information about specific problems it was facing, no information about costs or revenue potential, and no opportunity to talk with the insurance company staff at the start of the project. With so little information, my chances of demonstrating exciting results were slim.

I knew that my client was also speaking with other consultants, and that all of them would focus on fraud detection. Fraud is a big problem in the insurance industry, and many consultants and software vendors specialize in fraud detection. But it's a tricky example for analysis, especially when you have no way to know for sure which, if any, of the sample cases are fraudulent.

I wanted to find another angle to create value. I had an idea for how the data could be used to demonstrate the potential for improvements to existing business processes. But I didn't know if the insurance company executives would care. So I did some research and spoke with an industry insider who confirmed my suspicion that

everyday claims processing costs outweighed fraud losses. (In fact, he did so in very strong and colorful terms that won't be quoted here.)

Next, I needed a little help to get estimates of the costs associated with processing insurance claims. For that, I turned to a resource that many data miners neglect: the local reference librarian. With that information in hand, I put together a story for my presentation that made a convincing case for a good return on investment for data mining.

While all my competitors talked fraud, fraud, fraud, I was the only data miner who presented a story about how data mining could be used to improve routine business processes to lower costs and improve service for all customers. The diverse skills and knowledge of my team (a data miner, an industry expert, and a librarian) helped make mine the standout presentation.

A diverse team enhances your work by introducing differing skills, experience, and viewpoints, adding depth and breadth to the information you can obtain, increasing awareness of potential pitfalls you might not anticipate on your own, and stimulating creative thinking.

Oh, the people you'll meet!

As a data miner, your place in the organizational chart may be in a special group devoted to analytics, or within any conventional business unit. No matter where you're placed, whether you're dabbling in data mining or making a full-time job of it, you will be most productive if you are familiar with the roles of other business units and on good terms with appropriate staff members in each of them.

Marketing and Sales

When businesses decide to give data mining a try, the driving force usually comes from Marketing. For most data miners, the first project is a marketing project. (And marketing is not just for business. Nonprofits and government agencies all have similar roles.)

Get to know the scope of the marketing and sales functions where you work. In most cases, marketers are responsible for converting members of the general public into sales leads, and salespeople are responsible for converting those leads into closed sales. You can find variations, though, especially for companies involved in online or catalog sales.

Many marketers have some experience with traditional data analysis, so it won't be a big leap for them to understand the important concepts of data mining. They'll understand your questions and the reasoning behind them. And they will likely point out some issues that you would have missed. You can expect them to ask challenging questions about your processes, and you should give those questions serious consideration.

Marketers are usually good communicators, too, so you stand to discover a lot about the business from them.

Business Administration and Finance

Finance people don't get close to data mining nearly as often as marketers, but when they do, pay attention. These are the people who control the flow of money in the organization.

Finance experts can be particularly valuable for helping you understand which potential solutions to a problem are feasible, and which aren't. They can spot problems with cash flow, accounting, and legal concerns that might not be obvious to others.

Although finance and other administration units are not often the executive sponsors of data-mining projects, they do care about the results. Chief financial officers (CFOs) can be powerful advocates for data mining if they see a concrete connection to increased revenues, cost savings, or better cash flow.

Product Development

Product developers can be makers of physical or virtual products, even services. They may be engineers, programmers, designers, product managers, or any of a long list of other specialties.

Product developers possess invaluable knowledge! They know what they can and can't make and why. They know how long it takes to produce things. They know how much labor is involved and what skills are required. They know about union and other work rules. They know why things have been done in certain ways and whether changes are technically feasible.

You'll also find that members of the development team have knowledge of data that you're not aware of. The product engineer may have devoted hours to reviewing warranty claims. A designer may have interviewed (or even video recorded) users in the field. A software engineer may be keeping a personal file of new feature requests.

Information Technology

Data miners absolutely, positively must have a constructive working partnership with the Information Technology (IT) team to do the job right. So it's sad that in many cases, these two roles don't work well together. It's not unusual for information technology and data mining (or any type of data analysis team) to have a downright adversarial relationship.

People resist working through IT for a number of reasons. Access to data through approved channels is often slower than analysts would like. IT may impose rules on how data can be accessed, used, or shared. And they may require some electronic paperwork. It's all stuff that many data analysts perceive as a waste of time.

And IT isn't always dying to deal with us, either. Data mining sometimes requires a lot of data (a customer service representative opens one case at a time, while a data miner might use thousands or more). One big query from a data miner can grind everyday operations to a standstill.

So data miners around the world resort to work-arounds to avoid dealing with IT. They obtain data from any source they can, often without clearly understanding the source or quality issues. Then they don't share results. Why not? They don't want anyone asking questions. How is this behavior supporting data-driven decision making? Poorly, very poorly.

If data mining is to have a truly meaningful impact, data miners must make nice with IT, because

- ✔ Management can't put the results of an analysis into action if the details aren't available to the folks who manage your IT.

- ✔ Data and analysis aren't your personal property. They belong to your organization. You have to share.

- ✔ Data stores are growing large. You may need a sheer quantity of data that can't be kept surreptitiously in a personal file.

- ✔ Management (at least in some places) is getting smart enough to ask details. You'll need to document where, when, and how your data was obtained.

- ✔ Sidestepping IT puts you at risk of violating data privacy laws or failing to meet other important business obligations.

When you plan data-mining projects, talk with IT up front about what you're trying to accomplish. Get feedback on the data management issues you will face and your obligations regarding data privacy and other matters.

If someone in IT tells you that a problem exists with obtaining the data you need, ask about the reasons and listen carefully to the replies. You may be asking to do something that violates a law or contractual obligation. Explain your goals and ask about possible alternatives. Get these conversations going early in the process so that you won't find yourself making commitments that you'll later find out you cannot keep.

Starting a conversation with IT

If you're lucky, no history of conflict exists between data analysts (data miners, statisticians, marketers, or other roles) and IT at your company. But you might not be so lucky. Either way, make a point of reaching out to build an atmosphere of cooperation and respect with IT. Your livelihood depends on it.

Start with lunch.

Yes, you read that right. Start with lunch, your treat. Invite your IT counterparts to lunch with your team, order a few pizzas, and chat. You don't have to talk business the first time around; just be nice and give them the chance to do the same.

After the lunch, ask for tours of the IT area, talks on the function of IT, data privacy, and whatever they need you to know. Ask about the issues faced by your counterparts in IT, and you'll see them differently. (Remember that data you couldn't get? Someone in IT would have been fired if you had.) Offer to do the same so that IT staff can understand what you do. Show respect and talk like civilized people, and you'll build a good working partnership.

Addressing the data privacy challenge

Morgan Hunter, COO and cofounder of Intreis, a solutions integrator specializing in service management and compliance automation, understands why it can be so hard for you to get access to the data you want. In her own words, "For the majority of the time I've been in IT, I have focused on risk management and compliance. In essence, I am the person who makes up all those crazy forms, rules, and processes. Having worked in multiple market research companies, I am particularly sensitive to how businesses use data, in particular customer data. There are hundreds of laws governing the handling of protected data (healthcare, financial, data privacy, etc.) and when you collect and process that data on behalf of your customers, you must have the controls (read rules) in place to adequately protect the data and you must track and manage who has access to that data."

Morgan explains that a conversation about obtaining data you require may mean discussing issues like these:

✔ **What data do you need?** Describe your requirements as specifically as possible.

✔ **Who is the original owner of the data?** For example, was this data supplied to us by a customer for use in a project? What project was that? What are the data privacy requirements specified in the contract? If the data was collected internally, does it include any personally identifying information (PII)?

✔ **Who on your team would handle this data?** Restrictions may exist on who can handle which data.

✔ **Where is the data going?** Laptop, Internet, cloud, crossing international boundaries, email — all of these have legal and other implications.

✔ **If the data will be moved, how will copies be destroyed at the end of the project?** (Yes, you may have legal obligations to do this.)

Working with Executives

Most data miners are in staff or first-line management roles. You may go a lifetime without encountering an executive who's a hands-on data miner. Why? Doesn't data mining appeal to executives? On the contrary. Executives who see demonstrations of data-mining tools in use are often quite engaged. They like the work flow and the intuitive appeal of the graphics. But they rarely go on to do data mining themselves.

It comes down to the fundamental requirements that data miners must have the patience and time to devote to the data-mining process. Not every executive is patient, and none of them have time to spare. That's why they need you.

Businesses pay for analytics to support decision making, to provide them with information that gives the business the best shot at the biggest profits. Yet C-level executives frequently ignore or undervalue the analytics available to them.

Data miners do two things to turn off executives, and you can avoid both of them. First, data miners don't always focus on the problems that executives care about, and second, they present their results in the wrong way.

The next two sections help you get your focus aligned with your executive. Then you move forward and find out how to present results for maximum impact.

Greetings and elicitations

Have you ever walked into a store and found that a salesperson was trying to sell you something before asking questions about what you wanted? Some auto dealers show every woman the car's makeup mirror, even women who aren't wearing any makeup. Certain computer salespeople can't resist showing off the latest "really sweet" gaming machine to everyone, even people who haven't expressed the slightest interest in gaming. Awful, huh?

Here's something else that's awful: Some data miners treat executives pretty much like that. They don't ask what's important; they assume. And they usually assume wrong.

Every data-mining investigation should kick off with a good heart-to-heart talk between you and your executive, the person who'll be making decisions down the road. Just don't call it a heart-to-heart talk. Call it a project briefing, or something corporate like that.

This meeting shows your respect for the decision maker's authority, and it does something even more important. It provides you with an understanding of what's really valuable to this executive. That understanding will guide your work and ensure that you produce information of real value.

Ask questions and seriously listen to the answers. Clarify things you don't understand immediately, because you may not have another opportunity to speak with the executive again before the work is completed. Ask open-ended questions to give the executive the chance to raise issues that you neglected. And here's a good trick: Ask whether there are questions that you should have asked, but didn't.

What if you have no opportunity to meet with the decision maker from the start, or if you need information later, but can't reach the decision maker? Then talk with knowledgeable people from throughout your organization, asking questions in the same way.

Lining up your priorities

After you have an understanding of the issues of greatest interest to the decision maker, you can begin to plan your data-mining project. The idea here is pretty simple: Put your effort into the issues that the executive finds important. Align your priorities with the decision maker's.

Although this idea is not complex, many data miners find it difficult. Perhaps they fail to discover the decision maker's preferences, disagree with executive priorities, or get deeply engaged with a side issue discovered along the way. These are formulas for a short career in data mining.

But what if you discover something unexpected, something that might be really important? First, do what you've committed to do, and complete the work you've promised, the work the executive wants. If you have time to spare, use it to explore the new issue you've found. If you make a great discovery, wait until the after the main work has been presented and the executive is satisfied, and then present your extra discovery as a bonus. This approach marks you as an extraordinary data miner.

Talking data mining with executives

You're not getting into data mining just for the fun of playing with numbers. You want action. You want to see things done right, and you understand that it's important to base business decisions on solid evidence from data.

But you're not the one with the power to make the decisions. So you'll need to exercise your influence with the people who have authority. Don't expect them to learn your language; it's up to you to learn theirs.

And it's not enough to just speak in plain language. You also have to appreciate the executive's feelings. Executives don't win their jobs in a lottery. They fight for them. They are driven to rise to executive roles because they are people who need to feel

- ✔ Important
- ✔ Confident
- ✔ Powerful

So you must play to those elements of the executive personality.

Consider these four principles for talking data mining with executives:

✔ **The only numbers that interest executives are numbers with dollar signs in front.** (Pounds, yen, euros, and so on are also acceptable.)

Don't mention model fit measures, sensitivity analysis, significance, or any other data-mining technical term when presenting to an executive. Use plain words, and explain everything you possibly can in terms of money:

- *Bad:* "I've developed a stable model with optimized parameters for scoring customer credit records. The pseudo r-squared is 0.5519, and the p values for the input variables are all less than 0.02."

  Why is it bad to use technical language? Your executive won't fully understand it and won't feel confident. Your message won't sound like a solid basis for taking action.

- *Good:* "We can identify an additional 2 percent of the customer database who meet our acceptable loan risk criteria, offering a potential of $2 million in added revenue for next fiscal year."

  Now you're speaking in language that the executive fully understands! This inspires confidence.

✔ **Executives have very short attention spans: Get to the point.**

The most effective way to get an executive to make time for you and your message is to assume that the executive won't have time for you. Sound backward? Having many people competing for time and being free to choose the most interesting and compelling activities make the executive feel important. Compel the executive to linger with you by offering a compelling message quickly.

Imagine that the executive will have only 60 seconds to spend with you. What would you say? Just the things you care about most, right? And the most compelling reasons to believe you. If you had five minutes, you'd add more information, but still it would be carefully selected. Plan your presentation with this in mind. Open with 60 seconds of the most important and convincing thoughts you have to offer. Then briefly add a little detail. Be prepared to continue in steps. Stop to answer questions. Know your material well and be prepared to change the sequence or to go into more or less detail in response to the executive's interest.

✔ **Beware of details.**

You'll find two types of executives: those who have no interest in details and those who have far too much interest in details. The first type is easily bored; if you provide too much detail, you'll lose that executive's interest entirely. The second is easily sidetracked; the executive may take notice of something small and become strongly engaged, just not in the point you are trying to make.

Keep your presentations, and especially your visuals, spare and simple. Focus on the point you are making and the information that supports it.

Don't introduce distracting details. If you are trying to make a point based on the behavior of 90 percent of shoppers, don't display a huge scatterplot that includes 100 percent of the shoppers on the screen behind you. Choose another type of image, one that won't draw attention to outliers and extremes and distract from your point.

✔ **Striptease holds attention better than full disclosure.**

Nothing makes an executive feel more powerful than discovery. The executive wants to feel clever, even brilliant. He'll get no thrill in witnessing an information dump. Reveal only a little at first and let your executive feel powerful by asking questions and treating the responses as discoveries.

As you plan your layered presentation, build in opportunities for the executive to ask questions. You have anticipated the questions, created the paths that lead to the questions, prepared responses to the questions (in fact, you desire these questions), and you know the responses will lead the executive to the conclusion you have in mind. But never, ever reveal your plan.

Asking open-ended questions and having them answered enable the executive to draw conclusions, conclusions that are the executive's alone. You know that your presentation has guided the executive to the only reasonable choice, but keep that your little secret. Let the executive feel important, confident, and above all, powerful.

Part II

Exploring Data-Mining Mantras and Methods

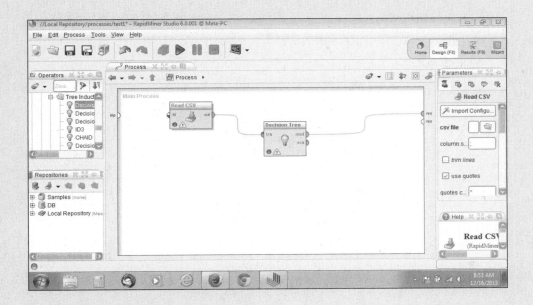

Find out about preventing data privacy disasters at www.dummies.com/extras/datamining.

In this part . . .

- ✔ Unveiling the principles of data-mining practice
- ✔ Exploring the data-mining process
- ✔ Establishing a case for data mining
- ✔ Revealing your secret plan for preventing data-mining failure
- ✔ Acquiring the tools of the trade

Chapter 4

Learning the Laws of Data Mining

Musicians have notes, scales, and music theory. Drivers have the rules of the road. Physicists have Newton's laws of motion. Every profession has its guiding principles, ideas that provide structure and guidance in everyday work. Data mining is no exception.

In this chapter, you find out about nine fundamental ideas to guide you as you get down to work and become a data miner. These are the 9 Laws of Data Mining as they were originally stated by the pioneering data miner, Thomas Khabaza. This chapter shows you what each of these laws means to your everyday work.

1st Law: Business Goals

Here's the 1st Law of Data Mining, or "Business Goals Law": *Business objectives are the origin of every data-mining solution.*

We explore data to find information that helps us run the business better. Shouldn't this be the mantra of all business data analysis? Of course it should! Yet novice data miners often focus on technology and others details which may be interesting, but not aligned with the needs and goals of executive decision-makers. You've got to develop a habit of identifying business goals before doing anything else, and focusing on those goals at every step in the data-mining process. It's significant that this law comes first. Everyone should understand that data mining is a process with a purpose. Real miners don't play in dirt; they follow a methodical process to uncover specific valuable material. Data miners also follow methodical processes to search for the specific information they need.

2nd Law: Business Knowledge

Here's the 2nd Law of Data Mining, or "Business Knowledge Law": *Business knowledge is central to every step of the data-mining process.*

Data mining gives power to the people — businesspeople — who use their business knowledge, experience, and insight, along with data-mining methods, to find meaning in data.

The million dollar model that nobody used

One well-publicized example shows a lot about what can go wrong when an analytics project isn't planned to suit all the needs of the organization. It began with an idea that seemed reasonable: Define a metric, make data available, and offer a reward for the algorithm that meets a specific performance criterion.

By 2006, Netflix, an online DVD-rental company, had nearly 10 million subscribers, many of whom had volunteered ratings for the movies they saw. Netflix developed a model for predicting ratings, but wondered if others could create even more effective models. So it sponsored a contest, open to anyone, offering a million dollars to the first scheme that proved to be at least 10 percent more accurate than Netflix's own.

The folks at Netflix are no dummies. They have expert analysts in house, and they have a lot of experience using analytics within the organization. Yet the Netflix prize experience shows us that even smart people aren't smart enough to anticipate every issue and prevent every problem.

Netflix made user data available to anyone interested in competing for the prize. Privacy advocates pointed out that the data wasn't as anonymous as it was supposed to be, and in 2009, a group of subscribers filed a class action lawsuit against the company.

And other issues existed. The contest rules rewarded accuracy, not simplicity, so the models they got were not simple or easy to use. In 2009, an international team of researchers called "BellKor's Pragmatic Chaos" achieved the 10 percent improvement and won the prize. However, Netflix never used this algorithm, in part because it was too complex for practical use and in part because the nature of Netflix's business had changed over the intervening years, making ratings less important than they had been at the start of the competition.

How can you avoid costly and embarrassing misadventures in analytics? Don't have the illusion that you are so smart that you know what everybody needs. Get out and talk with all the interested parties. Find out what people expect to do with results. How will management use the information to make decisions? What will IT have to do to deploy a model? Who can explain the relevant privacy concerns? Map requirements beginning from the desired final result, working backward to the data-collection process. Share your process and invite comment and criticism. You may be able to involve professionals who are process experts, such as product managers or business analysts.

It's easy to believe that you know what's important and can define the best approach on your own. But it's smarter to accept your own limitations, open your mind, and reach out to gather information from others at the start of every analytics project.

You don't have to be a fancy statistician to do data mining, but you do have to know something about what the data signifies and how the business works. Only when you understand the data and the problem that you need to solve can data-mining processes help you to discover useful information and put it to use.

Data mining produces useful results only in the context of the available data. You have to know what the data means. (If someone sends you unlabeled data, explain that you are a data miner, not a magician. You need to know what the fields and cases are.)

Data mining is no substitute for business understanding. Your own business knowledge has more value than any data-mining tool. Tools mean nothing alone; they merely add speed and power to aid your own thought process. If you know nothing about the domain of the problem, you must team up with someone who has that knowledge.

3rd Law: Data Preparation

Here's the 3rd Law of Data Mining, or "Data Preparation Law": *Data preparation is more than half of every data-mining process.*

Traditional statisticians often have the opportunity to collect new data to address specific research questions. They may use rigorous processes to plan experiments, design survey research questionnaires or otherwise gather high-quality data that is well targeted to specific research goals. Yet after all that, they still spend a lot of time cleaning and preparing data for analysis.

Data miners, on the other hand, almost always have to work with whatever data is available. They use existing business records, public data, or the data they can buy. Chances are, all that data was gathered for some purpose other than data mining, and without any rigorous plan or careful data-collection process. So data miners spend a lot of time on data preparation.

How much time? Pretty much every data miner will admit to spending more time on data preparation than on analysis. Some report that 80 or 90 percent of their time is spent on data preparation. It's not glamorous, but it's a vital element of the process.

4th Law: Right Model

Here's the 4th Law of Data Mining, or "NFL-DM": *The right model for a given application can only be discovered by experiment.*

This law is also known by the shorthand NFL-DM, meaning that there is No Free Lunch for the data miner.

First, what's a model? It's an equation that represents a pattern observed in data. At least, it represents the pattern in a rough way. Mathematical models of real things are never perfect! This is a fact of life, and it's just as true for nuclear physicists as it is for data miners.

A nuclear physicist might have theories about the underlying mechanism of a particular real-life process. Those theories might lead the physicist to select a specific type of mathematical model as the most appropriate one for a particular situation. Data miners, however, don't work that way.

Meet the data miner: Tom Khabaza

How did Tom Khabaza come to lay down the laws of data mining? There's something to be said for being first on the scene. Khabaza started data mining in the early 1990s, when few people had even heard of data mining, let alone tried it.

He began his career in psychology and gravitated to the study of cognition, human learning. Data mining has its roots in the attempt to simulate the complex process of human learning.

In truth, data mining is pretty crude compared to real human learning. But it's fast and consistent.

Tom got involved in the development of some of the earliest software designed for data mining (software that grew into a commercial product still widely used today). He put data mining to work in practical applications, lots of them. And he was one of the first people to make a career as a data miner.

Tom has broken a lot of ground for the rest of us. Are you interested in using data mining to predict customer *churn* (turnover)? Tom was a pioneer in that application. Perhaps you're intrigued by the potential of data mining for law enforcement. Tom was one of the first to do that, too.

Then Tom delved into his data-mining experience and knowledge of psychology to define the guiding principles of data mining. His 9 Laws of Data Mining were an instant hit in the data-mining community (such a big hit that now you may come across articles about the 9 Laws that don't even mention the originator). That's how Tom Khabaza became the Isaac Newton of data mining, a leader who provides inspiration and structure for others in the profession.

In data mining, models are selected through trial and error. You will experiment with different model types. The selection of models that you try will depend on the characteristics of the variables involved (Are the variables categorical or numeric? How many categories do you have?) and the modeling options available through the tools at hand. (For more about this process, see Chapter 15.)

You won't be able to defend your choice of model based on theory. Instead, you'll test. First, you'll test models using data that you have reserved just for testing. Then, you'll use your model in the field on a small scale and get new data to evaluate how well your model performs in the real world.

5th Law: Pattern

Here's the 5th Law of Data Mining: *There are always patterns*.

Think of any famous explorer, and you'll realize that successful exploration begins with a goal. Frederick A. Cook and Robert E. Peary explored the northernmost region of the planet in search of the North Pole. Richard Burton and John Speke explored Africa in search of the source of the Nile River.

As a data miner, you'll explore data in search of useful patterns. In other words, you'll be looking for meaningful relationships among the variables in the data. Understanding these relationships provides better understanding of the business, and better predictions of what will happen in the future. Most importantly, understanding patterns in the data enables you to influence what will happen in the future.

Here's an example: A computer dealer would like to increase profit margins by cultivating add-on sales. The dealer can make more money if computer buyers also purchase peripherals (like printers and keyboards), software, and small items like computer screen wipes.

You investigate the data with the aim of understanding the characteristics of customers who buy those items. Perhaps you'll discover that people who buy Acme brand computers also buy a lot of additional items, more than buyers of any other computer brand. That's a pattern, and the pattern guides the dealer's action. Cultivate buyers of Acme computers as clients, get more add-on sales. At least, that's the expectation. To prove it, you must test.

You always find patterns. The data always has something to tell you. Sometimes, it confirms that what you've been doing is right. That may not seem exciting, but at least it tells you that you've been on the right track. Other days, the data may tell you that your current business practices don't work. That's exciting, and though it might not be pleasant in the short run, knowing the truth is an important step toward improvement.

Like other great explorers, you'll always have a specific goal in mind. Keep your focus, and don't spend a lot of time investigating patterns that aren't relevant to your business goal. Christopher Columbus explored the oceans in search of a superior route to Asia, but never found it. In that case, his management ended up very happy anyway. Don't count on having the same luck yourself.

Data mining is still a young field, something that's brand new to most people. You can be a pioneering explorer in your own field by using data mining to investigate issues that are important to you. (And unlike the other explorers mentioned in this section, you can be an explorer in your own safe, warm office.)

6th Law: Amplification

Here's the 6th Law of Data Mining, or "Insight Law": *Data mining amplifies perception in the business domain.*

Yes, the wording of this law is kind of fancy-schmancy. I'll put it another way: Data-mining methods enable you to understand your business better than you could have done without them.

If important information was written in small print, you might be able to read it on your own, but you'd find it easier with the help of a magnifying glass. If the print was extremely tiny, you might not see it at all unless you had a microscope. Data-mining methods help you like a magnifier or a microscope, enabling the discovery of effects that would be difficult or impossible to detect through ordinary reporting.

Data mining is not instant (see Figure 4-1). Discovery and learning through data mining is an interactive process (see Figure 4-2). You'll make discoveries, find out a bit from each of them, and use what you've discovered to take action. The results of each action you try will produce more data, and that data lets you understand something more. It's a cycle of discovery, and the cycle continues as long as you continue to explore and experiment.

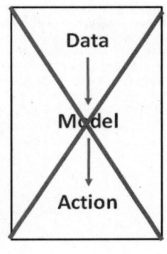

Figure 4-1:
Data mining isn't a straight-line path to perfect information.

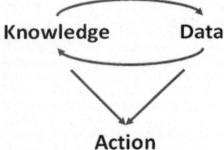

Figure 4-2:
Data mining supports an iterative learning process.

7th Law: Prediction

Here's the 7th Law of Data Mining, or "Prediction Law": *Prediction increases information locally by generalization.*

Yup, another fancy one.

Here's another way of stating this law: Data mining helps us use what we know to make better predictions (or estimates) of things we don't know.

A customer enters your store. How much will that customer spend? If you don't know any specifics about the customer, the best estimate you can make is that the customer will spend the average amount that other customers spend. But maybe you know something more. The customer heads for the electronics department. That might lead you to expect a higher spending level. Or maybe the customer heads for the restrooms, leading you to expect that the customer isn't there to make a purchase. Data mining uses data and modeling methods to replace your informal expectations with data-driven, consistent, and more accurate estimates.

8th Law: Value

Here's the 8th Law of Data Mining, or "Value Law": *The value of data-mining results is not determined by the accuracy or stability of predictive models.*

Data miners don't fuss over theory. As a data miner, you may never even know the theory behind the statistical models you use. Maybe that's just as well, because in data mining, you're going to use those models in ways that don't necessarily line up with the theory behind them.

Statisticians do fuss over theory. In that context, it makes sense for them to evaluate models based on accuracy (model fit to experimental data) and stability (producing consistent model structure from different data samples). Accuracy and stability are good things, but a model can be both accurate and stable, yet not offer much value to the business.

You, the data miner, must use a different approach. You'll look for models that produce correct predictions (and you'll use testing, rather than statistical theory, to judge that), yes. But you may be more concerned with other issues, such as whether the model makes business sense, enlightens you about unexpected predictive factors or is practical to use in your workplace.

9th Law: Change

Here's the 9th Law of Data Mining, or "Law of Change": *All patterns are subject to change.*

The world is always changing. The model that gives you great predictions today may be useless tomorrow. This is a fact of life for all data analysts, not just data miners.

The 0th Law of Data Mining

Duncan Ross, another respected data miner, has suggested an addition to the 9 Laws of Data Mining.

To understand Ross's Law Zero, you'll need a little background. Consider the *data scientist,* a new analytics job title that has been taking hold in some organizations, especially some larger, web-based businesses. The title means different things to different people. Sometimes it's a person who has a degree in statistics, but more often not. Applications, experience, training, and tools vary. The one constant is that these roles lean on programming skills. Some describe them as part statistician, part programmer, and part storyteller, and sometimes a few additional parts are required, creating an unrealistic ideal for the profession.

But, in any case, the data scientist title and the concept of data science are hot.

So, here's Law Zero: *The 9 Laws of Data Mining are equally relevant to Data Science.*

Q: Is Law Zero true?

A: Approximately.

Most of the 9 Laws are universals for any type of data analysis. Think about the first law, the Business Goals law. That's a basic for any kind of data analyst. Classical statisticians and operations researchers can work with specific business goals in mind, just like data miners.

Researchers who use classical methods might see room for discussion about the 4th Law, which says that the right model can only be found by experimentation. And they'd certainly have a few choice thoughts on the 8th Law, which downplays model fit and stability. Statisticians and scientists like their models to be stable, and they have reasons for that preference. The degree to which you accept these parts of the 9 Laws depends upon your approach to data analysis, not the name you call it. You can read more about Law Zero and why it's important in Duncan Ross's article "The 0th Law of Data Mining," at `http://strata.oreilly.com/2013/02/the-0th-law-of-data-mining.html`.

Chapter 5

Embracing the Data-Mining Process

Data mining doesn't have official rules. You have tremendous flexibility to define and refine your own work methods. Still, you'll find benefits to understanding and following the approaches that work well for others.

The *Cross-Industry Standard Process for Data Mining* (*CRISP-DM*) is the dominant process framework for data mining. It's an open standard; anyone may use it. This chapter explains each phase of the process.

Whose Standard Is It, Anyway?

The CRISP-DM process model is a step-by-step approach to data mining that was created by data miners for data miners. Participants from over 200 organizations (mainly a diverse group of businesses with an interest in using data mining internally or in promoting far-reaching use of data mining) provided input to develop the framework, which outlines key data-mining tasks in business terms and leaves users free to make their own choices about specific mathematical and computational approaches, and other technical matters.

The explanation of the CRISP-DM process in this chapter follows the original published version very closely. However, differences exist, such as changes in terminology or a diagram, intended to make the information clearer for data-mining novices. Also, the explanations in this book are briefer and lighter in style. If you would like to read the undiluted original (all 76 pages of it in small print), you can get it online (for free) at

```
ftp://ftp.software.ibm.com/software/analytics/spss/support/Modeler/
                 Documentation/14/UserManual/CRISP-DM.pdf
```

Approaching the process in phases

The CRISP-DM process model has six primary phases. These are

1. **Business understanding:** Get a clear understanding of the problem you're out to solve, how it impacts your organization, and your goals for addressing it.

2. **Data understanding:** Review the data that you have, document it, and identify data management and data quality issues.

3. **Data preparation:** Get your data ready to use for modeling.

4. **Modeling:** Use mathematical techniques to identify patterns within your data.

5. **Evaluation:** Review the patterns you have discovered and assess their potential for business use.

6. **Deployment:** Put your discoveries to work in everyday business.

Each of these phases involves several major tasks, and each task calls for several deliverables — primarily reports that summarize the work done and the information learned in that phase of the data-mining process. However, CRISP-DM does not define templates for these deliverables. You must plan and create them to suit the specific needs and style of your own workplace.

CRISP-DM defines the data-mining process primarily from a business stand-point. It tells you a lot about what you need to do, but it doesn't lay out all the technical details.

Cycling through phases and projects

Data mining is not something you do once and then forget. It's an ongoing cycle of activity. In any given project, you may address just a small element of a large and important problem, but you'll come back to that problem again and again with new projects. Because your work can also be applied to new projects, you'll revisit your past projects often, to see whether the models you developed in the past are still effective and to look for opportunities to improve on what you've done. Recycling your work in this way minimizes effort and helps you avoid confusion.

The CRISP-DM *process model* (not a mathematical model, but a set of guide-lines for data-mining work) is a cycle often represented by a diagram like the one shown in Figure 5-1. Each project begins with business understanding and steps through each of the five phases of the process. Within the cycle, you find smaller cycles, so you may make several passes back and forth as you work to understand the business and the data, or to prepare data and build models. The cycle repeats as your project evaluation and experience during deployment add to your understanding of the business and inspire new projects.

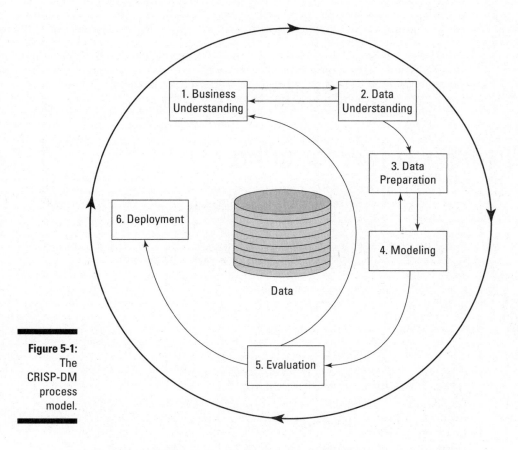

Figure 5-1:
The
CRISP-DM
process
model.

Documenting your work

When you are in the midst of a project, deeply involved with your data and the issues you've set out to address, you can easily get so familiar with the details that they seem obvious. You may not write things down because you don't see any need. Later, though, when you've moved on to other projects, spent time thinking about different datasets and different issues, and then returned to this project, you'll find that these details aren't obvious at all. You'll wonder what your sparse notes mean, be unsure of exactly where and how you got and prepared the data, and find other holes in your information.

Inadequate documentation leads to many problems. You may end up repeating work, and making others repeat work as well. You may fail to detect errors in your work. Your management or coworkers may become frustrated (and even angry) if you haven't prepared the documentation that they need. Failure to document your reasons for making certain decisions, or the proof that you met data privacy obligations, may even have legal consequences.

That's why much of the CRISP-DM process model is focused on reports and other documents that data miners create in the process of their work. These documents are your means of preserving information about what you've done so that you and others won't have to wonder later.

Business Understanding

In the first phase of a data-mining project, before you approach data or tools, you define what you're out to accomplish and define the reasons for wanting to achieve this goal.

The business understanding phase includes four *tasks* (primary activities, each of which may involve several smaller parts). These are

- Identifying your business goals
- Assessing your situation
- Defining your data-mining goals
- Producing your project plan

Task: Identifying your business goals

The first thing you must do in any project is to find out exactly what you're trying to accomplish! That's less obvious than it sounds. Many data miners have invested time on data analysis, only to find that their management wasn't particularly interested in the issue they were investigating. You must start with a clear understanding of

- A problem that your management wants to address
- The business goals

✔ Constraints (limitations on what you may do, the kinds of solutions that can be used, when the work must be completed, and so on)

✔ Impact (how the problem and possible solutions fit in with the business)

Deliverables for this task include three items (usually brief reports focusing on just the main points):

✔ **Background:** Explain the business situation that drives the project. This item, like many that follow, amounts only to a few paragraphs. Here's an example of a Background item:

> *Our client, a regional planning commission, seeks to influence property use to enhance the quality of life for local residents. The planning commission has a broad charter which allows it to consider wide-ranging issues including employment, recreation, environment, and many other aspects of community life; however, the commission's role is purely advisory. It has a great deal of latitude to select issues for study, conduct research, and make policy recommendations to local lawmakers and staff, but does not have independent power to set regulations or influence property owners.*

> *Commission members (and others in local government and civic organizations) believe the best opportunity to influence property use occurs when the property changes hands. This implies that local government planning efforts can achieve greatest impact by focusing on properties which are about to change ownership. This poses a problem: the best time to act is before property changes hands, but the local government doesn't have dependable information about which properties are likely to be transferred. (Commercial real estate listings may be useful, but they do not cover all property transfers, and the best time to act may be before the property is listed.)*

> *Earlier research has identified a number of factors believed to indicate impending change of ownership; these include nonlocal ownership, multiple building code violations, and foreclosure, among others. While commissioners have good reason to believe that these factors influence the likelihood of property to change hands, their effects have not been quantified.*

✔ **Business goals:** Define what your organization intends to accomplish with the project. This is usually a broader goal than you, as a data miner, can accomplish independently. For example, the business goal might be to increase sales from a holiday ad campaign by 10 percent year over year.

✔ **Business success criteria:** Define how the results will be measured. Try to get clearly defined quantitative success criteria. If you must use subjective criteria (hint: terms like *gain insight* or *get a handle on* imply subjective criteria), at least get agreement on exactly who will judge whether or not those criteria have been fulfilled.

Task: Assessing your situation

This is where you get into more detail on the issues associated with your business goals. Now you will go deeper into fact-finding, building out a much fleshier explanation of the issues outlined in the business goals task.

Deliverables for this task include five in-depth reports:

- ✓ **Inventory of resources:** A list of all resources available for the project. These may include people (not just data miners, but also those with expert knowledge of the business problem, data managers, technical support, and others), data, hardware, and software.

- ✓ **Requirements, assumptions, and constraints:** Requirements will include a schedule for completion, legal and security obligations, and requirements for acceptable finished work. This is the point to verify that you'll have access to appropriate data!

- ✓ **Risks and contingencies:** Identify causes that could delay completion of the project, and prepare a contingency plan for each of them. For example, if an Internet outage in your office could pose a problem, perhaps your contingency could be to work at another office until the outage has ended.

- ✓ **Terminology:** Create a list of business terms and data-mining terms that are relevant to your project and write them down in a glossary with definitions (and perhaps examples), so that everyone involved in the project can have a common understanding of those terms.

- ✓ **Costs and benefits:** Prepare a cost-benefit analysis for the project. Try to state all costs and benefits in dollar (euro, pound, yen, and so on) terms. If the benefits don't significantly exceed the costs, stop and reconsider this analysis and your project.

Decision makers often feel more comfortable allotting resources to projects that reduce costs than those that aim to increase revenue, so always look for cost-savings potential, and state savings opportunities first in your costs and benefits report.

Task: Defining your data-mining goals

Reaching the business goal often requires action from many people, not just the data miner. So now, you must define your little part within the bigger picture. If the business goal is to reduce customer attrition, for example, your data-mining goals might be to identify attrition rates for several customer segments, and develop models to predict which customers are at greatest risk.

Deliverables for this task include two reports:

- ✔ **Data-mining goals:** Define data-mining deliverables, such as models, reports, presentations, and processed datasets.

- ✔ **Data-mining success criteria:** Define the data-mining technical criteria necessary to support the business success criteria. Try to define these in quantitative terms (such as model accuracy or predictive improvement compared to an existing method). If the criteria must be qualitative, identify the person who makes the assessment.

Task: Producing your project plan

Now you specify every step that you, the data miner, intend to take until the project is completed and the results are presented and reviewed.

Deliverables for this task include two reports:

- ✔ **Project plan:** Outline your step-by-step action plan for the project. Expand the outline with a schedule for completion of each step, required resources, inputs (such as data or a meeting with a subject matter expert), and outputs (such as cleaned data, a model, or a report) for each step, and dependencies (steps that can't begin until this step is completed). Explicitly state that certain steps must be repeated (for example, modeling and evaluation usually call for several back-and-forth repetitions).

- ✔ **Initial assessment of tools and techniques:** Identify the required capabilities for meeting your data-mining goals and assess the tools and resources that you have. If something is missing, you have to address that concern very early in the process.

Data Understanding

In the second phase of a data-mining project, conducted after you have defined goals and made a plan, you obtain data and verify that it is appropriate for your needs. You might identify issues that cause you to return to business understanding and revise your plan. You may even discover flaws in your business understanding, another reason to rethink goals and plans.

The data-understanding phase includes four *tasks*. These are

- ✔ Gathering data
- ✔ Describing data
- ✔ Exploring data
- ✔ Verifying data quality

Task: Gathering data

You've just set goals and defined a data-mining plan. Every step of the plan depends on having the right data. Better make sure that you really have that data!

Just one deliverable exists for this task: the initial data collection report. In your report, you need to verify that you have acquired the data or at least gained access to the data, tested the data access process, and verified that the data exists. You'll also need to load data into any tools that you will be using for data mining to verify that the tools are compatible with the data.

You may do a lot of work to assemble the data you need before you can write this report. First, you will make your plan, as follows:

- **Outline data requirements:** Create a list of the types of data necessary to address the data mining goals. Expand the list with details such as the required time range and data formats.

- **Verify data availability:** Confirm that the required data exists, and that you can use it. If some of the data you want is unavailable, decide how you will address that issue. Consider alternatives such as

   • Substituting with an alternative data source

   • Narrowing the scope of the project

   • Gathering new data

- **Define selection criteria:** Identify the specific data sources (databases, files, documents, and so on.) you will use. Within those sources, specify the tables, fields, and case ranges that are relevant to this project.

Once you've gone through these steps, you must actually obtain the data. At this stage, import the data into the data-mining platform you'll be using for the project to confirm that it is possible to do so and that you understand the process. In the course of this trial you may discover software (or hardware) limitations you had not anticipated, such as

- Limits on the number of cases or fields, or on the amount of memory you may use

- Inability to read the data formats of your sources

- Difficulty dealing with imperfections in the data (for example, you might encounter products that won't import or analyze incomplete datasets)

Finally, summarize the gathering process in a report. The report should describe your requirements, and explain in some detail exactly what data you have gathered and from what sources. Here you confirm that you have actually obtained the data and that it is compatible with your data-mining platform. If you have run into difficulties, you'll explain what they were and how you have addressed them (using alternative sources, revising plans, changing formats).

The deliverable for this task is just a simple report, but the work that you need to do before you can write that report won't be simple! Data access can be one of the most challenging and frustrating parts of the data-mining process, rife with both technical and business challenges.

Task: Describing data

Now that you have data, prepare a general description of what you have.

The deliverable for this task is the data description report. In it, you describe the source and formats of the data, the number of cases, the number and descriptions of the fields, and any other general information that may be important. You also make a brief evaluation of the suitability of the data for your data-mining goals. For example, verify that the data includes the fields that you expect and need to be there and sufficient cases for analysis.

Task: Exploring data

In this task, you examine the data more closely. For each variable, you look at the range of values and their distributions. You'll use simple data manipulation and basic statistical techniques for further checks into the data. Data exploration supports several purposes:

- ✔ Get familiar with the data.
- ✔ Spot signs of data quality problems.
- ✔ Set the stage for data preparation steps.

The deliverable for this task is the data exploration report. It's the place to document any hypotheses or initial findings that you have developed during data exploration. This report should include a more detailed description of the data than the data description report, including distributions, summaries, and any signs of data quality problems.

Task: Verifying data quality

You have the data and you've examined it, and now you have to determine whether it's good enough to support your goals. You will often have some quality problem to address yet still be able to move forward, but at times the data quality is so poor that it cannot support your plan and you'll have to look for alternatives. Some of the worst data problems would include

- ✔ The data you need doesn't exist. (Did it never exist, or was it discarded? Can this data be collected and saved for future use?)

✔ It exists, but you can't have it. (Can this restriction be overcome?)

✔ You find severe data quality issues (lots of missing or incorrect values that can't be corrected).

The deliverable for this task is the data quality report. This summarizes the data that you have, minor and major quality issues that you have found, and possible remedies for quality problems or alternatives (such as using an alternative data resource). If you are facing any really serious data quality issues and can't identify an adequate solution, you may have to recommend reconsidering goals or plans.

Data Preparation

Data miners spend most of their time on the third phase of the data-mining process: data preparation. Most data used for data mining was originally collected and preserved for other purposes and needs some refinement before it is ready to use for modeling.

The data preparation phase includes five *tasks*. These are

✔ Selecting data

✔ Cleaning data

✔ Constructing data

✔ Integrating data

✔ Formatting data

The CRISP-DM step-by-step guide does not explicitly mention datasets as deliverables for each of the data preparation tasks, but those datasets had darn well better exist and be properly archived and documented. Datasets won't correspond one-to-one with tasks, but information about the data used should be included in each deliverable report.

Task: Selecting data

Now you will decide which portion of the data that you have is actually going to be used for data mining.

The deliverable for this task is the rationale for inclusion and exclusion. In it, you'll explain what data will, and will not, be used for further data-mining work. You'll explain the reasons for including or excluding each part of the data that you have, based on relevance to your goals, data quality, and technical issues — such as limits to the number of fields or rows that your tools can handle, or the suitability of the data formats for your needs.

Task: Cleaning data

The data that you've chosen to use is unlikely to be perfectly clean (error-free). You'll make changes, perhaps tracking down sources to make specific data corrections, excluding some cases or individual cells (items of data), or replacing some items of data with default values or replacements selected by a more sophisticated modeling technique. You may choose to use only subsets of the data for all or some of your data-mining work.

The deliverable for this task is the data-cleaning report, which documents, in excruciating detail, every decision and action used to clean your data. This report should cover and refer to each data quality problem that was identified in the verify data quality task in the data-understanding phase of the process. You report should also address the potential impact on results of the choices you have made during data cleaning.

Task: Constructing data

You may need to derive some new fields (for example, use the delivery date and the date when a customer placed an order to calculate how long the customer waited to receive an order), aggregate data, or otherwise create a new form of data.

Deliverables for this task include two reports:

- **Derived attributes:** A report that describes what new fields (columns) you have constructed, how you did it, and why.
- **Generated records:** A report that describes what new cases (rows) you have constructed, how you did it, and why.

Although the merge data and format data tasks are listed last in this phase of the process, they don't always come last, and they may not come up just once. You might have to do some merging or reformatting early in the data preparation phase.

Task: Integrating data

Your data may now be in several disparate datasets. You'll need to merge some or all of those disparate datasets together to get ready for the modeling phase.

The deliverable for this task is the merged data. (And it would not hurt to document how the merge was performed.)

Task: Formatting data

Data often comes to you in formats other than the ones that are most convenient for modeling. (Format changes are usually driven by the design of your tools.) So convert those formats now.

The deliverable for this task is your reformatted data. (And a little report describing the changes you have made would be a smart thing to include.)

You should end the data preparation phase of the data-mining process with a dataset ready for modeling and a thorough report describing the dataset.

Modeling

This is the part of the process that most data miners like best. Your data is already in good shape, and now you can search for useful patterns in your data.

The modeling phase includes four tasks. These are

- Selecting modeling techniques
- Designing test(s)
- Building model(s)
- Assessing model(s)

Task: Selecting modeling techniques

The wonderful world of data mining offers oodles of modeling techniques, but not all of them will suit your needs. Narrow the list based on the kinds of variables involved, the selection of techniques available in your tools, and any business considerations that are important to you. (For example, many organizations favor methods with output that's easy to interpret, so decision trees or logistic regression might be acceptable, but neural networks would probably not be accepted.)

Deliverables for this task include two reports:

- **Modeling technique:** Specify the technique(s) that you will use.

- **Modeling assumptions:** Many modeling techniques are based on certain assumptions. For example, a model type may be intended for use with data that has a specific type of distribution. Document these assumptions in this report.

Statisticians are well-informed, strict, and fussy about assumptions. That's not necessarily true of data miners, and it's not a requirement to become a data miner. If you have deep statistical knowledge and understand the assumptions behind the models you select, you can be strict and fussy about assumptions. But many data miners, especially novice data miners, don't fuss much over assumptions. The alternative is testing — lots and lots of testing — of your models.

Task: Designing tests

The test in this task is the test that you'll use to determine how well your model works. It may be as simple as splitting your data into a group of cases for model training and another group for model testing. Training data is used to fit mathematical forms to the data model, and test data is used during the model-training process to avoid *overfitting:* making a model that's perfect for one dataset, but no other. You may also use *holdout data,* data that is not used during the model-training process, for an additional test.

The deliverable for this task is your test design. It need not be elaborate, but you should at least take care that your training and test data are similar and that you avoid introducing any bias into the data.

Task: Building model(s)

Modeling is what many people imagine to be the whole job of the data miner, but it's just one task of dozens! Nonetheless, modeling to address specific business goals is the heart of the data-mining profession.

Deliverables for this task include three items:

- ✔ **Parameter settings:** When building models, most tools give you the option of adjusting a variety of settings, and these settings have an impact on the structure of the final model. Document these settings in a report.

- ✔ **Model descriptions:** Describe your models. State the type of model (such as linear regression or neural network) and the variables used. Explain how the model is interpreted. Document any difficulties encountered in the modeling process.

- ✔ **Models:** This deliverable is the models themselves. Some model types can be easily defined with a simple equation; others are far too complex and must be transmitted in a more sophisticated format.

Task: Assessing model(s)

Now you will review the models that you've created, from a technical standpoint and also from a business standpoint (often with input from business experts on your project team).

Deliverables for this task include two reports:

- ✔ **Model assessment:** Summarizes the information developed in your model review. If you have created several models, you may rank them based on your assessment of their value for a specific application.

- ✔ **Revised parameter settings:** You may choose to fine-tune settings that were used to build the model and conduct another round of modeling and try to improve your results.

Data mining, like an onion, a Dobos torte, or a sedimentary rock, has lots of layers. When you are just getting started in data mining, you can start by leaving parameter settings at their default values (in fact, you might not even notice options unless you make an effort to look for them). As you get comfortable in your new data-mining career, it will make sense for you to find out about model parameters and know how you can use them. Your options will vary widely with the type of model and specific tool that you are using. The details are beyond the scope of this book, so when you are ready, refer to Chapter 19 for information about resources for discovering more about data mining.

Evaluation

You've explored data and you've found patterns, and now you have to ask: Are the results any good? You'll evaluate not just the models you create but also the process that you used to create them, and their potential for practical use.

The data-understanding phase includes three tasks. These are

- Evaluating results
- Reviewing the process
- Determining the next steps

Task: Evaluating results

At this stage, you'll assess the value of your models for meeting the business goals that started the data-mining process. You'll look for any reasons why the model would not be satisfactory for business use. If possible, you'll test the model in a practical application, to determine whether it works as well in the workplace as it did in your tests.

Deliverables for this task include two items:

- **Assessment of results (for business goals):** Summarize the results with respect to the business success criteria that you established in the business-understanding phase. Explicitly state whether you have reached the business goals defined at the start of the project.

- **Approved models:** These include any models that meet the business success criteria.

Task: Reviewing the process

Now that you have explored data and developed models, take time to review your process. This is an opportunity to spot issues that you might have overlooked and that might draw your attention to flaws in the work that you've done while you still have time to correct the problem before deployment. Also consider ways that you might improve your process for future projects.

The deliverable for this task is the review of process report. In it, you should outline your review process and findings and highlight any concerns that require immediate attention, such as steps that were overlooked or that should be revisited.

Task: Determining the next steps

The evaluation phase concludes with your recommendations for the next move. The model may be ready to deploy, or you may judge that it would be better to repeat some steps and try to improve it. Your findings may inspire new data-mining projects.

Deliverables for this task include two items:

- ✓ **List of possible actions:** Describe each alternative action, along with the strongest reasons for and against it.
- ✓ **Decision:** State the final decision on each possible action, along with the reasoning behind the decision.

Deployment

Deployment is where data mining pays off. It doesn't matter how brilliant your discoveries may be, or how perfectly your models fit the data, if you don't actually use those things to improve the way that you do business.

The deployment phase includes four tasks. These are

- ✓ Planning deployment (your methods for integrating data-mining discoveries into use)
- ✓ Planning monitoring and maintenance
- ✓ Reporting final results
- ✓ Reviewing final results

Task: Planning deployment

When your model is ready to use, you will need a strategy for putting it to work in your business.

The deliverable for this task is the deployment plan. This is a summary of your strategy for deployment, the steps required, and the instructions for carrying out those steps.

Task: Planning monitoring and maintenance

Data-mining work is a cycle, so expect to stay actively involved with your models as they are integrated into everyday use.

The deliverable for this task is the monitoring and maintenance plan. This is a summary of your strategy for ongoing review of the model's performance. You'll need to assure that it is being used properly on an ongoing basis, and that any decline in model performance will be detected.

Task: Reporting final results

Deliverables for this task include two items:

- ✔ **Final report:** The final report summarizes the entire project by assembling all the reports created up to this point, and adding an overview summarizing the entire project and its results.

- ✔ **Final presentation:** A summary of the final report is presented in a meeting with management. This is also an opportunity to address any open questions.

Task: Review project

Finally, the data-mining team meets to discuss what worked and what didn't, what would be good to do again, and what should be avoided!

This step, too, has a deliverable, although it is only for the use of the data-mining team, not the manager (or client). It's the experience documentation report. This is where you should outline any work methods that worked particularly well, so that they are documented to use again in the future, and any improvements that might be made to your process. It's also the place to document problems and bad experiences, with your recommendations for avoiding similar problems in the future.

Data mining is a team activity. So if this process seems to include a lot of steps, realize that it may not be your personal responsibility to do every one of them, and that it's always appropriate to ask for help from others when you need it. (At the start of the project, you made a list of people who are resources for the data-mining project. That's your little directory of helpers!)

Chapter 6

Planning for Data-Mining Success

I have good and bad news about data mining. The bad news is that data-mining programs can and do fail. In fact, it's pretty common for organizations to report that they have not achieved positive returns on their investments in data mining. The good news is that this kind of failure is preventable. Taking a few simple, common-sense steps at the start will put you on track for data-mining success and documented value.

Data miners who consistently and thoughtfully plan for success routinely produce results that lead to positive return on investment and satisfied executives. Preparing a business case maximizes your chances for producing information that decision makers can and will use to yield good outcomes. Planning lets you reduce risk for the business while building your own credibility.

This chapter shows you how to build a business case and establish a plan for data-mining success.

Setting the Course with Formal Business Cases

Data mining has costs — costs for software, costs for labor, costs for servers, and perhaps costs to obtain data as well. Expenses can run up to tens of thousands of dollars, even hundreds of thousands of dollars.

To justify paying for all of this, you may be required to prepare a *business case*. A business case outlines a specific business problem, a proposed plan to address it, and the associated benefits and costs. A business case can help a company or organization's decision makers understand the situation and come to an appropriate decision. Any type of organization may use formal business cases to support decision making. Publicly traded or large businesses and government agencies generally require them for all significant expenditures.

Business cases can help you, too. Preparing a good business case clarifies your own thinking about plausible goals and your path to reaching them. It documents the reasoning behind your plan. And you can use your business case to set realistic expectations for management and your peers. So, even when a business case isn't a formal requirement, it's still a good idea to prepare one for your data-mining program or project.

Satisfying the boss

You have limits to your authority to set priorities and allocate resources. Almost all data miners answer to a supervisor. Even the self-employed have clients to satisfy. If you want access to a substantial or expensive resource, you'll need your boss's approval to get it.

How can you get this access? A business case. Your business case is your means for securing approval (permission and resources) for data mining.

But why go to so much fuss? Your boss knows and trusts you. Why not just tell your boss which option you recommend and leave it at that? It's all about reducing risk.

You may think a certain approach is the way to go, and your boss may believe you. But your boss has a boss, too, and your boss's boss doesn't know you as well or trust you as much.

Neither of these bosses wants to risk a bad decision. If questions arise about why resources were devoted to a particular project (and not to another), or if something goes wrong, they won't be able to defend their decisions without a documented case. So help them out!

You boss needs your business case to

✔ Get a thorough understanding of your recommendation and the reasoning behind it

✔ Address the concerns of higher-level managers

✔ Have adequate documentation to address concerns that may come up later

Minimizing your own risk

A business case doesn't just lower the risk for your boss. It lowers your risk as well.

The process of preparing a business case requires that you devote thought and research to the business problem you want to tackle. You'll prepare the business case before you begin data mining — in fact, before you commit any resources to the project. As you do so, you'll have the opportunity to spot issues that you might not have considered otherwise, questions that your management may ask, and ways to improve on your own ideas.

So when you go to your boss with a real business case instead of just a recommendation, you'll be more confident and better prepared to defend your recommendation.

Making a business case lowers your risk because

- ✔ You'll be more persuasive when explaining you proposal and its benefits.
- ✔ Some potential problems will already have been identified, and the proposal will include steps to prevent them.
- ✔ Documentation of the business case will be important if questions arise later. The decision will be based on the business case, not your personal opinion.

Building Business Cases

As a data miner, you want data-mining tools, time to devote to a worthwhile data-mining project, or maybe just the opportunity to do something new and different from the usual routine.

But none of that matters to your management, your shareholders, or your customers. They have a problem that's costing them money, interfering in their lives, or maybe both. All they want is a solution to that problem.

That's where your business case comes in. Your business case will be devoted to that problem: what it is, how big it is, and how much it hurts. It's meant to make them feel that pain and to understand how only your proposal can relieve it. In your business case, you're not setting out to make anyone and everyone desire data mining. You're setting out to convince a specific group of people that their pain is too much to live with, that your plan can make that pain go away, and that you can be trusted to do that. You must convince them that your proposal is more valuable than the money they have to spend.

Elements of the business case

The elements of a data-mining business case are . . . the elements of a business case. Nothing is unique about a data-mining business case other than the fact that the solution it proposes will call for data mining.

If your management is unfamiliar with data mining, be prepared to provide sufficient details to make a convincing case that your proposal will work. But you should be doing that anyway!

Because a business case is an evidence-based document, you'll need to collect some evidence.

Before you sit down to write your business case, gather materials that you will need for reference. You'll need to explain the problem and how it is affecting the organization. Look for reports, records of complaints, and other documentation that describes the nature and the magnitude of the problem.

You may already have explored some options for addressing the problem. Did you conduct interviews, obtain literature from vendors, or find industry reports that you'll use to make your recommendation? Get all of that material together where you can find it easily to use for reference. Don't worry about what's missing yet. You can always obtain additional information as you work through the process.

Table 6-1 shows you the elements of a business case, arranged in the order that they should appear. This is the information that you should be gathering and the questions that you should be asking as you conduct your research.

Table 6-1	The elements of a business case
Topic	*Questions to ask*
Situation	
Background	What organization(s) is involved? What is its business?
Problem statement	What's going wrong? When did it start? Whom does it affect? Is the cause known? Is this a common or unusual type of problem? Have we or others fixed problems like this before?

Topic	Questions to ask
Options	
Action alternatives	What solutions have been suggested to address the problem? What are the advantages and disadvantages of each alternative?
Preferred action	Which alternative do you judge to be the best? Make your case for it above all others.
Connection of preferred action with strategic goals	Some organizations emphasize such goals and some don't. If yours does, you must explain that your proposal aligns with at least one of those goals, and how.
Benefits	
Expected benefits	What value will the proposed solution yield? This should be expressed in dollars, even if the benefit isn't cash. If you expect to save labor, for example, get an estimate of labor costs per hour and multiply by the expected hours saved to translate the benefit to a dollar figure.
Mechanism	How will the proposed action cause the expected benefits?
Metrics	How will the benefit be measured? (In other words, how can management check the results later?)
Costs	
Costs	What's the proposed action going to cost? Provide a detailed budget with cash and noncash costs, and a timeline.
Costs of taking no action	How much will the problem cost if we take no action at all?

What if you're missing an important piece of information? Don't leave it out! Go find out what you need to know. If you can't find exactly what you want, get the best substitute that you can manage. (For example, if you don't know how long something will take, estimate a reasonable range of person hours for the task.)

Putting it in writing

Gathering information is the most time-consuming part of the creation of a business case. After you've collected the supporting information and taken time to think over each element of your business case, writing it down should be quick and simple by comparison. You can write the same information, organized in the same order, that you have just reviewed. You don't need to be fancy. You're writing a business case, not poetry.

You also have some freedom to change the structure of the business case when you write it. If you feel that the case would be expressed more clearly with some changes in organization, that's fine. For example, you may want to put the cost of the problem early in the report, with the problem statement. Or you may want to state costs and benefits immediately after each alternative option that you describe. As long as all the elements are included and your business case is easy to read and understand, you're doing fine.

Any business case that is more than a couple of pages long must have an executive summary. That's a one page (no longer) summary of the key points, especially the conclusion (your recommendation and the benefits). The executive summary should be the very first page of your business case. Don't forget it, because this may be the only part that a busy executive reads.

The basics on benefits

In a business case, it all comes down to money. Even if the benefit your business case offers isn't obviously money related — that is, if your business case merely saves time, improves working conditions, or provides better information — be sure that you've phrased that benefit in terms of money. You must get in the habit of defining a cash value for the advantages that your business case offers and in all your discussions with decision makers.

When you look at it that way, you find only two kinds of benefits:

- ✔ Increased revenue
- ✔ Decreased costs

A key part of preparing your business case, then, is to identify and quantify all the ways that your proposed solution will do either of those two things.

It's a little known dirty truth that a business case that balances project costs with cost savings is more convincing, by far, than one that promises revenue increases.

This is mostly because estimates of revenue increases require more guess-work, and often, more things go wrong along the way. Many executives have learned from experience that it takes more cooperation from others to achieve revenue increases, and you may not get the cooperation that you are expecting. That's not to say that revenue increases aren't desirable. In fact, greater potential value often exists in a revenue increase. You can only save as much as you spend, though, which is a limiting factor. Revenue, on the other hand, has no limit.

Still, make it a priority to identify cost-savings potential and build your business case on that, even if your personal goal is to increase revenue. (If you're successful, nobody will turn down bonus revenue!)

Avoiding the Failure Option

If you check out the latest business news reports, you'll have a good chance of finding a couple of business success stories that involve data mining. Failures don't often make the news. Nobody hires a publicist to get a failure story placed in the media. But if you speak privately with people who've tried out data mining, many will admit that it didn't go so well for them.

It would be ideal to begin a discussion of the evidence against data mining with some nice, solid data. If only adequate studies existed to confidently state that a certain number of businesses made an investment in data mining last year, and that x percent experienced significant returns, y percent broke even, and z percent failed to break even. However, that data doesn't exist.

An assortment of surveys have been taken on this topic. Some paint a rosy picture of analytics' return on investment. Others have yielded very different results, indicating that only a minority of those who invest in data mining (or predictive analytics, or a similar concept) break even, let alone achieve significant returns. Why such different results? Some surveys involve only the customers of particular vendors, and the respondents are all customers selected by those vendors. Others may be relatively independent of vendor influence. However, those studies haven't necessarily been conducted under the highest standards of survey research. Some of the survey results in circulation never cite a source other than "a recent industry study."

Because you won't find a dependable source of hard data, here's an assessment based on extensive personal experience with data miners and the data-mining industry. The case against data mining can be summed up in one sentence:

Most organizations that make a data-mining investment never break even.

Why is this true? What does this imply for you? Is data mining only right for certain special situations? Are some people born to be data miners, but not others?

No, it's much simpler than that. It so simple, it's dumb. Here it is, the number-one cause of data-mining failure (drum roll, please):

Lack of planning.

Pretty anticlimactic, huh?

So, the secret is out. Data miners fail because they fail to make plans to succeed. Most failed data-mining programs never started with any plan for success.

You might feel disappointed by that revelation. It's like saying that most English majors fail to become best-selling writers because they fail to write any books.

But it's also wonderful news! Because you now have a tremendous advantage over most novice data miners. You know what they don't know: To maximize your chances of data-mining success, you must make a plan that connects the dots from a problem to data mining to a solution.

Does that sound familiar? Sounds a lot like a business case, doesn't it? And you found out how and why to develop your business case earlier in this chapter.

The business case isn't the whole plan. You'll also need to prepare a step-by-step work plan, a road map for carrying out the commitments that you made in your business case. That concept might sound familiar to you, too. If not, refer to Chapter 5 to read about the CRISP-DM process for data mining.

Chapter 7

Gearing Up with the Right Software

In This Chapter

▶ Waiting for the right moment

▶ Determining software requirements

▶ Avoiding risks

▶ Dealing with vendors

People getting into data mining often have many questions about software. At data-mining conferences and presentations, most every speaker is asked, "What tools do you use?" And you hear lots of talk about pricing and negotiating with vendors. Media coverage of data mining and other types of analytics also puts heavy emphasis on software.

With so much attention focused on software, it can seem that your data-mining career begins with getting your hands on the right tools, but that's the wrong place to start. You'll get better results and a more positive experience by putting your business goals first, and letting business needs direct your software selection process.

That's where this chapter comes in. In this chapter, you find out how to put your own business goals first, and use them to guide you as you gear up for data mining. The focus here is process: assessing needs, prioritizing, comparing products, and working with software vendors. (Refer to Appendix B for a list of major data-mining software suppliers, including commercial and open source options.)

Putting Data-Mining Tools in Perspective

If you needed a place to live, you wouldn't start by dashing off to the store for new power tools, and you wouldn't just move in any place where you could get a free room. You'd start by considering your needs. You'd think about who is going to live in your home and the lifestyle you desire. You'd review the strengths and weaknesses of the current home for meeting those needs, and form some ideas about what is really required to meet your needs.

With your requirements defined, you'd make a plan. Budget and other factors might cause you to make your plan a little different from what you had imagined at first. Perhaps you would start with a modest dwelling that meets your most pressing needs, while leaving room for future additions and improvements.

It would not make sense to select tools, materials, or services until you have a plan, because the plan guides your understanding of what you will need and when, to build your house. Your data-mining projects also begin with plans. Until you have defined what you intend to accomplish and your own working requirements, don't focus on software.

Avoiding software risks

Think about what could happen if you selected a home without thinking your choice through carefully. When you moved in, you might find that the layout didn't suit your lifestyle. You might discover equally nice houses in the same neighborhood for sale at lower prices. Or you might find that the house is harder to maintain than you expected. Rushing your choice of software comes with similar risks.

Good preparation protects you from these common risks:

- ✔ **Inadequate software capabilities:** New data miners often find that the software they've selected doesn't have the full set of capabilities they require. Although it's tempting to blame the problem on the software provider, that excuse probably won't satisfy your boss or client.

  The first and most important way to avoid selecting products that don't meet your requirements is to delay the selection of software until you have completed a thorough assessment to determine what those requirements will be. After you have a good understanding of what you need, it makes sense to plan appropriate tests before committing to a purchase. Always test software before settling on a product.

  Evaluate a variety of products. Free products are, of course, easily accessible, and most commercial software vendors will let you test their products for a short time at no charge. Make the most of these trials by preparing a test plan and defining success criteria before you begin.

If your software test demands a significant amount of technical assistance from a vendor, such as bringing a support person to your site for several days, you will likely be asked to pay a fee for that service. (Keep this in mind when considering free software. Companies that distribute their software free often make money selling services.) Vendors will sometimes apply those fees toward your software purchase. If that isn't offered, ask.

Sometimes, the problem isn't really that the software lacks a necessary capability, but that the data miner hasn't learned enough about how to use it. Plan on training for any product you acquire, and start training as soon as you bring a tool in-house.

✔ **Overpaying:** People often do not even realize that they have bought a more expensive product than they needed. While the most cost-effective choice for you is not necessarily the one with the lowest price tag, there is no point in paying for product features that you will not use.

Your best defense against paying too much is to do some comparison shopping — with your list of requirements in hand. If a sales representative encourages you to select a more expensive product than you think you need, ask questions. Ask what additional capabilities are provided in the pricier product, and how they are relevant to you. Get enough information to let you determine whether the upgrade would actually be more valuable to your organization, or just increase the sales representative's commission.

✔ **Unnecessary complexity:** When data miners sit down to carry out a project with a new tool, they sometimes find it harder to use than they expected. Sometimes, it's clear that the tool can do what's needed, but not easily. In other cases, it may appear that the product simply can't meet a requirement.

One way to avoid unnecessary complexity is to try products before making a selection. Always give software a through trial before committing to use it in a real application.

Good data-mining tools are designed to help business users discover useful patterns in data quickly. At least, that's the goal. The real-life truth, though, is that it still takes effort to understand new tools and complete projects.

Focusing on business goals, not tools

It's important that you focus on business goals first, and throughout the data-mining process. Your boss is never going to respond to a persuasive presentation by asking, "What tools did you use?" Never, ever.

Your boss is interested in increasing product sales, decreasing warranty claims, getting more technical support problems resolved on the first contact, or preventing the problems so that technical support won't be needed in the first place — stuff like that. So talk about stuff like that. And think about stuff like that.

Good data miners often produce perfectly useful results using tools that aren't the best. You can have the fanciest software on the market yet not produce good results. Your attention to business goals and the thought you put into the data-mining process are far more important than the toys, er, tools you have on hand.

Focusing on software too early can lead you to choose the wrong software, but that's the least of your problems. The real problem with a "tools first" mentality is that it isn't a "business goals first" mentality. Addressing the business goals is what data mining is all about.

So keep your eyes on the prize and let your software choices, and every choice you make while data mining, be guided by business goals that you set from the outset, based on input from your management, and your own business knowledge.

Keep these principles in mind:

- **Focus on issues that are important to the business and your management.** Tools, techniques, and interesting patterns in the data that are not related to the business goal may fascinate you, but they mean nothing to a manager under pressure to address a specific business problem.

- **Respect deadlines.** Do first things first. Missing a milestone means that you are preventing others from doing their work on time.

- **Make the most of your resources.** Software selection is only one area where forethought and planning prevent waste. Your time and the time of other team members are even more valuable.

- **Build credibility step by step.** Each time that you help management achieve an important business goal, you build trust. Managers respect analysts who speak their language, so talk about dollars and cents, not fancy math. Keep your presentations brief and on topic. Present only information that is directly related to the business goal.

Determining what you need

You can't make a rational choice of software until you have thought through business needs. A thorough review of your goals, work environment, and the needs and preferences of the team sets the stage for making a smart choice.

Data doesn't mine itself, and great models won't look so great if nobody will use them. Getting input from everyone involved in the process helps you to understand what software capabilities you will need and why, but more importantly, it helps you build bridges and find out how to work with others to put data mining to work. While you may have only one or just a few people using data-mining software hands-on, many others contribute to the process. You'll need data, for example, so talk with Information Technology staff about data access. Models are no use unless you can integrate them into business operations. Learn the options for doing that and the technical (as well as legal and political) requirements for the process.

Talking with staff members about the processes they use can be a great way to make connections. Here are some tips to keep in mind:

- **Be inclusive when seeking input.** Reach out to people in every functional role that may need to support your process. Seek diversity in work experience, education, and points of view. This isn't just a nicety. Getting input from a diverse group of people helps you avoid blind spots that could cause unforeseen problems and stand between you and your goals.

- **Show respect.** It's important to show respect for each person you interview and listen thoughtfully. Still, listening is not enough. Most people are not expert communicators. They may not know exactly how to explain their concerns in a way that's easy for you to understand. So it's up to you to ask good questions. If you don't understand the responses clearly, say so (politely) and ask for clarification. Explain what you need from each person, and ask about what is expected in return. If it's data that you want, describe what you need and ask what it takes to get it. Starting with broad questions may help you discover issues that you would not have thought of on your own (maybe you're thinking of technical specs but aren't aware that you'll need management authorization). Work gradually toward more specific questions as you proceed.

- **Share your data.** When your review of goals and staff interviews is completed, summarize and share your findings. Circulating your summary gives everyone a chance to correct you on anything you may have misinterpreted, and point out issues (or people) that you may have missed. Let the team know that you welcome these corrections. It's better to find out about these now than later when the project is under way and you bump into a problem.

Comparing tools

Now comes the fun part, or the icky part, depending on your personal taste. It's time to make a list of your software requirements, based on your business goals, working conditions, and the preferences of the team.

Develop your software checklist. Review your findings and determine the ways in which software can help you achieve your goals. Keep the following in mind:

- ✔ **Functions:** What do you need your software to do? The following list shows some of the more common data-mining software functions:

  - *Data access and import:* You won't get to square one if your tool can't import data from the database or files where it is stored.

  - *Data preparation:* Data manipulation needs are not always obvious from the outset, so look for tools that offer broad data manipulation capabilities.

  - *Exploratory techniques:* You'll need to create tables and a variety of graphs.

  - *Modeling:* You don't know yet exactly what model will perform best for you, but you do know, based on your business requirements, what kind of variables (fields) will be inputs (predictors, independent variables) and outputs (targets, dependent variables). Your tool should offer not just one but several appropriate model types.

  - *Reporting:* You'll save time if results from the tool can be easily incorporated into your written reports and presentations.

  - *Data export:* Data miners produce new data. You'll need a good process for exporting that from your tool to use elsewhere in the business.

  - *Deployment:* A good model means nothing if you can't deploy it into everyday business. Some tools offer more or easier options for deployment than others.

  - *Keeping track of what you've done:* Compare capabilities for creating audit trails, organizing your work, and collaboration.

- ✔ **Interface:** The most appropriate user interface for data mining is one that uses visual programming, where major steps (such as importing data or constructing a model) appear as icons that take the place of many lines of written code. (See Figure 7-1.) It may be helpful to have a product that offers the option of using code for specific tasks.

- ✔ **Services:** Be sure that your needs for training, technical support, and customer support can be met. You may also need consulting help to learn how to address your specific business needs with the tool.

- ✔ **Information resources:** Look for resources that will help you to understand and use your tool, including documentation, user groups, and books.

Figure 7-1:
A visual pro-
gramming
interface
uses icons
rather than
menus or
code.

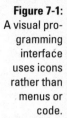

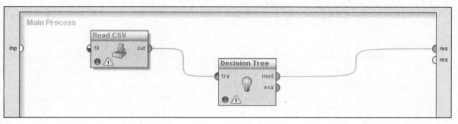

Figure 7-1: A visual programming interface uses icons rather than menus or code.

Shopping for software

Keep these tips in mind when you're shopping for software:

- ✔ **Do prioritize requirements.** It's likely that you won't be able to get every single capability you desire at once. Prepare yourself to make good choices by giving thought to what matters most and what can slide.

- ✔ **Do test the tools you are considering.** Data-mining software should not be complex to install, and it should be reasonably easy to import a small amount of data and experiment with a few functions.

- ✔ **Do insist on getting satisfactory answers to your technical questions.** Vendors should have technically competent staff available to address questions thoroughly.

- ✔ **Don't assume that sales representatives have actually used the products they sell.** In most cases, sales representatives have little or no hands-on experience with data-mining tools.

- ✔ **Don't rely on any vendor for information about the offerings of a competing vendor.** Vendors generally don't have in-depth, up-to-date knowledge about competitors. Claims about competing products are often outdated, misleading, or simply wrong. This isn't deliberate; it's just hard to keep up.

- ✔ **Don't use vendors as your sole information source, even for information about the vendor's own products**. The vendor's job is to make you a customer. The responsibility for getting good and unbiased information is yours.

- ✔ **Don't skimp on training.** You won't get good value out of tools that you don't know how to use well.

- ✔ **Don't ignore warnings.** If a representative tells you that a particular product is unsuitable for your application or a poor fit, give the warning serious consideration.

Evaluating Software

When you shop for a car, you look at more than the purchase price. You take fuel efficiency into account, as well as costs for necessities such as maintenance and insurance. You might pass up a low-priced car for one that costs more, if you expect that the more expensive one will be easier to maintain or use less fuel. It's rational to consider the total cost of ownership when you make software choices.

Choosing software works the same way as choosing a car. Select something that lets you get where you need to go for a reasonable cost. Take into account all costs, not just the initial price. Among the most common costs you will encounter are

- **Technical support:** Ask whether technical support is available, whether it is included with the software, and whether it will be sufficient for your needs. Are higher levels of support available, and if so, what is the cost?

- **Training:** Review the training options that are available — these may include built-in tutorials, online training libraries, or live classes. Find out what each option costs. If you have several people who will need training, ask about discounts for multiple participants.

- **Labor:** Some tools require much more time and effort to perform common tasks than others. The cost of skilled labor is an important element of your total cost of software ownership.

Many free software packages are available today, including several data-mining workbench products, as well as related tools like statistical programming languages. That sounds like a bargain, and in some respects, it is.

But getting your work done always means more than just downloading software. You'll still need software with the right capabilities to do your work, something that is reasonably easy to use and compatible with other tools that you use. You'll need technical help and training.

So evaluate free software as you would any other option.

Free software isn't always free!

Wait, what?

That's right, products that are free for some situations may not be free for others. You may be required to pay for a license to take advantage of certain high-value capabilities, to use the software for commercial purposes, or for other reasons. Read user agreements and make sure that you understand and respect them. Be sure that you know what license you will require and account for license costs when selecting software for your projects.

Don't fall in love (with your software)

Many people grow so attached to their software that it becomes central to their identities. You may encounter programmers, for example, who identify themselves by the language in which they program, or database architects who identify themselves with a specific kind of database. Heaven forbid that one day the best tool for a task will be, well, a different one.

A data miner probably won't walk up to you and say, "I'm a [Brand X] data miner," but that doesn't mean that the loyalties are any less strong. People get attached to their tools and sometimes resist change.

If you get tools that meet your needs from the start, it's likely that you'll be able to use them for a long time. Changing tools takes effort, so you don't want to make frequent changes.

But conditions are also changing. Your current software may not look like such a great pick a couple of years down the road when your needs become more complex. Competing products may make improvements that are attractive to you. Perhaps you will bring in new staff who require something easier to use or more flexible. So keep an open mind, and review your needs and the products that are on the market from time to time.

And there are other reasons not to become too attached to your favorite software. Your employer may insist on a change, or you may change employers and need to adapt to a new way of doing things. Your colleagues may not share your enthusiasm for a particular tool, and your personal preference may not win out. Stubborn devotion to any particular product may narrow your options, make you look foolish, and needlessly annoy your colleagues. Remember, no perfect software exists, and you'll always find more than one way to get a job done. What you know and do will always be more important than what tools you use.

If you are considering a tough test of your software (often called a "proof of concept"), such as completing a small project, develop success criteria before beginning the test. Define your requirements for a successful test: Spell out what tasks must be performed, and what results must be achieved, to call the test a success. These requirements, known as "success criteria," help to keep your test on track and get you past the test stage and on to productive work. Success criteria are also helpful if you are asking vendors to provide you with evaluation copies of costly products, or with support from their staff for your test, because defining and sharing success criteria indicate that you are a serious prospective buyer.

Engaging with sales representatives

When you begin data mining, you may be a lot more involved in selecting and sourcing your tools than usual. Your employer may not give you any choice about what computer or office applications to use, but when it comes to data mining, end users usually get actively involved in identifying products for consideration, testing, and evaluation, and even negotiating with sales professionals. You'll have more productive interactions with software vendors if you understand what's going on at their end of the conversation.

Hold on, what's all this about sales professionals? Why deal with sales professionals when software is available free? Here's why:

- **Licensing:** Free software licenses don't necessarily cover all uses. The product you like may not be free for the use you have in mind.
- **Capabilities:** Free products are often feature limited. These limitations may be strategic choices designed to get you to pay for an upgrade.
- **Services:** Vendors who offer software free often make their money by charging for services.

You can skip the rest of this chapter if you've found a free data-mining application that you love, and

- You don't require technical support, training, or a warranty.
- You feel confident that you can be just as productive with that application as any other.
- Your organization's IT policies allow you to use that product.

You may have long-term goals and a strong personal commitment to the type of work you do. A long-term outlook may be strongly encouraged by your employer, or if not, then by your peers. Sales representatives are almost always judged on short-term performance. So, all sales representatives are very interested in opportunities that are likely to lead to sales quickly, and the larger the sale, the better.

A really good sales representative will make an effort to understand your business and long-term goals. Why? A productive long-term business relationship maximizes the potential to make many sales to you over time.

The sales representative's work life runs in cycles — with goals for each quarter of the year, and also for the fiscal year as a whole. No goals are set more than one year in advance. Sales representatives change roles frequently, often changing territories within a company yearly, and moving from one company to another every few years.

Be aware of sales cycles when dealing with vendors. Representatives are busy and under a lot of pressure to meet sales quotas in the final month of each quarter (March, June, September, and December). If you will be investigating products over several months, it's better to initiate discussions with vendors early in the quarter, when representatives have more time and patience. If possible, plan on completing purchases late in the quarter, when pressured representatives may be more motivated to offer discounts.

Sales representatives are required to meet sales quotas by the end of each quarter of the year, so the closer it is to the end of the quarter, the more likely it is that you'll be offered a good deal. Late March, June, September, and December are the best times to get discounts, but to get them, you must be ready and able to purchase immediately.

The sales professional's mantra — BANT

Sales representatives ask a lot of questions.

Your vendor's sales rep's chatter isn't just talk. The object is to balance two interests — your needs and the vendor's. No sale will happen until you're convinced that the product meets your requirements, so the rep will probe for information about your goals and expectations. And the vendor needs to know whether you are a serious prospective customer.

The combination of Budget, Authority, Needs, and Timeframe (BANT) is widely accepted as a standard for "qualifying" a sales lead. In other words, BANT is the method that salespeople use to determine whether a legitimate opportunity exists to sell something.

Expect to address questions about these topics:

- **Budget:** You'll need to know whether a budget has been allotted for the purchase and how much money is available. Exact budgets may be something you want to keep private. That should not pose a problem, but you should plan to share enough information to let the representative know whether you could realistically afford to purchase the products under discussion.

- **Authority:** Understand your organization's process for purchasing software and related services before starting discussions with sales representatives. Software purchases are often delayed when people who thought they had authority to make a purchase independently discover that their employer won't issue a purchase order without elements such as obtaining competitive bids or approval from the Information Technology department.

- **Needs:** Sales representatives ask about your needs so that they can identify and offer appropriate products, and provide you with relevant information. But you'll find another side to the discussion of needs. The representative knows that no need equals no sale, and that the products and services offered must be kept in line with the magnitude of the problem you face. There's no point in offering a $1 million solution to a $100,000 problem.

- **Time frame:** Your time frame is an indication of whether and when you intend to make a purchase. In most cases, the closer your deadline, the more serious you will appear. A target purchase date more than 12 months in the future hints that your interest is grounded in curiosity rather than serious interest, because software budgets are rarely established more than one year ahead.

You may be tempted to share no information at all. Although you may have legitimate concerns about privacy and about establishing a negotiating position, total secrecy isn't the best strategy for protecting your interests when purchasing software. Without adequate information about your needs, vendors may be unable to identify the most appropriate tools or pricing schemes for you, and without evidence that you are a serious prospect, they may be unable to offer the support you need.

Part III

Gathering the Raw Materials

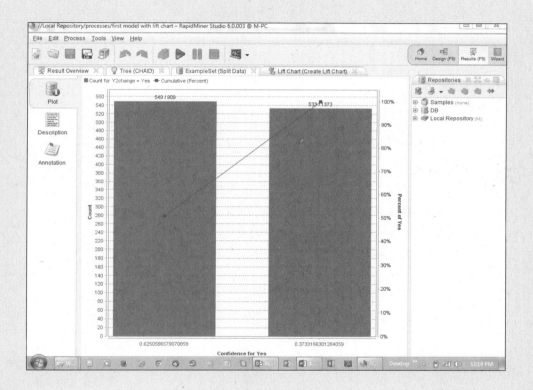

Find out how to start your search for data in the federal data portal at www.dummies.com/extras/datamining.

In this part . . .

- Making the most of the data you have
- Obtaining unique new data to fill gaps in your information
- Taking advantage of government and other public data resources
- Finding out what to expect from government agencies
- Building awareness of commercial data options

Chapter 8

Digging into Your Data

Many organizations possess a mountain of data that's been collected in the course of routine business, and they're adding new data each day. As a data miner, you'll use this internal data as your primary natural resource.

This chapter focuses on framing a problem and finding relevant data within your existing resources. If you have more data on hand than you know what to do with, you're in the very situation that data mining was created to address. But on the other hand, if your data resources seem skimpy, don't worry. The ideas in this chapter still apply to you. Make the most of whatever you have! (See more about expanding your data resources in Chapters 9, 10, and 11.)

Focusing on a Problem

A data-mining project begins when you identify a specific business issue to investigate. The narrower and better-defined the question, the more effectively it can be answered. The more clearly the question is defined, the more clearly the data requirements can be understood, as well as the limitations of the answer. If you're faced with an issue that is very broad (such as "Why are we not selling enough?"), it helps to first break the question down into manageable bits. You don't have to cover the whole topic at once; just take one narrow part of the big problem and start with that.

Take, for example, one retailer's initial question, "How much repeat business are we getting?" That sounds at first like a simple, straightforward question, but it's actually a broad question that encompasses many smaller, more specific questions, like these:

- ✔ How many new customers come back?
- ✔ How many second-time customers return a third time?
- ✔ Do customers who first buy suits come back for shoes?
- ✔ Do those who make a small purchase return for larger purchases?

Answering these questions doesn't require a lot more than counting. It's just not that difficult to calculate how many customers return a second or third time, if you have some way to identify individuals. That's easy for online stores, where shoppers can be tracked by an account login or email address. Traditional retailers can identify customers by house credit cards or loyalty cards, although not every customer uses those.

From here, as the retailer got more familiar with data mining and the potential of predictive analytics and data-mining tools, his questions became more sophisticated and action oriented:

- ✔ How does the amount spent in the first visit relate to long-term spending?
- ✔ What behaviors or characteristics are indicators of high future spending? If so, what are they?
- ✔ Would additional information (for example, demographic data) improve our ability to predict a customer's spending behavior?

The object of data mining is to move beyond simply knowing what has already happened and understand how you may influence what will happen in the future.

Building on business knowledge

The most fundamental data needed for any data-mining project isn't the kind of data that is stored in electronic files. It's the business knowledge that you and others on your team have accumulated from your own experience and training. You don't have to be the foremost expert in the field you're investigating, but you do have to understand the basics of the business. You need to know the definitions of the fields in the data, and a little about how the data is collected and what flaws might occur in the data. If you know more, so much the better.

One client's unrealistic expectations

Some people have unrealistic expectations about data mining. To put it simply, they think it is magic, and expect results that only magic could provide. But it's really a down-to-earth practical process that helps you leverage your business knowledge and a few good tools to quickly extract useful information from data, so that you can use that information to address a specific business problem.

Here's a real-life example of an unrealistic expectation for data mining, and how that got in the way of the data-mining process. A large insurance company sent me a data sample and asked for results. But the insurance company didn't state any business concern that needed to be addressed. In fact, it didn't even label any of the data. I looked at the data file and found that it was nothing but unmarked columns and rows of data. The insurance company's staff thought that was all I needed. Situations like this are not rare, and they pose a challenge that data miners must patiently address. I contacted the client to explain that I could do nothing without knowing what the variables in the data

were. I explained that, no, data mining really did not work that way, made a case for the client to provide the missing information, and then waited for it to be assembled and sent me. All of that took time. Even then, the client wasn't willing to reveal any specific business problem to address, so I had to guess. I suspected that claims processing would be an important cost and customer satisfaction issue, and confirmed that with an industry expert, which took more time. When the work was done (a focused analysis of the time required to process claims, identifying offices that processed claims more quickly than others, with the aim of investigating practices used by those offices to use as models for process improvement elsewhere), I wasn't sure that the client would value the results, because the client had never expressed any real interest in putting the information into action.

Think how much faster and better the process would have been if the client had begun with realistic expectations and teamed with me to discuss business issues from the start.

Managing Scope

Asking questions and exploring data can be fun. Now that you are a data miner, you'll find that you can ask and answer questions that were previously beyond your reach. Finding answers is motivating. You'll think of yet more questions. Perhaps you'll discover something so cool that you'll want to tell everyone about it.

It's all so exciting that it can easily get out of hand!

It's not just your own interests that can cause a project's scope to expand. As you work, you'll have discussions with coworkers, and they'll all have ideas and questions to inspire more exploration.

How a retailer got excited about data mining

Before people get enthusiastic about data mining, they're usually angry or frustrated about something else. As a data miner, your most satisfying moments, and your best opportunities to create loyal fans of your work, lie in addressing the problems that make managers lose sleep at night.

Earlier in this chapter, I told you about a retailer who began by asking simple questions such as, "How many first-time customers return for a second visit?" and gradually evolved into more sophisticated, action-oriented questions, such as, "What customer characteristics are associated with high levels of long-term spending?" What was on that retailer's mind when the process started? Just one thing: the lack of certain desired reports.

The retailer had invested in some very expensive software, with the goal of producing routine reports on a handful of simple metrics, such as the number of new customers returning for a second visit, but the software wasn't effective and the reports never materialized. Management was not happy.

So when the retailer went looking for a better solution, management wanted proof that the new solution would actually produce those reports. Just reports. Nobody asked for data mining. Nobody was thinking about asking questions that might give better guidance for action. Just give us our reports, please.

If you, as a data miner, heard about this retailer's situation, you might be tempted to shout, "Forget those old reports; data mining is better. You'll see that data mining is much more powerful than any report!" But that would be the wrong way to win over the retailer.

Here's an old adage: You must be equal before you can be better. So, if your manager or client wants something specific, you must first satisfy that want. You'll show that you are equal to the requirement. When you've done that, you will have earned the respect required to go forward, provide something additional and unexpected, and be . . . better.

And that's just what happened for this retailer. With the report completed, and the retailer's requirements satisfied, the data miner was free to dig a little deeper.

She had noticed that the data included some information obtained through the retailer's loyalty program, basic information about the customers, and details of their homes and interests. But this information was often left blank. She wondered, "Is it worthwhile to collect this information?" So, she quickly experimented with decision-tree models for predicting consumer spending (refer to Chapter 15 for more about decision-tree models). She tested combinations of behavioral data (what the customer bought) and demographic data (customer information collected with loyalty program registrations). She discovered that the loyalty program data was not only useful, but that by combining it with sales information for the customer's first purchase, she was also able to develop a surprisingly good prediction of the customer's long-term spending.

When the time came for a presentation, the data miner first presented the report that the retailer had requested at the start. Only when the retailer had reviewed and felt fully satisfied with that report did the data miner go on to show something more. And wow! The customer spending model was a great finale. The retailer became an instant fan of data mining.

You'll find no limit to the sources of inspiration available to the data miner. But a limit exists to your available time.

As you work, you must have specific goals in mind as well as a realistic plan for meeting them. The goals must be defined in business terms that suit your manager's or client's needs. Your plan is your assurance that you will produce something of value, not just something that you find interesting. Your plan is your guide for deciding which questions to address now and which questions must be set aside for later.

So focus on specific goals, refer to your plan, and don't let your project's scope expand or wander before you complete your goals. (Refer to Chapter 6 for a detailed discussion of planning for data mining.)

What if you've completed your project goals and still have time before your deadline? Fantastic! Now you have the opportunity to investigate one or more of the best new questions that have come to mind, and add a valuable extra to your final presentation.

Using Your Organization's Own Data

A data miner has nothing without data. And if you work in a large organization, you'll have hundreds, perhaps thousands, of existing data resources potentially available for data mining. Every activity generates records, and those records can become your raw material. Table 8-1 shows the variety of commonly collected data in a number of business activities.

Table 8-1	Data collected from common business activities
Business activity	*Data collected*
Research	Competitor product information experimental and test data
Manufacturing	Process data; procurement records production records inspection and test records
Marketing	Competitor marketing information and sales data campaign data marketing cost data
Sales	Sales activity sales data customer information

(continued)

Table 8-1 *(continued)*

Business activity	Data collected
Fulfillment	Packaging records shipping records shipping complaints
Customer service	Customer interaction records product and service complaints service issues
Technical support	Support requests product problem reports design and other product suggestions
Training	Staff training records customer training records certification and other credentialing records
Accounting	Bills payments audit records taxes collected and paid

That's a pretty long list, yet it's really only a tiny sample of the activities and related data that's already waiting somewhere within your business.

But knowing that data exists is not the same thing as being able to access and use it for data mining. For one thing, you'll need much more specific information about exactly what internal data is relevant to the specific business problem you're investigating. Who collects it? Who controls access? What variables (fields) are recorded, and for what range of time or activity? Where can you find documentation?

Appreciating your own data

You and your manager might choose from a number of options when selecting which project to tackle with data mining. You always have a choice of tools. But when it comes to data, you may have no choice at all: You use the data available to you or your company right now.

You may have doubts about this data. You are sure to know something about its flaws. And you may have heard about other organizations that have larger quantities of data or different types of data than your own. Nonetheless, your organization's internal data, the information collected in the course of everyday business, is your most valuable resource. It's the very best data that you can have for data mining. It is superior to all external sources in a number of ways:

- ✔ **Unique relevance:** The data pertains to your own business, with all its distinctive characteristics. It's about your own customers, your own products, your own business practices. Whatever you may discover in this data will clearly also be relevant to the business. Nobody will be able to reject your results with the *but our business is different* excuse.

- ✔ **Transparency:** You know (or you can find out) the sources of your own data. No mysteries should exist about the definitions of variables, the data collection methods, the time, the place, or the people involved.

- ✔ **Detail:** You'll have *raw data,* collected in the finest possible level of detail.

- ✔ **Range:** Your data resources cover the full scope of activity taking place in your business.

- ✔ **Competitive advantage:** Only you have your own internal data. It is not available to your current or your upcoming competitors.

- ✔ **Development potential:** You can build on your own data in ways that would not be possible with data from any outside source. If you want to integrate information from multiple sources, your data will contain the identifiers you need to do that. If you want to know more about customers, you have their names and contact information, and you can refer to other records, survey them, or even call and have a personal conversation. If you need more detailed or additional data, you may be able to change a data collection practice.

Another nice thing about your own data: You own it. Any data collection costs were covered by the business unit that generated the data in the first place. You'll pay no fees and have no licensing issues to consider when using and reusing the data. (You may face data storage and other data management issues, but that's true for any data source.)

Your own data resources will not be perfect in every way. You might discover that some data you'd like to use has not been collected, or has been discarded. You're bound to encounter some data quality problems. And, of course, internal data has limits — it tells you about your own organization, but not your competitors. Still, internal data will always be your primary and most valuable data resource.

Handling data with respect

Data mining, like any kind of data analysis or reporting, uses a lot of data, much more than most everyday business activities. When you access data and perform analysis, you must be careful to do so in ways that stay within your company's guidelines and that don't interfere with routine business processes.

Data resources can be just as precious, and just as private, as cash. Get off to the right start in data mining by treating data with respect and discovering proper practices for data management and governance that affect your work.

Failure to follow legal and good business practices for data governance can lead to serious trouble. It's important that data isn't accessed by people who should not use it, that records not be improperly changed or destroyed, and that new data you create be properly archived. Documentation is a necessity. Many legal and good business practice requirements will be relevant to your work in data mining. (See Chapter 3 to learn about teaming up with others to get guidance and help with data management.)

This may not be simple. You'll have to discover things about what data is available, how to get access, and how to handle the data properly so that you don't get in the way of others. In short, you'll have to get involved with new things and new people. And it will be worth it, because you'll get more done and broaden your own horizons as a result.

You'll have to find out new things, but you won't have to become a data governance expert. You can rely on the others in your organization who are experts in data governance and data management. Work with them constructively, and they will help you to stay within the law and to follow good data management practices.

Data miners and data governance professionals don't always play nicely together. Data miners have been known to resent controls on access to data and sometimes resort to elaborate schemes to avoid playing by the data access rules. Data governance experts don't always understand why data miners need to use so much data; they've been known to stall. Frustrating experiences in the past can affect the way that either group deals with the other.

So, as you start your career in data mining, make it a point to reach out to people in your Information Technology department. Talk with them about your data-mining work and discuss how it will benefit the organization. Ask about data governance issues that relate to your work, and show that you care about good data management. This show of respect is the way to start a positive and absolutely necessary working partnership between the data-mining and data governance teams. (Refer to Chapter 3 for more about teamwork.)

Chapter 9

Making New Data

The best data is your own data. Your own stuff is more relevant to your organization and clients than any data you can buy, and it's often richer in detail. And only you have it! The better your private data resources, the greater your information advantage over competitors. (Refer to Chapter 8 for more on the wonders of your own internal data sources.)

But what if you need data that you don't already have? Is that your cue to look for a data vendor? Maybe . . . but probably not.

When you have made the most of the data you have, your next step is to build on what you've learned by adding additional depth and detail. You want to know more about your own clients, who they are, how they behave, and how they think. And you need information that is relevant to the business problems that you want to solve. In most cases, no vendor has data that addresses those specific needs.

When you don't have the data you need and nobody offers it for sale, it's time to start collecting your own new data. That's where this chapter comes in.

Fathoming Loyalty Programs

Retailers use data mining to get clues about how to get and keep customers, and encourage them to buy more, and in more profitable ways. Data mining can also be used to improve retail business processes, reduce costs, and improve customer experience. But you can't do any of these without the appropriate data.

As a data miner in the retail sector, you'll start by investigating customer behavior in a simple and general way, and over time you'll dig deeper, gradually adding more detail. You might start by looking at what products you sell and in what quantity. Every retailer keeps those records. Then you might investigate the combinations of products sold together within individual transactions. Most retailers have that information, at least for recent transactions. (This kind of data detail is sometimes discarded by IT staff who mistakenly believe it is not needed. If that's happening in your company, sit down with your IT team and explain your needs.) The next step would be to follow individual customers over time to gain an understanding of their behavior and purchasing patterns. But many retailers have not collected and preserved the necessary data to do that.

How can retailers get the data they need to understand customer behavior beyond individual transactions? The most widely used solution is a loyalty program.

Grasping the loyalty concept

A *loyalty program* is an agreement between a business and its customers. Customers agree to allow the business to track purchases (and possibly other actions as well), and in return, the business offers rewards. Typical rewards include lower prices or a free product or service.

You may be involved in several loyalty programs as a customer right now. Airline frequent flyer programs are loyalty programs. So are wholesale club memberships, preferred shopper cards, and even coffee shop punch cards.

Every loyalty program depends on the cooperation of the customer. The customer must first opt to participate in the program, and then follow up on every transaction. In the simplest cases, the customer might carry a simple paper punch card, which the business would mark each time a purchase is made. When the customer has made some required number of purchases (perhaps 10 or 12), the card can be handed in to the business in exchange for a free item. But punch cards don't provide the kind of information you need for data mining!

More sophisticated loyalty programs provide the customer with a card resembling a credit card that can be electronically scanned. When the customer forgets his card, he may have the alternative of giving a membership number, phone number, or name to locate the proper account. These programs are important for data miners, because they allow the business to track the customer's purchasing behavior in detail. Some businesses use this type of tracking specifically to get data for analysis. But others have a different motive: Paper cards and coupons can be easy to counterfeit. So some businesses choose these computerized tracking methods primarily to protect themselves from losses due to fraud.

Smartphone applications allow customers to identify themselves and receive coupons and other offers without the need to carry membership cards. These applications are popular with shoppers who find them convenient. For the retailer, smartphone apps can provide a depth of information that isn't available through any traditional loyalty program, including real-time browsing and geographic data. Smartphone-based loyalty programs also facilitate sharing by users. It's easier to share a great promotion on social media with your phone than to pass around paper coupons, for example.

Online retailers have special advantages. Their customers usually set up accounts when making a first purchase, and provide information that can be used for tracking, such as an email address. These retailers don't necessarily promise rewards for setting up an account, yet they can collect data on transactions and on all sorts of online behaviors. They can also track visitors using weblogs and *cookies*, tracking information associated with web browsing. They know when a customer visits the website and what products the customer views, even if no purchase occurs. Users may voluntarily add additional information to their own accounts, such as product reviews, wish lists, and user profiles. Every bit of this information has value for data mining.

Your data bonanza

Here are some of the data elements that may be available to you as a data miner in the retail sector:

- ✔ Customer location
- ✔ Products purchased
- ✔ Combinations of products purchased together
- ✔ Prices paid
- ✔ List or everyday prices (often different from the price the customer paid)
- ✔ Coupon or other discount offer used
- ✔ Time that a purchase took place
- ✔ Detailed product descriptions
- ✔ Pages/products viewed
- ✔ Time on site
- ✔ Timing of site visits
- ✔ Product reviews and information sharing
- ✔ Referrals (for example, did the customer come directly to the site, or via a link from another site, or a link in an email?)
- ✔ Offers or ads that the customer viewed
- ✔ Social network details, such as people the customer knows

This information is a treasure trove for marketing! As a data miner, you could hardly dream of a more valuable data source to help a business understand what and how to sell to individuals. But be wary. Boundaries exist on the appropriate use of this personal data. Some are defined by the law, and others by public sensibilities and the preferences of the individual customer. (Refer to Chapter 3 for more on partnering with your Information Technology team to address data privacy issues.)

Putting loyalty data to work

Now that you have a loyalty program and the data it produces, what are you supposed to do with it? As a data miner, it's your role to provide decision makers with analysis that supports the business. Some executives understand loyalty programs and may request specific information, perhaps more of it than you have hours to provide. But many others don't ask.

Some executives don't trust data, some don't like it, and many don't understand it, but the most common reason why executives don't ask you for information is that they just have a lot of other things on their minds. When management isn't asking for analysis, don't sit around waiting for a call. This is a good opportunity to take a proactive role. It's more than an opportunity; it's a necessity!

Your organization may have many executives, but you must treat each one as an individual. Your company may make 101 kinds of snacks, but the person in charge of corn chips only wants to hear about corn chips. He doesn't have authority to make decisions about chocolate, crackers, or fruit rolls, and he doesn't have time to think about them, either.

Focus on something that's important to a particular decision maker. If you don't know the executive's priorities already, here's how you can figure it out. Start by getting an understanding of the executive's responsibilities. These may be defined by elements such as specific product lines or geography. The executive will have specific strategic goals, and you need to know what they are. Next, find out what metrics are most important to the executive's survival. Executive compensation, for example, is often tied to business performance metrics. When you know what metrics define the executive's pay, you'll know exactly where to focus your data-mining efforts.

Consider that you want to provide some useful analysis for the executive in charge of marketing corn chips in Canada. You've narrowed the scope a lot just by knowing these responsibilities; you have no need to consider any product lines except corn chips, or any geography except Canada. Next, look at goals. Maybe the executive has a goal to increase sales by 7 percent this year.

Here's the key: Executives already know what has happened, and they need you to show them how they can influence what happens next.

Data mining maximizes warehouse club profits

Perhaps you have shopped at one of the *warehouse clubs,* retail chain stores that offer members-only shopping in large, no-frills stores. Warehouse clubs have bare concrete floors, plain functional shelving, and limited choices of products and package sizes. Their check-out lanes don't offer bags, let alone baggers, to pack up your purchases.

Warehouse clubs set themselves apart from typical retailers by opening their doors only to shoppers who are willing to pay annual membership fees. Why create this barrier to entry? Some point out that the membership creates a bond between the shopper and the store, a motivation to return and maximize the value returned for the membership fee. And then, you have the data.

Because warehouse club shoppers must present membership cards to make a purchase, these retailers know exactly who buys what. They can track every transaction in full detail. They know the identity of the shopper, because prospective members must provide proof of identity. They know what the shopper buys. They know the time and location of each purchase. They know the prices the shopper paid and whether any special promotions were involved.

So, warehouse clubs have more accurate and complete information about their shoppers than any other physical stores. In fact, they may have better information than their online competitors.

Rich resources of consumer shopping data, as well as identity and demographic data, enable warehouse stores to mine their data and provide exceptionally high-quality information to support decision making. Mining shopper data can reveal

- **Characteristics of high-spending shoppers:** How often and when they shop, which products they purchase, and other demographic details.

- **Product affinities:** Groups of products frequently purchased together.

- **Relationships among different offerings:** Do people who come in for gas stick around to buy groceries? Do they spend more or less than others? Do they buy similar or different products? What about those who purchase gas, eyeglasses, or prescription drugs? Which transaction comes first, and does that say anything about subsequent purchasing patterns?

- **Geographic details:** Where do the shoppers live? How far do they travel to shop? How do product preferences and behavior patterns vary from region to region?

Good data-collection and data-mining practices provide warehouse stores with accurate and detailed information about shopper behavior, which they can use to make informed decisions about which products to offer in each store, what prices to charge, and other matters. They can also combine shopper data with other business data to learn about productivity, process improvement, and product quality. (Benefits extend beyond data mining when the data is used to inform customers about product recalls, or to simplify returns and other customer service matters. Certain data — like , for example, aggregate data about purchasers'

(continued)

(continued)

demographics associated with specific product categories — can even be sold to create an additional revenue stream.)

What does this mean to a warehouse club financially? The Costco warehouse club chain now has more than 70 million members and reported revenues of over $100 billion for the 2013 fiscal year. Nobody claims data mining is the only reason for that (Costco publicly emphasizes the importance of good hiring, treating employees well, and training and promoting from within), yet data mining enables Costco to build on those fundamentals based on detailed information about customer behavior and preferences, at a local and even individual level.

So don't go to the executive and explain that corn chip sales are up 4 percent so far this year. Somebody else has already done that. Instead, mine the data for clues about what actions could increase sales. Become your decision maker's data-miner hero by discovering actionable information such as

- ✔ Characteristics of customers who buy large quantities of a product
- ✔ Characteristics of customers who are increasing the amount they buy
- ✔ Growing customer segments
- ✔ Combinations of products that are often bought together
- ✔ Promotions that work better than others
- ✔ Marketing channels that are more cost-effective than others
- ✔ Shopper behavior patterns (in-store and online) that affect sales
- ✔ Unexpected factors (or combinations of factors) that influence sales

Testing, Testing . . .

Remember those science classes you took way back when? You know what scientists do when they need data for their research, don't you? They make the data they need by conducting experiments and recording the results.

You probably conducted a few experiments yourself back then. Maybe you experimented with the effects of temperature on fungus growth, or the effect of a catalyst on a chemical reaction.

Scientists like chemists, biologists, and physicists conduct controlled experiments all the time. Chemists and physicists have a lot of control over the conditions for their experiments. It's harder for biologists, and harder still for anyone who does research on people, to have perfect control over an experiment.

But lucky for us, we data miners don't demand perfection. Sometimes we take data that we already have and that wasn't collected under controlled conditions, and we analyze it like experimental data. If we discover something interesting, we try the same approach with another sample of data, or new data, and see whether we get consistent results.

When you don't have appropriate data to address a particular question, or you want to get some fresher or better data than what you have, you can still do what you did in school: conduct an experiment.

Experimenting in direct marketing

When you think of an experiment, you may imagine a person wearing a white lab coat and goggles who is peering at a test tube full of some mysterious substance. This image, and the absence of lab coats, goggles, and test tubes in your workplace, may lead you to believe that experiments are something done by other people in other places, people who are different from you. But experiments are conducted every day by people who don't fit that image at all, people who are nearer to you than you may realize.

Perhaps the most common application for experiments, legitimate controlled experiments much like the ones that scientists use, is *direct marketing.* When you see an ad on television, on a billboard, or in a magazine, that's *mass marketing,* delivering a broad message to a broad audience, without reaching out to specific individuals or even knowing who they are. Direct marketing involves contacting individual people. When you get a text or an email from a retailer, that's direct marketing. Traditional mail order catalogs, phone calls from charities, and campaign letters from political candidates are all forms of direct marketing. Successful direct marketers are aggressive experimenters. They may call their experiments *A/B tests, split tests,* or just plain *tests,* but these are simply industry terminology for controlled experiments.

Here's a simple and common example of a direct marketing test:

An online retailer sends emails to follow up with customers who have viewed a specific product but haven't purchased it after 24 hours. Would changes to the email message improve the response? Perhaps a different subject line would lead more customers to open the message.

This theory can be tested by taking a sample of customers, separating the sample into two groups that are as similar as possible, and sending one group the message that's already in use, while the other group gets a test message that is identical, except for the subject line. Analysis of the response to each message reveals whether any difference existed in the performance of the two subject lines, and if so, which worked better and by how much.

Spying test opportunities

A lot of everyday business activity in commerce, nonprofits, and some government work amounts to direct marketing. If you are calling upon specific individuals (even if there are millions of them) to take specific actions, you're doing direct marketing. Direct marketing is not only for selling but also for uses like these:

- Fundraising
- Getting out the vote
- Separating recyclables from other trash
- Promoting public health
- Promoting the use of public services
- Removing inefficient appliances from the power grid
- Collecting taxes

Whenever you have a list of people and an action you want them to take, think about testing. Any aspect of your direct marketing that you can change and control is testable. Common examples of things you can test include

- **Copy:** Short versus long, messaging, or variations in wording
- **Layout:** Images, white space, fonts
- **Envelope:** Colors, shape, paper stock
- **Printing:** Color, text, images
- **Enclosures:** Gifts (such as address labels, greeting cards, cash, or other items of value), return envelopes, thank-you notes, giving/purchasing history
- **Subject lines:** Topic, wording, use of recipient name
- **Offer:** Price, packaging, shipping

Testing online

Online environments present data miners with a unique mix of challenges and advantages for data collection and analysis.

Here's the bad news. Web data formats can be difficult to import and manipulate in data-mining applications. Systems that serve web pages are often poorly integrated with sales tracking systems, making it hard to identify connections between the visitor's experience and the resulting actions. Web designers and webmasters don't always have testing in mind when they develop designs or select web technology. Even if no big technical challenges exist, people can be reluctant to open web platforms for experimentation.

There's good news, too. Special tools are available that greatly simplify the process of serving web pages properly for testing, and provide analysis capabilities as well. So, no matter what tools you generally use for data mining, consider using a specialty tool for web page testing. (You can find information about these by searching for terms such as *A/B testing tool, multivariate testing tool,* and *split testing tool.*)

Just one thing: To test online, you first must have cooperation with the people responsible for your organization's website. If you don't have that now, it's time to open that discussion.

Tools designed for data mining are not necessarily ideal for A/B testing of email or web pages, and you may encounter challenges integrating the two. But you may be able to sidestep those issues altogether. Many email service providers offer built-in A/B testing capability. If you use any of the major email services, you probably have this available right now. For web design testing tools, use your favorite search engine and the keywords *A/B testing* or *multivariate testing.*

Microtargeting to Win Elections

Most political campaigns depend on consultants to provide voter research, or else get by with very informal assessments of voter attitudes and interest in voting for a particular candidate (or voting at all). But in recent years, certain political campaigns, including both candidate and issue campaigns, have begun to use *microtargeting,* organized programs of survey research and message testing, to develop and deliver personalized campaign messaging tailored to individual voters.

Treating voters as individuals

Think of the difference between shopping at a mall and shopping on your favorite online store. At the mall, everyone sees the same signs, the same flyers, the same items on display. The shopper has access to everything that's available but has to make the effort to discover the most appropriate items. Your favorite online store doesn't show the same ads and products to everyone. It uses your past history to tailor the presentation. In the online store, you see ads that were selected specifically for you based on factors such as the items you've purchased before, the products you've looked at, and the products purchased by others whose buying or browsing history resembles yours. And that online store tests every element of the presentation (offer, text, images, layout, and more) to find out what works best.

A typical political campaign might use a program of political polling to identify key messages for voters as a whole, or large segments of voters, such as
women, seniors, or youth. Microtargeting examines each voter as an individual and, like the online store, uses information about individuals to personal-
ize the campaign.

Looking at an example

Consider that two candidates, Fred Mertz and Lucy McGillicuddy, are running
for office. Fred will use traditional campaign techniques. Lucy's campaign will
use microtargeting. How will the two campaigns differ?

Both campaigns will make use of publicly available voter records. These
records provide each candidate with a list of registered voters, addresses,
and voting history. The records don't reveal how individuals vote! The ballot
itself is always secret. But they do tell if and when someone has voted, and
may include details such as party affiliation (some regions require this information for voting in primary elections).

Even Fred, the traditionalist, understands that people are not all identical.
But he has little or no information about the attitudes of individuals. So, he'll
mail the same brochures to everyone in the district and use the same few
messages in all his advertising. He'll get out to shake hands in every neighborhood. Although he understands that people in different neighborhoods
have differing concerns, he'll have only his intuition to guide him in speaking
with individuals. At best, he'll be making educated guesses about what to say
to each person.

Enhancing voter data

How will Lucy's microtargeted campaign be different? For her, the public
voter records are only the heart of the data resources. Lucy's voter database
will include lots of information that Fred's does not, such as

- Demographics
- Occupation
- Political and charitable contribution history
- Memberships
- Home, auto, and boat ownership status
- Permits and licenses
- Magazine subscriptions
- Political volunteer history and other indicators of political views

How does Lucy get all this information? Her political party, private sources, and her own team enhance the voter database with additional information about each individual voter. Some of this information is available through public records and some can be purchased from commercial data vendors, but the most valuable information for a political campaign comes from one-on-one contact with prospective voters.

Gaining an information advantage

Assembling Lucy's voter database involves a lot of work! Even a candidate who has the money and know-how to obtain data from disparate sources and match it to individual voters would still need a lot of patience and labor to integrate data sources. Few campaigns have such resources. Fortunately for Lucy, her party has already developed an enhanced voter database that she can use as a starting point. So she starts her campaign with a significant information advantage over Fred. But plenty of data gathering is still ahead for the microtargeted campaign.

What about Fred? Why isn't his party providing data to help his campaign? Major political parties in the United States, Canada, and the United Kingdom now all have voter databases for their own candidates, so many candidates could launch campaigns with data resources similar to Lucy's. If Fred isn't doing this, perhaps he's unaware of what his party offers, doesn't know how to use it, or just doesn't appreciate the value of the data.

Developing your own test data

Although Lucy now knows a lot about the voters, she doesn't yet have the information that she needs to tailor messages to individual voters. To get that, Lucy and her campaign team must conduct an ongoing program of developing and testing specific messages.

First, her team will identify some major voter segments using the enhanced database. Perhaps they have data from some preliminary surveys that they will use to divide voters into three groups to start: firm Fred Mertz supporters, firm Lucy McGillicuddy supporters, and undecided (or persuadable) voters. Within the undecided voters, they might next choose a narrower segment, such as Latina working mothers.

They could then brainstorm about the issues and messages that might appeal to Latina working mothers. The marketing team would develop some sample scripts, each focusing on one specific issue and message. The messages must be consistent with the candidate's position on the issue, but plenty of options will exist for investigating which issues to highlight and which messages are most persuasive.

The only way to know what works is to test. In a typical test scenario, volunteers would be given lists of voters to call and alternate scripts to use, such as one focusing on public schools and another on health clinics. The volunteers would read from the script and also ask questions about the voter's likelihood to vote for Lucy. At the end of the test, Lucy's campaign will have new data, the survey responses gathered during these test calls.

Lucy's campaign now has unique survey data. Using this data, Lucy's campaign now discovers which of the test messages was most persuasive to a specific group of voters.

The survey may uncover details that were not specifically part of the test. Voters may reveal something unexpected in their comments. Some of this group might mention that they are not so concerned about public schools because they send their children to parochial schools. That information helps the candidate to understand why certain messages work better than others. It also hints at the opportunity to get even deeper in understanding individuals. The next survey might compare Latina working mothers whose children go to public schools with Latina working mothers whose children go to parochial or other private schools.

Taking discoveries on the campaign trail

Now that Lucy knows something about a message that appeals to Latina working mothers, she and her volunteers are going to use that information in everything from Lucy's speeches to flyers to talking points for volunteers canvassing neighborhoods.

Lucy's team will conduct surveys like this, on the phone, by email, and face to face, throughout the campaign. Her database will be augmented on an ongoing basis with new voter data and new tests. As the depth of Lucy's information grows, she and her volunteers will become better equipped with each passing day to present individual voters with messages that are relevant and appealing to that specific voter.

Sounds like a lot of work! And it is a lot of work. A serious microtargeting campaign conducts surveys and tests daily, and uses the results to inform the actions of the candidate, campaign staff, and volunteers each day as the campaign progresses.

A billion-dollar A/B testing success story

How much value can test data deliver to your organization? It could be worth a billion dollars, or something even more precious.

The 2012 United States presidential election was more expensive than any previous election. Campaign budgets had been rising over the decades, and this election stood to be contentious: In 2008, the presidency had shifted from Republican to Democratic control, while in 2010, Republicans had increased their numbers in Congress.

The reelection campaign of incumbent U.S. President Barack Obama set an unprecedented fundraising goal: $1 billion.

Obama's previous campaigns were known for certain strengths: attracting new voters, engaging donors and volunteers who had not previously been politically active, bringing in small contributions from many people, and effectively mixing traditional campaign methods like door-to-door visits with new tactics in social media.

To meet its fundraising goal, the Obama campaign would build on existing strengths in attracting new and small donors through an aggressive program of email solicitation. In other words, they used a modern direct marketing campaign. And the campaign maximized the value of its email solicitations with the help of a technique that had been a favorite of direct marketers for nearly a century: A/B testing.

Just as a retailer tests subject lines, copy, offer, and other aspects of each ad, Obama's campaign team tested the elements of its fundraising emails. They found that more messages meant more money, that copy mattered, and that a lot of people could not resist opening a message from Barack Obama with the simple subject line "Hey."

In the end, the campaign raised $1.1 billion, nicely exceeding its already unprecedented goal. It coupled exceptional fundraising with a microtargeted political campaign and novel use of analytics to maximize the impact of its ad spending. And, in case you haven't heard, Obama was reelected in 2012.

Analytics cannot buy anyone a presidency, but they can go a long way in helping any organization to make the most of its resources.

Surveying the Public Landscape

Surveys may be the most common and familiar approach for obtaining your own unique data from people. Anybody can write a few questions, present them to some people, and there you have it . . . a survey. Good surveys, though, require thought and effort.

Eliciting information with surveys

In survey research, people are asked to answer questions, usually about themselves. Typical survey questions are about

- ✔ **Demographics:** Age, gender, occupation
- ✔ **Behavior:** Purchasing or using specific products, spending patterns, participating in social or athletic activities
- ✔ **Intentions:** Vote or not vote, candidate A or B, hire fewer or more new staff members next year
- ✔ **Attitudes:** Often concerning current political or social issues

If the data that you want has to do with people's feelings or actions that they may take in the future, a survey may be your only option for getting data. But surveys are also used for getting information that is simply easier to obtain by survey than other options. For example, a lot of information exists about spending contained within credit card records, but getting access to those records through either the individual account holder or banks is all but impossible (and not without reason). But you can ask people how much they spent on your product (or a competitor's or a specific class of products) last year, or how much they intend to spend next year, and many people will tell you.

Good survey research offers you the advantages of

- ✔ **Flexibility:** You pose questions about any topic you choose. So you can always get information that is relevant, even for topics where no other data sources are available to you.
- ✔ **Speed:** Surveys are quick to set up and conduct, so your data will be up to date.
- ✔ **Depth:** Use surveys to fill in the information gaps that other data sources leave open.
- ✔ **Privacy:** You're not obliged to share the results with anyone. You'll have an information edge over competitors.

But it's not as simple as jotting down a few questions and asking a few people to answer. Questions must be written properly to be understood and obtain responses that are accurate and relevant for your needs. And you must get responses from people who are representative of those you aim to understand.

Using surveys

Surveys are useful for collecting data about almost any aspect of human life. You can only ignore surveys if your profession has nothing to do with people, like say, astrophysics. Then again, astrophysicists need people to fund their research and want people to visit planetariums, so they might need surveys, too! Here are examples of the varied uses of surveys:

- ✔ **Government:** Assess the economic, physical, and mental state of people and businesses to support government activity. Nearly 200 national statistical agencies exist around the world, all using survey research to better understand their people. States, counties, and cities conduct local surveys for the same purposes.

- ✔ **Psychology:** Study mental health and the working of the human mind.

- ✔ **Sociology and political science:** Understand public attitudes regarding current issues.

- ✔ **Public health:** Find out how people care for themselves, what choices they make regarding health options, and why.

- ✔ **Marketing and advertising:** Measure brand awareness, product preferences, and other factors that impact purchasing behavior.

- ✔ **Advocacy and campaign management:** Identify characteristics of supporters and detractors, and test campaign messaging options.

- ✔ **Media:** Obtain information about public attitudes to include in reports and predict election outcomes.

- ✔ **Customer service:** Assess customer satisfaction, and identify problems and possible solutions.

Developing questions

A good survey question should be

- ✔ **Specific:** Deal with just one idea.

- ✔ **Narrow:** Limited to a specific time frame, location, or whatever scope is appropriate for your needs.

- ✔ **Neutral:** The wording should not lead the respondent to an answer.

- ✔ **Clear:** Easily understood by anyone who might take the survey.

Often, it makes sense to offer options for responses. Response options should be

- ✔ **Simple:** So that all respondents can understand them.

- ✔ **Consistent:** All response options should have the same structure.

- ✔ **Complete:** The full range of options must be covered.

- ✔ **Distinct:** Options must not overlap.

These last two items, covering all possibilities and not overlapping, are often neglected. The result is confusion and frustration for respondents, and flawed data for you. So, put care into developing your survey questionnaires.

Conducting surveys

Now that you've developed your survey questions and assembled them into a questionnaire, you can reach out to people for answers. You will have to select one or more channels for reaching your respondents:

- ✔ **Face to face:** An interviewer meets personally with the respondent, asks questions, and records responses. This method is often used for complex surveys, such as medical surveys or surveys where respondents are reluctant to respond, as with some government surveys.

- ✔ **Paper or kiosk:** A respondent is given a form (or simply picks up a form left in a convenient spot) or is directed to an electronic kiosk to take the survey. Often used for customer service surveys.

- ✔ **Mail:** The survey is mailed to the respondent, who fills it out and returns it by mail.

- ✔ **Telephone:** An interviewer calls the respondent, asks the questions, and records the responses.

- ✔ **Internet:** Respondents are recruited and take the survey online.

Your choice among these options depends on many factors. Your desired respondents may prefer some channels over others. Some cost more than others: A face-to-face interview in the respondent's home costs far more than presenting the same questions online. And the time required to complete your survey varies with the way that you conduct it.

Recognizing limitations

Despite the many desirable aspects of survey research, you also find limitations. It's difficult to get good data when the subjects are people, no matter how you go about it. Even scientific researchers, who make every effort to conduct controlled studies, cannot control experimental conditions with human subjects as they do with lab animals.

Reaching the right respondents for your survey isn't always easy. Some people are hard to reach; others are reluctant to participate. People who are available and willing to respond might or might not have the same behavior and attitudes as those who are not.

After you have a satisfactory pool of respondents, don't think that your troubles are over. You may not get answers to all your questions. People don't always know the answers. A question that seems simple to you may not seem simple to the respondent. Perhaps you've asked about the respondent's income. Did you mean that one person's income or the household's? Would that include the children's income? Nontaxable income as well as taxable?

What about losses? What if the income varies? The respondent might wonder whether the right answer would be the level of income she's had recently, expects soon, or typically earns, and those might be three different things.

Survey researchers sometimes seem to forget that respondents are less interested in the survey topic than they are. You may be very interested in ketchup, ketchup purchasing habits, ketchup flavor and texture preferences, and all things ketchup, but most people aren't. So even a willing respondent may be unable to answer all your in-depth ketchup questions. He may buy ketchup, but not recall when or how often, or what price he paid or what brand he bought, let alone how that brand compares in flavor and texture with each of the major competing ketchup brands. So don't kid yourself about the level of depth you can expect in survey responses.

And then the worst survey problem of all is this: not asking the right questions. You can ask every question you can think of and still miss the point. The most important issue in a customer's (or patient's, constituent's, or member's) mind could be an issue that you just haven't given any thought to. That's why many surveys end with an open-ended question, such as "Is there anything else we can do to improve your experience?" While it is a good idea to ask such questions, you have no guarantee that you'll get all the information you need.

Bringing in help

You are busy becoming a data miner. If you're like most data miners, that means that you are already working at your profession, and you are finding out about data mining to help you do your work better. You're busy! You have limits to the time and energy that you can put into doing survey research to get the data you need. Do the simple stuff on your own if you like, but when it gets tough, bring in expert help.

Survey research firms come in large and small sizes, general-purpose and niche types, and local to international. The names and details are always changing, but you'll always be on the right track if you look to the survey research industry's professional societies for a good starting point. Here are a few of the major industry associations:

- ✔ **American Association for Public Opinion Research** (www.aapor.org) focuses on informing policy makers.

- ✔ **American Marketing Association** (www.marketingpower.com) covers a wide spectrum of marketing interests.

- ✔ **Advertising Research Foundation** (www.thearf.org) members include academics as well as advertising professionals interested in the impact of advertising and media.

- **Marketing Research Association** (www.mra-net.org) members provide the research used by manufacturers, retailers, and others to make marketing decisions.

- **European Society for Opinion and Marketing Research** (www.esomar.org) is also an organization of professional researchers, and more international than Marketing Research Association.

Getting into the Field

You don't have some of the data, and you can't download, buy, or get it by asking for it. Sometimes, the only way to get the data you need is to get out into the world, observe, and measure. Or get someone to do that for you.

Going where no data miner has gone before

Now that you are a data miner, you're also a primary researcher. Sounds more scientific, doesn't it? Your research is primary because you will begin from raw (basic, unprocessed) data and analyze it to add something new to the world's knowledge.

You'll probably also integrate some secondary research into your work. In other words, you'll also make use of analyses that you or someone else did earlier. You might review internal documents to get up to date on what's been done in your own organization or visit a library to read research papers. You might obtain data that isn't in its raw state but that has already been subjected to some processing analysis. For example, when you use recent census data, you don't get information about individuals, but rather aggregate data that describes groups of people within some geographic region. Using that kind of data is also a form of secondary research.

In fact, you should never go out to collect new data by any means until you've looked into your options — not just for getting raw data, but also for taking advantage of any analysis of your subject that has already been done.

 Primary research is what you do when nobody else has already done the work to develop the information you need. Make a habit of reviewing internal and external sources before you start any project so that you won't end up wasting resources re-creating information that already exists.

Doing more than asking

It's remarkable how much data you can get by asking for it. Loyalty programs are based on asking participants for their data, and millions of people around the world agree to participate. Surveys are nothing more than asking people for data, and you'd have a hard time finding any adult who hasn't responded to at least one survey. And these are valuable approaches to primary research. But some types of data still exist that you either can't get or where you would not get good data quality just by asking for the information.

Paco Underhill, author of *Why We Buy: The Science of Shopping* (published by Simon & Schuster), described his research into customer behavior within stores. He could have asked people about their shopping paths or the reasons why they lingered in or avoided particular spots. But if you were asked, on entering a store, what path you were about to take, how well do you think you could foresee that? If you were asked the same question on departing, would you be able to remember? How much patience would you have for thinking it over and explaining the details? Underhill and his colleagues decided not to ask shoppers about their behavior, but to observe it directly, using video and other methods. The *San Francisco Chronicle* declared him "a Sherlock Holmes for retailers."

Software designers need to know how users view their designs. They may want to know where users focus their attention on a page, whether they are able to perform tasks in the intended manner, and how long it takes them to do things. The designers could ask, but the users would probably have a hard time giving really effective feedback on these details. So software designers watch people using their software. They may do this directly by setting up stations where they can watch the users live and in person. Or they may use remote options based on the user's keystrokes or video recording through web cameras.

If your government agency wants to know where in the world bomb-making, military training, or some other suspicious activity might be going on, you certainly won't get the information by phoning all the world's heads of government and asking for it. That's why spies love satellites!

You may not need anything as fancy as a satellite to get the data you need, but you might benefit from down-to-earth data collection techniques like these:

- Want to know where the shoppers at your mall have come from? Walk the parking lot and note the states on the license plates.
- Don't believe the foot traffic estimates from your local chamber of commerce? Stand on the street and count the passersby.
- Aspire to make clothes that fit women better? Get out the measuring tape . . . please!

Getting a fresh angle on your problem

When you've examined and analyzed all the data that you can get, but still can't solve a problem, maybe it's time to get out of your office and seek inspiration from others. A group of surgical nurses did just that and made a discovery that led to a 50 percent increase in productivity for their facility, with no sacrifice in quality.

These nurses were no strangers to data. They understood and used accepted statistical methods for quality improvement in healthcare. But they were also willing to do something that many people would not have done: They left the hospital and made a field trip to observe outstanding professionals in a very different industry.

They went to an auto race track to watch a pit crew in action.

Pit crews work very quickly and yet very well. Even a single wasted second can mean the difference between a driver winning or losing a race. But quality cannot be sacrificed for speed, because poor-quality work could lead to the driver's death.

Pit crews practice. Just as musicians play the scales and ballerinas exercise at the barre, pit crews practice tasks over and over to develop speed and skill. The nurses did their jobs, but they had never practiced. They decided to give it a try.

Practicing enabled the nursing team to do their work more quickly, yet just as well. The capacity of their facility rose from two procedures per day to three per day as a result. Patients got shorter wait times for surgery, the hospital got more revenue, and the nurses got great performance reviews, all because the nurses opened their minds and tested a fresh approach to their work.

One Challenge, Many Approaches

Sometimes obstacles exist to obtaining the data that you want to address a particular business issue. You may face technical challenges, legal issues, or high costs. When you're up against a big obstacle, try not to invest a lot of time trying to overcome it. Instead, look for alternative (and easier) ways to solve your problem.

Perhaps you want to know how much money your customers make, but you can't get access to that data. Maybe it exists but you can't get permission to use it, maybe company policy forbids asking that question on a survey, or maybe the customers just won't tell. Don't worry about the reasons; just look for another angle.

You might be able to estimate income based on census data or purchase estimates from a data vendor. Better yet, you might reconsider whether income is really such a valuable bit of data. What do you really want to know?

Maybe you're not as interested in what people make as what they spend. Asking people how much money they made last year is a touchy question; asking how much they spent on dish soap is not.

Any data-mining project can be approached in more than one way. Most things can be measured in many ways. If your project is stalling, use your best creative thinking to consider alternatives about the kind of data that you can use and the ways that you might obtain it. But your methods don't have to be original, so pay attention to the ways that others get data, and not just other data miners. Scientists, marketers, spies — everybody gathers data, so you could discover a new approach from anybody.

Consider the following case: Researchers at Ansell (a manufacturer of health-care products), Indiana University, and Turkey's Ministry of Health were each faced with the same data challenge. Each team of researchers had a different goal — including improving product design, understanding body image issues, and protecting public health, all important matters — but no dependable source existed for the data they needed. Each team then set out to create new data, and each went about it in a different way.

What were they looking for? Each of these organizations needed measurements of the human penis.

You may never need data that is as elusive, as emotionally charged, or as awkward to measure as this. And that's the point. If you find many good ways to get *this* data, many good ways exist to get the data that you need, too.

Here's how they did it:

- ✔ **Ansell:** As the manufacturer of Lifestyles condoms, Ansell's goal was to ensure that its products would be both functional and comfortable. Ansell wanted measurements made by medical staff for accuracy. The staff set up private tents outside a nightclub and recruited volunteers, who were measured by medical personnel. (Lesson learned: This might not be such a great approach. Many of the men were not able to do what had to be done for measurement. One wonders how much they had to drink in the nightclub, and whether they felt comfortable doing this in a tent.)

- ✔ **Indiana University:** The team at the Center for Sexual Health Promotion partnered with Church and Dwight, makers of Trojan condoms, so they were also interested in condom fit. But in this case, a larger study was involved. The study covered a variety of issues, including contraceptive and disease prevention practices as well as body image. This team believed that men could self-report honestly and accurately, and offered an incentive to do so — a custom-fit condom.

✔ **Ministry of Health, Turkey:** This study focused on body image and concerns that men may be seeking unneeded medical interventions. The study was conducted under the supervision of a hospital review board, and subjects were screened to exclude those with certain medical issues. All measurements were made by the same medical professional (for consistency) in a controlled environment (temperature, lighting, and so on) using a technique developed for earlier studies by a U.S.-based urologist and medical researcher. These subjects were offered the option of watching videos to help prepare for measurement.

Each of these teams collected data in the best way it could identify for its own specific needs. You may observe that there are imperfections and limitations in the datasets that each has collected. Yet the fact that each team has clearly defined and documented its measurement practices and taken significant steps to ensure consistency in measurement means the quality and usability of these datasets is better than many that you will encounter in business environments.

Other teams around the world are also gathering similar data. And they have found even more ways to approach the problem. Some are employing professionals to do the measuring, but they are not medical professionals. While the researchers in Turkey offered videos, some of their counterparts in the United States use pharmaceuticals.

If multiple ways of getting data like this exist, multiple ways of getting data to meet your needs are available, too! Think creatively, look to others for ideas, and make peace with imperfection. Data mining is all about getting useful information now, not perfect information at some time in the future.

Chapter 10

Ferreting Out Public Data Sources

*W*hen you need data that you don't already own, look for public sources first. Not only are these sources numerous and diverse, but in many cases, no commercial entity would be able to independently gather the same information. And public data is usually available free or at low cost.

Looking Over the Lay of the Land

Public data is primarily government data. Government agencies collect and share data about people, activities, and resources. In the U.S., you have the right to request information from any part of the federal government (though not all parts are equally responsive). Every state, county, and city collects and maintains data that may be available to you. Countries around the world have their own statistical agencies, as do a number of intergovernmental organizations.

Public data is a by-product of everyday government work; no government collects data for the purpose of sharing it with data miners. Obtaining relevant government data in a form you can use isn't always easy. You can develop a good sense of what to expect if you make an effort to understand why and how governments collect and share data:

▶ **Why governments collect data:** Every business keeps records of its activity, such as contracts, purchases, and sales; payments to employees and suppliers; and interactions with customers. These records are needed to support everyday business, because what we do today depends on what we did and agreed on yesterday, and keeping records ensures that we will have clear information about past activity when we need it. Governments have the same needs, so governments also keep records of their activities. In fact, record-keeping may be even more important in government than in industry, because every constituent has an interest in what the government does (or does not do). This type of data is also known as transactional data, and most government data is of this type.

Data miners (and other sorts of data analysts) are often more interested in data about people: who they are, what they do, and how they live. With that kind of data, you can discover behavior patterns and other aspects of human life that are relevant to your own business goals. Governments collect that kind of data too, because they also need to know about their constituents, how they live, and their needs for government services.

Perhaps you recall filling out a census survey form in the past. Your responses become government data. The census is only one of many surveys that the government uses to obtain data for analysis. This type of data is also known as statistical data. The purpose of these surveys, and other government research, is to provide data that government staff can analyze to provide information for lawmakers and other officials. Statistical data is a relatively small part of all government data, but it's important.

✔ **Why governments share data:** Governments sometimes share data to get a job done. If an initiative exists to encourage exercise, discussing survey data about current exercise patterns might help. They also share data to persuade. If you want funding to build a bridge, that case is more persuasive if you share data that indicates a need for a bridge, competitive costs for construction, and so on. And finally, governments share data because they must. Constituents expect it, and the law requires it.

Not every bit of government data is available to the public. Some information is protected for security reasons, and some is kept secret to protect the privacy of citizens. When you respond to the census, your individual responses are not shared, but *aggregates,* information about groups of people, become public. (So, an individual's income is private, but the average income for a community is public.)

Exploring Public Data Sources

Public data resources are vast, but they have been tailored for specific government purposes, not your needs. You face certain challenges when you look to public sources for the data you need, so be prepared. Before you begin your search, make sure you first

✔ **Define your needs:** You'll need to know specifically what data you need, and in what form. You must be prepared to explain this, in writing or verbally, in the course of your search.

✔ **Find the right source:** You'll familiarize yourself with government agencies and find out which ones are likely sources for the data that you require.

✔ **Know how to obtain the data:** Sometimes getting the data you need will be simple; you'll just download it or obtain a report. But if the data you need is not already distributed through such simple channels, getting it can involve a complex and slow process.

Hundreds of governments and quasi-governmental organizations around the world collect, analyze, and share data. It may be shared as machine-readable data in files or via an application programming interface (API); it may be found in written reports, complete with sophisticated analysis; and it may even show up in small bits found in news reports.

Don't think of data only as fields and cases that you can work with in your data analysis software. Any form of data, raw or analyzed, may be useful to help you improve your understanding of the business issues that you face. You may even find that some agency or organization has already explored certain issues that affect you, collected data, analyzed it, and made a report available. If so, take advantage of what's already been done, discover, and move on to the next stage.

Data or statistics?

In this book, and in everyday situations, I talk about getting and using data. But, strictly speaking, that's not always the proper term. Often, what I'm really using are *statistics*. Most of the time, you can use any term you like and it won't matter, but at times, you'll need to know the difference.

Perhaps you measure the height of each child in a school. The individual measurements are data. And because they are just what you've measured and haven't been processed in any way, those measurements may also be called *raw data*.

You might calculate the average height of all the students in a classroom, or all students in

the school; those averages (calculated values) are statistics. But people still call them data. And most of the time, that's not going to cause any confusion.

But maybe you're looking over a government agency website. You may see that the agency shares statistics. But it doesn't seem to share data. Or you may get into a conversation with an agency staff member and find yourself in a quibble over whether the agency releases data. The agency's staff may be much stricter than you in its choice of words. So remember that the proper term for what you want may be statistics, not data.

United States federal government

The U.S. government includes over 100 statistical agencies, agencies with a primary purpose of collecting and analyzing data for some government use. The result is a vast resource of professionally collected, managed, and analyzed data, much of which is available to you.

This section explains the purpose and data offerings of some major federal statistical agencies. It will also introduce you to Data.gov, a portal that helps you locate government data sources to match your needs.

Dozens of additional statistical agencies are not described individually here. You can find a list of them, with links and descriptions of the agencies and the kinds of data provided, at FedStats.gov, the portal to federal statistical agencies. FedStats (www.fedstats.gov) lets you find an agency by name or subject, find information by geography, and even find links to kids' pages on agency websites.

The federal data portal: Data.gov

If you're looking for data that the federal government might have, but you aren't sure which agency is involved, start your search on the federal data portal www.data.gov. There you will find a searchable catalog of data from all federal agencies. You can search for datasets by keywords and get information about what's available, the source for each dataset, the formats available, and where to find the data.

The data portal isn't a source for data, just information about what data is available and where to get it. And the portal doesn't cover every bit of government data available. So, if you find something that's useful to you on Data.gov, follow up by investigating the website of the agency that actually provides that data to search for additional information and data. If you need something you can't find, contact the agency directly. You may be able to speak with someone who can help you locate what you need, or at least find out why the data you want is unavailable.

While nothing is new about public data, the portal facilitates certain new initiatives. All newly generated federal government data is required to be made publicly available in open, machine-readable formats, while maintaining privacy and security. The key concept here is machine readability, providing data in formats that are appropriate for computing use, especially use in developing applications.

Top-ten hits on America's data portal

Over 100,000 datasets are available through the federal data portal. Of course, some are more widely used than others. A look at a few of the most popular examples will give you a sense of the variety of information that's available to you.

Don't assume that the most popular sources on Data.gov are necessarily the most popular overall. Many people obtain data directly from the agencies that produce it, or indirectly through third parties, such as news reports and data vendors.

So what's hot? Here's a list of the ten most popular datasets on Data.gov (at the time this was written).

Name	Source	Format	Description
Climate Data Online (CDO)	National Oceanic and Atmospheric Administration, Department of Commerce	HTML	Provides access to climate data products through a simple, searchable online web-mapping service.
Consumer Complaint Database	Consumer Financial Protection Bureau	CSV, JSON, XML	Complaints received about financial products and services.
NOAA National Weather Service - National Mosaic of Weather Radar	National Oceanic and Atmospheric Administration, Department of Commerce	N/A	National Weather Service's radar imagery allows interactivity with the display.
Federal Student Loan Program Data	Federal Student Aid, Department of Education	XLS	Quarterly recipient and disbursement information for the Direct Loan and Federal Family Education Loan Programs by postsecondary school.

(continued)

(continued)

Name	Source	Format	Description
State Education Data Profiles	National Center for Education Statistics, Department of Education	XLS	Searchable information in elementary/secondary education, postsecondary education, and selected demographics for all states in the United States.
Social Media Monitoring Metrics	U.S. Department of Health & Human Services	CSV, JSON, XML, RDF, XLS, XLSX	Basic social media metrics aggregated on a weekly basis. Metrics include SAMHSA's Facebook fans, comments, likes, and posts and Twitter followers and mentions.
Food Access Research Atlas	Department of Agriculture	HTML, JSON, XLS	A spatial overview of food access indicators for low-income and other census tracts.
U.S. International Trade in Goods and Services	U.S. Census Bureau, Department of Commerce	XLS, TXT	Monthly U.S. trade data, including imports, exports, and balance of payments for goods and services.
Campus Security Data	Office of Postsecondary Education, Department of Education	CSV, XLS	Rapid customized reports for public inquiries relating to campus crime data.
State Dropout and Completion Data	National Center for Education Statistics, Department of Education	CSV/TXT, SAS, XLS	The number of dropouts from each grade 9–12 and the relevant event dropout rates.

Agencies are also required to

- ✔ **Create a single agency data inventory:** They must document and track data assets as they do equipment, furniture, and other assets.

- ✔ **Publish a public data listing:** The listing must be posted on the agency's web pages, including all data assets that are public or that could be made public.

- ✔ **Develop new public feedback mechanisms:** They must provide ways for the public to provide feedback related to data-sharing priorities.

The federal data portal also allows local governments to add their datasets to the portal's catalog. This is not mandatory and not many cities are ready to participate, but you may come across some local data in the catalog, and you can expect to see more in the future.

While this portal can lead you to a large and diverse range of data, none of it was created specifically for data-mining use. All of it was originally collected for government use; sharing with the public is secondary. Privacy and security requirements prevent some data from being made public, and some data can only be shared in aggregate form. (For example, an individual's income may be private, while the average income of a group of people is public.) And open data initiatives are driven by programmers, not data miners, so the data may not be organized or formatted as you prefer.

The data portal is a starting point, not a final destination, in your search for data. Not all government datasets are included in the catalog, and some that are may not be tagged with the keywords that you choose for your search. But Data.gov can guide you to many useful datasets and provide leads to agencies that may have more to offer. You may even discover some unexpected gems to enhance your data-mining work.

Bureau of Economic Analysis

The Bureau of Economic Analysis (BEA) (www.bea.gov) is a part of the United States Department of Commerce. The Commerce Department's job is to "help make American businesses more innovative at home and more competitive abroad." The Department is made up of 12 agencies that deal with matters as diverse as weather, communications, and patents. It's the BEA's job to "promote a better understanding of the U.S. economy by providing the most timely, relevant, and accurate economic accounts data in an objective and cost-effective manner."

BEA gathers economic data, conducts research and analysis, and makes the results available to the public. It provides information on matters such as economic growth, relationships among industries, and the nation's position in the world economy. It produces information on a national, international, and regional basis, and also for specific industries.

Here are some of the widely used types of data available through BEA:

- Balance of payments
- Foreign direct investment
- Gross domestic product (GDP)
- Gross domestic product by state
- Industry data
- International trade
- National income and product accounts (NIPAs)
- Personal income
- Personal income by state
- Gross domestic product by metropolitan area
- Gross domestic product by industry
- Personal income by county and metropolitan area

Bureau of Justice Statistics

The Bureau of Justice Statistics (BJS) (www.bjs.gov) is part of the Office of Justice Programs in the U.S. Department of Justice. The Justice Department's job is to "enforce the law and defend the interests of the United States according to the law; to ensure public safety against threats foreign and domestic; to provide federal leadership in preventing and controlling crime; to seek just punishment for those guilty of unlawful behavior; and to ensure fair and impartial administration of justice for all Americans." That's a lot! To do all that, the Justice Department has dozens of agencies, with wide-ranging responsibilities including antitrust matters; alcohol, tobacco, and firearms; civil rights; tribal justice; and a whole lot more.

BJS collects, analyzes, and shares information on crime, criminals, and victims, as well as the operation of the justice system. It also provides technical and financial assistance to state governments to develop their criminal justice statistics, criminal history records, and information systems.

BJS is the key source for data about

- Crime and victims
- Drugs and crime
- Criminal offenders
- Courts and sentencing
- Corrections
- Expenditure and employment
- Criminal record systems
- Firearms and crime
- Law enforcement

Bureau of Labor Statistics

The Bureau of Labor Statistics (www.bls.gov) is part of the U.S. Department of Labor. The Department of Labor's job is to "foster, promote, and develop the welfare of the wage earners, job seekers, and retirees of the United States; improve working conditions; advance opportunities for profitable employment; and assure work-related benefits and rights." It has more than two dozen agencies, whose responsibilities cover a range of issues including wages and benefits, occupational safety, occupational training, disability, and many others.

BLS is responsible for measuring and tracking the labor market, price changes, and working conditions. It collects, analyzes, and shares information on these and related matters.

BLS provides data such as

- Compensation
- Consumer expenditures
- Consumer price index
- Contingent workers
- Displaced workers
- Employee benefits
- Employer-provided training
- Employment
- Employment cost trends
- Employment projections
- Foreign labor
- Import-export prices
- Industry employment
- Job injuries
- Labor force
- Locality pay

- ✔ Longitudinal surveys
- ✔ Occupational projections
- ✔ Producer price index
- ✔ Productivity
- ✔ Real earnings

- ✔ State and area employment
- ✔ Unemployment
- ✔ Union members
- ✔ Wages
- ✔ Weekly earnings

Bureau of Transportation Statistics

The Bureau of Transportation Statistics (BTS) (www.rita.dot.gov/bts) is a part of the Research and Innovative Technology Administration (RITA). RITA has four agencies that deal with matters of transportation issues pertaining to safety, intermodalism, cost-effective regulation, compliance, training, and research.

It's BTS's job to "to create, manage, and share transportation statistical knowledge with public and private transportation communities and the Nation," to help advance the strategic goals of the Department of Transportation.

BTS shares transportation-related data on topics such as

- ✔ Airlines: On-time performance and financials
- ✔ Economics and finance
- ✔ Commodity Flow Survey
- ✔ Freight
- ✔ Household travel
- ✔ International travel and transportation
- ✔ Transportation snapshot
- ✔ Publication: National Transportation Statistics
- ✔ Ferry operators

Census Bureau

The United States Census Bureau (www.census.gov) is a part of the United States Department of Commerce. The Census Bureau's job is to "serve as the leading source of quality data about the nation's people and economy." This may sound something like the role of BEA, but while BEA focuses on whole industries and regional economies, the Census Bureau focuses on the characteristics and well-being of people and businesses.

If you use, or are even aware of, any government data, it's probably data from the Census Bureau. This is the agency that reports on how many Americans exist, who we are, and where and how we live. It tells us about the number and health of businesses. It tells us what's being built and what's being made in the United States.

The Census Bureau provides information on matters including

- Business ownership
- Construction
- Governments
- International trade
- Income and poverty
- Manufacturing
- Population estimates
- Population projections
- Social and economic characteristics
- Retail and wholesale trade

Economic Research Service

The Economic Research Service (ERS) (www.ers.usda.gov) is a part of the United States Department of Agriculture (USDA). The USDA's job is to "provide leadership on food, agriculture, natural resources, rural development, nutrition, and related issues based on sound public policy, the best available science, and efficient management." It is made up of more than 20 agencies and offices that deal with matters such as marketing of U.S. agricultural products, ensuring the health and care of animals and plants, and agricultural policy.

ERS "communicates research results and socioeconomic indicators via briefings, analyses for policymakers and their staffs, market analysis updates, and major reports."

Examining the American Community Survey

The Census Bureau's American Community Survey is one of the most widely used sources of public data. If you hear a news report that mentions demographics of your local region, that data came from the American Community Survey. If your congressman posts district facts and figures on his website, the data came from the American Community Survey. If a commercial source offers you data with income estimates and related information about individuals, it's based on data from the American Community Survey. Data miners, especially those involved in marketing and social sciences, depend on the American Community Survey every day, yet most are unaware of the data's origins.

The American Community Survey (ACS) is an annual survey conducted by the U.S. Census Bureau. The primary purpose of the survey is to provide communities with information they need to plan services and investments. Community governments need to know about the number of people in the community, who they are, and what they need, so each year, a sample of Americans are asked about themselves, their families, and how they live. The survey includes questions about the respondents' age, sex, and race; their family, education, income, and benefits; getting to work; veteran status; disabilities; and cost of living.

Government decisions at every level are made based on information obtained through the American Community Survey. And because data from the survey is available to the public, it is also the basis of business decisions. (Privacy concerns prevent sharing information about individual people, so the shared data is always aggregated. You can't get the survey data of an individual, but you can get information about groups based on geography or other factors.) This data is so widely used, analyzed, and integrated into reports and other information sources that users often are not aware of the primary source.

The American Community Survey enhances general census data (the survey that reaches out to every American once every ten years) to provide greater depth and more timely information that is vital to support government and business decisions.

With so many users and decisions depending on this survey, you'd think its future was assured, but it isn't. Open data initiatives oblige agencies to share the data they have in certain ways, but not to collect data. The budgets of statistical agencies are at risk. And the American Community Survey has opponents. Some lawmakers oppose the survey, citing budget and privacy concerns. (One public data user told a story of reaching out to a congressman who opposed ACS, and noticed that he had data from ACS posted on his website. Apparently, the congressman was unaware that even he depended on ACS data to do his work.)

Data made available through ERS includes

- Agribusiness/industry concentration
- Biotechnology
- Chemicals and production technology
- Crops
- Diet, consumption, and health
- Farm financial and risk management
- Farm structure, income, and performance
- Farm/rural finance and tax
- Food and nutrition assistance programs
- Food market structures
- Food prices, spreads, and margins
- Food safety

- International agriculture
- Livestock, dairy, poultry, aquaculture
- Macroeconomics in the agricultural and food economy
- Natural resources, environment, and conservation
- Policy topics
- R&D and productivity
- Rural America
- Trade
- U.S. state fact sheets with information on population, income, education, employment, federal funds, organic agriculture, farm characteristics, farm financial indicators, top commodities, and exports

Energy Information Administration

The Energy Information Administration (www.eia.gov) is a part of the United States Department of Energy (DOE). The DOE's job is to "ensure America's security and prosperity by addressing its energy, environmental, and nuclear challenges through transformative science and technology solutions."

EIA's job is to collect, analyze, and share "independent and impartial energy information to promote sound policymaking, efficient markets, and public understanding of energy and its interaction with the economy and the environment." By law, the data and analysis produced by EIA is independent; it's not subject to approval by any other employee or officer of the government.

EIA provides data on topics like these:

- Coal
- Coal supply and disposition
- Commercial
- Consumption
- Diesel prices
- Electricity
- Energy, forecasts
- Energy, statistical overview
- Environmental data
- Forecasts
- Gasoline prices
- Fuel economy
- Natural gas
- Nuclear
- Oxygenates
- Petroleum
- Power plants
- Prices, monthly all sources
- Refinery capacity
- Renewables
- Residential
- State energy profiles

Environmental Protection Agency

The Environmental Protection Agency (EPA) (www.epa.gov) is an independent agency whose job is to protect human health and the environment.

EPA provides data on environmental pollution. EPA's Envirofacts online database (www.epa.gov/enviro) is a central starting point for EPA data.

Office of Research, Analysis and Statistics

The Office of Research, Analysis and Statistics (RAS) (www.irs.gov/uac/Tax-Stats-2) is a part of the Internal Revenue Service (IRS). The IRS is "the nation's tax collection agency."

The job of the RAS is to provide "leading research, analytical, and technology services" to support the IRS.

RAS provides data on taxation, such as

- Corporation tax
- Estate and gift taxes
- Excise taxes
- Exempt organizations and bond tax

✔ Individual tax

✔ International or foreign-related tax

✔ Partnership economic data

✔ Sole proprietorship tax

National Agricultural Statistics Service

The National Agricultural Statistics Service (NASS) (www.nass.usda.gov) is a part of the United States Department of Agriculture (USDA). The NASS's job is to provide "timely, accurate, and useful statistics in service to U.S. agriculture."

NASS offers data on an extensive range of agricultural matters, including

✔ Crop progress and condition

✔ Dairy production

✔ Field crops

✔ Fruits, nuts, and vegetables

✔ Poultry production

National Center for Education Statistics

The National Center for Education Statistics (NCES) (http://nces.ed.gov) is a part of the United States Department of Education (ED). It's ED's job to "promote student achievement and preparation for global competitiveness by fostering educational excellence and ensuring equal access."

NCES collects, analyzes, and shares data about education in the United States and around the world.

NCES provides data on educational matters such as

✔ Early childhood education

✔ Education assessment

✔ Elementary and secondary education

✔ Finance

✔ International comparisons

✔ Libraries

✔ Other education subjects

✔ Postsecondary education

National Center for Health Statistics

The National Center for Health Statistics (NCHS) (www.cdc.gov/nchs) is a part of the Centers for Disease Control and Prevention (CDC). It's CDC's job to "protect America from health, safety, and security threats, both foreign and in the U.S."

NCHS's job is to "provide statistical information that will guide actions and policies to improve the health of the American people."

NCHS provides data on health-related topics, such as

- Asthma
- Births/Natality
- Child and infant health
- Deaths/Mortality
- Diabetes
- Disabilities/Impairments
- Divorces
- Health insurance coverage
- Heart disease
- Home health/Hospice care
- Hospital utilization
- Hypertension
- Influenza
- Leading causes of death
- Life expectancy
- Mammography/Breast cancer
- Marriages
- Men's health
- Nursing home care
- Occupational health
- Overweight prevalence
- Prenatal care
- Prescription drugs
- Sexually transmitted diseases
- Smoking
- Teen pregnancy
- Women's health

National Science Foundation, Science Resources Statistics

The National Science Foundation (www.nsf.gov/statistics) is charged with promoting the progress of science, advancing the national health, prosperity, and welfare, and securing national defense. The National Science Foundation provides data on topics such as

- Science and engineering education
- Science and engineering workforce
- Research and development

Office of Management and Budget

The Office of Management and Budget (OMB) (www.whitehouse.gov/omb) is part of the Executive Office of the President of the United States.

It's OMB's job to "serve the President of the United States in implementing his vision across the Executive Branch." This is the agency that manages the nation's budget and oversees other federal government agencies.

OMB shares the current and historical information about

- Budget of the U.S. government
- Fact sheets on government and social issues

Office of Retirement and Disability Policy

The Office of Retirement and Disability Policy (www.ssa.gov/policy) is a part of the Social Security Administration (SSA). It's SSA's job to administer retirement and disability benefits for Americans. It is the principal advisor to the Commissioner of Social Security on major policy.

Research and policy analysis for SSA is done by three parts of ORDP: the Office of Research, Demonstration, and Employment Support; the Office of Research, Evaluation, and Statistics; and the Office of Retirement Policy.

ORDP provides data on matters such as

- Income of the aged
- Social Security (Old-Age, Survivors, and Disability Insurance, OASDI) beneficiaries and benefits
- Supplemental Security Income (SSI) beneficiaries and benefits
- Trends in Social Security and disability programs
- Income of the Population 55 or Older
- Workers covered under Social Security and Medicare
- Congressional statistics

Governments around the world

The United States is only one of many governments that share data with the public. While you won't find exactly the same range or types of data from every country, you will find that most nations have some data to share. This section also includes some intergovernmental and nonprofit organizations that offer international data resources.

OFFSTATS

University of Auckland's OFFSTATS database (`www.offstats.auckland.ac.nz`) is a portal to statistical agency sources around the world, like an international version of the United States' FedStats portal. It has links organized by country, region, and subject. (International agencies do business in the local languages, and many don't have English-language versions.)

Organisation for Economic Co-operation and Development

The Organisation for Economic Co-operation and Development (OECD) (accessible through the statistics portal at `www.oecd.org/statistics`) aims to promote policies to improve the well-being of the world's people. The OECD measures productivity, global trade, and investment. It analyzes data on trade and everyday life.

The OECD also offers resources targeted for use by statisticians at `www.oecd.org/statistics/statisticalresources.htm`. These are also valuable for data miners. And the OECD has a portal to data sources around the world at `http://stats.oecd.org/source`.

U.S. open government portal

You can find lists of open data portals for international sources (as well as U.S. states, counties, and cities) on Data.gov at `www.data.gov/open-gov`.

United Nations

The United Nations (UN) is the world's most influential intergovernmental organization. The UN offers a portal to its statistical sources at `http://data.un.org`.

European Union

The European Union, which includes most of the Western European nations, has a portal to its statistical sources at `http://europa.eu/publications/statistics/index_en.htm`.

The Open Data Institute (`http://theodi.org`) promotes sharing and use of open data around the world. It's a key source for news on open data, as well as a center for research and education.

United States state and local governments

Finding the data you need from state and local governments can be very challenging. Some states are more interested in sharing data than others. You can't count on every state or local government to have an open data portal, or on finding someone in the local government to help you find what you need or address your questions.

U.S. states

Start your search for state-specific data the easy way with an online search for your state's data portal. If that turns up nothing, check the federal data portal (www.data.gov/states/page/states-data) and look for a link for your state.

If you find no sign of a portal, that doesn't mean that your state doesn't have data to share. You'll just have to work harder to find what you need. Check the state's website for information about your state agencies. If you don't find what you need online, start calling agencies by phone. Be prepared to explain what you need.

Your state may have a librarian who can help you understand how to locate information. Librarians at your local library may also be able to advise you on navigating government information sources. Be polite and persistent; state agencies are not always responsive about data requests.

Every U.S. state, as well as the District of Columbia, has an open records law similar to the federal Freedom of Information Act. If you're having trouble getting data that you know (or have good reason to believe) exists, you can request the information through the rights guaranteed to you by these laws.

Pew Charitable Trusts

The Pew Charitable Trusts (www.pewstates.org/states) is a good non-profit source for research and other information about U.S. states. It conducts research and reporting across all states and the District of Columbia.

U.S. counties

Most counties don't yet have centralized open data portals, but some, like Illinois' Cook County (see Figure 10-1), do. Try an online search for one when you start looking for data. The next place to check is the county open data portal list on Data.gov at www.data.gov/counties.

Figure 10-1: Data portal for Cook County, Illinois (United States)

Chances are, your county won't make it easy for you, so it may take some time to locate the data you seek. Call county offices and explain your needs. Don't be surprised if you have trouble reaching someone who seems to understand your request, but keep asking around. Try speaking with a local librarian for advice on obtaining local government data.

If all else fails, talk with the staff at the office of your local government representatives (local to the source of the data you need). Many of them deal with similar challenges obtaining data all the time and can offer advice or other help with the process. Remember that these offices exist to serve constituents, so if you don't live in the area, mention a little about how your work helps the locals. If your work might lead to new businesses, employment, or any economic benefit for the area, be sure to say so!

U.S. cities

Many cities are establishing open data portals now. You may find yours easily in an online search, especially if you are interested in a large city. You can also find a list of city portals on Data.gov at www.data.gov/cities.

Here are some of the established big-city data portals:

- **Chicago:** https://data.cityofchicago.org
- **New York:** https://nycopendata.socrata.com
- **Boston:** https://data.cityofboston.gov
- **Seattle:** https://data.seattle.gov
- **San Francisco:** https://data.sfgov.org

County and city governments collect a lot of transactional data — records about government activity such as building permits, property transfers, licenses, and tax payments. But they don't usually gather and share much information about people and how they live. If you are interested in demographics, cost of living, lifestyle, and so on, you may get more relevant data from the federal government or a commercial data supplier.

Getting user support for public data sources: An interview with Becky Sweger

Becky Sweger uses public data every day. She's director of Data and Technology at National Priorities Project (NPP), a nonprofit, nonpartisan research organization dedicated to making complex federal budget information transparent and accessible. NPP aims to help people prioritize and influence how their tax dollars are spent. It's Becky's responsibility to create research products that put the federal budget in context for partners, the media, and novice budget users.

Q: Tell us about a situation where you weren't able to get the information you needed. What you were trying to accomplish?

Sweger: I was trying to get a state-by-state breakdown of federal spending on a handful of programs — specifically, the Children's Health Insurance Program (CHIP) and Low Income Home Energy Assistance Program (LIHEAP). Both are administered by Health and Human Services.

Q: What agency was involved?

Sweger: Each federal agency is responsible for supplying information to USASpending.gov. I was working with data specific to Health and Human Services (HHS).

Q: What problem led you to ask for help? What kind of help did you need?

Sweger: For both CHIP and LIHEAP, I found records that were missing a field called "Place of Performance State." This field drives the maps displayed on USASpending.gov. As you might expect, it's a required field according to the data dictionary and data requirements published by the Office of Management and Budget (OMB).

Q: What kind of response did you get?

Sweger: The USASpending.gov help desk personnel did answer my email for this issue, saying that while they're not responsible for data issues that originate from the agencies, they would try to find out why the HHS data was able to get into the database without having all the required fields. Here's the answer, directly from the email sent by the USASpending.gov help desk:

"Health and Human Services is one of the agencies that does not require a Place of Performance Code. We are unaware of the policy behind this. You will need to contact someone from HHS for the policy explanation or to ask that they correct any existing awards that you believe should have a code. We do not have an HHS point of contact for you."

Q: So, you never got the data or a satisfactory explanation.

Sweger: It's clear that neither OMB nor some of the agencies have made it a priority to provide complete, accurate data to USASpending.gov, despite the 2006 law that requires them to do so, the Federal Funding Accountability and Transparency Act (FFATA). Ultimately, this is a people/process problem, not a data problem — I've found that to be the case most of the time.

Q: But you've also had good experiences. Tell us about one of those.

Sweger: Yes. Here's an example: I was trying to find the best source of state-level poverty data.

(continued)

(continued)

I was looking at several United States Census Bureau products that measure poverty (there are about six ways to get the number).

Q: What problem led you to ask for help? What kind of help did you need?

Sweger: As a novice user of this data, I needed help understanding the differences between the various poverty numbers to make sure that I chose the right one for our purposes.

Q: How did it go?

Sweger: The Census Bureau provides a description of each product and when it should be used. I learned that the poverty measure I'd been looking at was not, in fact, appropriate for doing year-over-year comparisons at the state level.

And there's a bonus from Bureau employees: If you still have questions after reading their documentation, the Census Bureau is happy to talk with you on the phone. They understand that the job entails more than just publishing data — it's also their job to make sure that people can use it appropriately.

Q: Any final advice for newbie public data users?

Sweger: Data published by entities that are solely in the data business (for example, Census, Bureau of Labor Statistics, or Bureau of Economic Analysis) is always accompanied by documentation. Read it. This will not only make you smarter than most of the other people who use that data, but it will also help you be smarter about using "exhaust" data (in other words, data that's generated as a by-product of doing business, like the stats published by the IRS). Entities that publish exhaust data aren't necessarily in the business of creating information that can be used for rigorous analysis.

When assessing a source of public data, find out who else uses it and for what. Don't be afraid to reach out — most people are happy to discuss their work.

Chapter 11

Buying Data

● ●

● ●

*E*ven if you have access to massive quantities of data in internal data-bases and invaluable public data resources, you may at times still find it worth your while to buy data from commercial suppliers. When the data you need is unavailable, or when it's available but isn't up to snuff, turning to private sources for data can make a lot of sense. Some of the advantages of commercial data are as follows:

✔ **Availability:** Some data is available only through private sources: data generated in the course of business or other nongovernment activity, for instance, such as consumer or business credit histories or lists of individuals with specific affiliations or interests.

✔ **Preparation:** Gathering data from disparate public sources, organizing it into consistent formats and exercising proper management control over that process can be time-consuming and costly. If, for example, you need real-estate transaction data from communities throughout the United States, you could get it by requesting transaction records directly from thousands of local governments all over the country and merge all the results yourself, but using a real-estate data service would certainly be much easier — and probably cheaper, too.

✔ **Enhancements:** Some private data sources offer enhancements that can add value to a data resource. Credit ratings for consumers and businesses may be the most familiar type of data enhancement. Others include scores for sympathy toward specific political causes or likelihood to make a purchase, and identification of the language or subject matter of text data.

This chapter discusses some of the advantages and disadvantages of buying commercial data.

No data is like your own data. Data generated within your own business is uniquely relevant for you, and you have the ultimate power to ensure that it is properly managed. Get more value from your data by using outside sources selectively to obtain information that complements or clarifies the data you own.

Peeking at Consumer Data

To introduce you to the kinds of consumer information available through commercial suppliers, I'll look at a detailed example. Table 11-1 includes all the data collected about one consumer by Axciom, a major vendor of consumer marketing data. This vendor provides marketing data about individual consumers and the households in which those consumers live, as follows:

- **Individual consumers:** For each individual, the vendor divides information into two data categories:

  - *Characteristic:* Demographics such as age, marital status, level of education attained, and whether the consumer has children. Data about household members that share the consumer's last name may also be included here.

  - *Home:* Information about the consumer's place of residence, whether it is a single family or multifamily dwelling, whether the consumer rents or owns, and the length of residence.

- **Households:** The vendor tracks four categories of household data:

  - *Vehicle:* Details about car ownership and insurance, including number of vehicles, makes and models, and insurance renewal dates.

  - *Economic:* Information about the household's financial activity. Estimated income, preferred spending methods and spending activity through various channels.

  - *Purchases:* Information about the household's buying habits, online and offline. May include information about the types of products commonly purchased — categories, amounts, and frequencies.

  - *Interests:* Hobbies and other interests such as cooking, sports, and home improvement.

Table 11-1   Sample data from Axciom for one individual

Characteristic data	
Date of Birth	01/23/1945
Gender	Female
Education	Completed Graduate School
Marital Status	Single
Small or Home Business	True
Home	
Home Information	No Data Found
Vehicle	
Auto Policy Renewal	October
Economic	
Estimated Household Income Range	$75,000–$99,999
Presence of Credit Card	Credit Card Holder – Unknown Type
Credit Card Use – American Express	Regular
Credit Card Use – Discover	Regular
Online Purchasing Activity	True
Number of Purchases – Cash	2
Number of Purchases – Credit Card	1
Number of Purchases – AMEX	20
Number of Purchases – Discover	1
Number of Purchases – Visa	1
Number of Purchases – Other	11
Purchases	
Mail Order Responder	Mail Order Responder
Mail Order Buyer	Mail Order Buyer
Gardening Products	Purchased
General Merchandise	Purchased
Total Dollars Spent	1502
Total Number of Purchases	9
Average Dollars Spent Per Offline Purchase	157
Total Offline Dollars Spent	1394

(continued)

Table 11-1 *(continued)*

Purchases	
Total Number of Offline Purchases	31
Total Offline Purchases – Under $50	25
Total Offline Purchases – $50–$99.99	6
Total Offline Purchases – $250–$499.99	1
Average Dollars Spent Per Online Purchase	101
Total Online Dollars Spent	304
Total Number of Online Purchases	3
Total Online Purchases – Under $50	3
Total Online Purchases – $50–$99.99	1
Total Online Purchases – $100–$249.99	2
Interests	
Interests	Fashion, Children's Items, Cooking, Gourmet Cooking, Health/Medical, Current Affairs/Politics, Crafts, Home Furnishings/Decorating, Home Improvement, Gardening, Other Pet Ownership, Reading, Reading Magazines, Aerobics

This is only a single example of the marketing data that is available for sale. (A few fields have been slightly altered for privacy reasons; otherwise the example includes all the complete data retrieved from Axciom.) Another example — even one from the same supplier — might look different, with different fields, additional family information, or more accurate (or inaccurate) results. And even complete records may not count if the consumer opted out of data sharing.

You can explore some of the data that is being shared about you. The data presented in this example was provided by Axciom, a major vendor of consumer marketing data. Through its About the Data website (`https://aboutthedata.com`), Axciom enables consumers to review their own data, get information about how the data is collected and used, edit the data, or opt out of data sharing.

Take a moment to think over the sources of information open to the data supplier. The supplier has to assemble its consumer marketing profiles from public or legally shareable private sources. Many data sources — personal paychecks, banking records, tax returns, and many others — are off limits. The example in Table 11-1 was compiled from three types of sources:

- ✔ **Public sources:** These include

    - Government information such as property and assessor's files and license records

    - Publicly available sources such as telephone and online directories

- ✔ **Survey research:** Surveys and questionnaires that consumers chose to fill out. Although data here is limited to those consumers who participated, it is sometimes used to estimate data for others.

- ✔ **Commercial opt-in data:** Information collected by commercial sources who obtained an *opt in* (permission) from the consumer to use the data.

In the marketplace, any data about people is likely to be described as *consumer marketing* data, regardless of whether you are interested in the "consumer" aspect of this data, or whether you intend to use the data for marketing purposes. Be mindful of how you intend to use the data, though, and make sure that your agreements with the data supplier are compatible with the intended use.

These sources may have many imperfections. The data may be out of date. You may find errors or incomplete data. Individuals might not be properly matched to other household members. Just as you must assess the quality and suitability of your internal data sources for any given use, you must carefully evaluate commercial data sources as well. But although you may be able to take action to improve the quality of an internal data source, you won't likely have that option with a commercial source. If the quality of the data or the documentation is very poor, don't waste money buying it. Look for alternate vendors, consider collecting your own data, or just live without it.

Beyond Consumer Data

Not all the data you may need is about people. Perhaps you're more interested in businesses or nonprofit organizations. Maybe you have an interest in thunderstorms, pineapples, or bridges. No problem. Commercial sources can provide data for all these things, and many more.

If data is available that you value enough to consider paying for it, somebody probably is out there ready to sell. This is true of data concerning people and organizations, and also true for data about myriad other things. Some widely used categories include data about

- ✔ Geography and locations
- ✔ Resources and products
- ✔ Weather and climate

Many of the kinds of data that we use to understand people and their behavior have equivalents for businesses and other organizations. Basic descriptive facts about people, such as age, gender, and income, are called *demographics*. Similar information about organizations is called *firmographics*. Information about an organization's financial status, financial transactions, or connections to people and things is also often available through commercial sources.

Richer data is often available for organizations than for individual people. Organizations, especially publicly held corporations and nonprofit organizations, are often obliged to make information about their finances and activities public, and even many private companies choose to share some information. In addition, data suppliers may have more liberty to research and share business information than information about people, and even those who offer opt-out options to consumers may not do so for organizations.

Desperately Seeking Sources

You can learn more about using commercially available data for business and consumer marketing by connecting with marketers and market researchers who share your interests, as well as data vendors. These professional associations are a good starting point for making contacts:

- ✔ American Marketing Association (www.ama.org)
- ✔ Direct Marketing Association (http://thedma.org)
- ✔ Advertising Research Foundation (www.thearf.org)

For a list of major data vendors and the types of data they provide, see Appendix C. Although this list represents only a small portion of the hundreds of data suppliers active in today's market, even these few provide a wide range of offerings, covering millions of individuals.

Sources for data concerning specific things are not always obvious, but you can usually find an obvious place to start inquiring. If you want data about a product — whether it's a raw material, a crop, a commodity, or a finished brand-name product — you can find an industry association for the people involved in the making and selling of that product. Some industry associations commission or conduct their own market research and sell reports and data directly. Even if the one you need doesn't, its staff or members will still be good contacts to ask about sources of data.

Specialty providers offer a range of other data types. Some categories are fairly easy to find through a simple web search, and may be dominated by one or just a few influential providers. For example, mapping and geographic data is dominated by companies such as ESRI and MapInfo, and weather data by The Weather Company.

Less popular types of data may require a good deal of effort to find. If you have difficulty finding providers through search or referrals, consider consulting a good, old-fashioned resource you may be neglecting: a reference librarian, especially if you can find one who regularly deals with business inquiries.

Assessing Quality and Suitability

The small data sample shown earlier in this chapter has some obvious flaws. No data about the consumer's home was retrieved. She must live somewhere! You see an insurance renewal month, but nothing about the car itself. In fact, a number of things in the data don't reflect a realistic picture of that consumer. If you followed the tip and retrieved your own consumer marketing data via Aboutthedata.com, you probably noticed some surprises in your own data as well.

Make sure you understand exactly what the vendor is offering to sell you. You'll want to know

- ✔ **What the data means:** What does each field (variable) and row (case) represent? What documentation is provided? Ideal documentation explains the source of the data and any refinements made by the vendor, in detail. In practice, data documentation is often skimpy.

- ✔ **How the data is offered:** Is the data offered on a subscription basis or one-time only? Will you get just an extract from the vendor's resources, or flexible access to a data source?

✔ **What uses are permitted:** Do the vendor's terms of service permit the use you have in mind? Will you be permitted to retain the data or use it only once?

✔ **How the data is delivered:** Will you receive a data extract, as a downloadable file or in some other form (such as a CD-ROM, DVD, or even on paper), use a self-service API, or some other interface? Is support available if you have difficulty using these interfaces?

✔ **How the data is structured:** Is the level of the data (raw or aggregate) suitable for the analysis you have in mind? Is the storage format (database or file format) convenient for you to use? If not, will the vendor convert it for you? Are database tables organized intuitively for your needs? If not, can the vendor provide some interface to simplify your data queries? (Try to minimize the data restructuring that you'll need to do later.)

Before making a significant investment in any data source, make an effort to assess the quality of the data and verify that it is suitable for the purpose you have in mind. Ask questions! Find out how the data is obtained. What are the sources? Is a trained research staff involved in data collection and preparation? Can you see how survey questions were worded and organized? Make sure that you understand the vendor's terms of use and whether they permit the use you need. In many cases, obtaining a small amount of data is a good first step, so you can examine and test the data in use. Remember to check the documentation for the data, which is sometimes inadequate and sometimes nonexistent.

Part IV

A Data Miner's Survival Kit

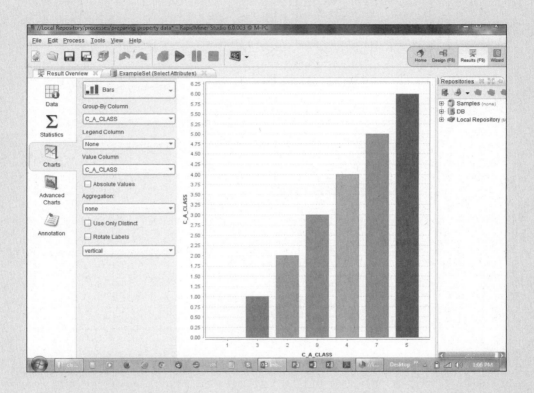

Discover more ways of mastering your data-mining toolkit at www.dummies.com/extras/datamining.

In this part . . .

- ✔ Getting data into your tool
- ✔ Manipulating data to suit your needs
- ✔ Preparing data for modeling
- ✔ Exploring data with graphs
- ✔ Building predictive models

Chapter 12

Getting Familiar with Your Data

*B*efore a French chef whips up a dazzling dish, she sets out all the ingredients and tools. She checks that the ingredients are fresh and good, and that the tools work properly. She does not begin to cook until she puts everything in place.

A data miner is no different. Before you whip up a dazzling predictive model, you get acquainted with the data that you will use. You put it where you need it. You make sure that you understand what data you have, how it's arranged and stored, and whether it is complete and correct.

This chapter shows you how to analyze and evaluate your data.

Organizing Data for Mining

Data mining has very strict requirements for data organization. They are not exotic, complex, or difficult requirements to meet, but they are strict.

Let me use an example to show how data must be organized for data mining. Figure 12-1 shows a sample of data viewed as a table in data-mining software. (See Chapter 2 for more about this data and an example data-mining application.) Each row represents one parcel of real estate. Information about the parcels of real estate is organized in columns. The first column contains the tax identification number (TAXKEY), the second column contains the assessed value of the land from a prior assessment (P_A_LAND), and so on. Every entry in any one row pertains to one specific parcel of land. Every entry in any one column is the same type of information. No rows or columns are left blank for reasons relating to style and readability. This data is properly organized for investigating differences among the parcels of real estate.

ExampleSet (162403 examples, 0 special attributes, 58 regular attributes)				03 / 162,403 examples):	all			
Row No.	TAXKEY	P_A_LAND	NR_UNITS	C_A_LAND	LAND_USE	C_A_CLASS	C_A_TOTAL	CHK_DIGIT
1	10001000	48200	1	48200	8810	1	229600	3
2	10011000	146200	0	150700	5093	3	602800	8
3	10021000	115000	0	115000	1794	2	384000	2
4	10022000	0	0	0	8880	9	0	8
5	18100000	100	0	100	6	4	37000	7
6	18101000	100	0	100	6	4	37000	2
7	19989000	0	0	0	4010	9	0	X
8	19990000	0	0	0	4010	9	0	5
9	19991000	0	0	0	4010	9	0	0
10	19992100	40600	0	40600	4010	2	40600	2
11	19996100	53400	6	53400	8830	7	179600	4
12	19996210	0	0	0	8885	9	0	8
13	19998200	47800	1	47800	8810	1	153700	1
14	19999100	139700	0	139700	4225	2	268800	0
15	20032000	495700	0	495700	5171	4	15729000	X
16	20051000	204100	0	204100	5171	4	475000	3
17	20052000	114700	0	114700	4225	4	120000	9
18	20071100	0	0	1734900	5172	4	12638000	9

Figure 12-1: Data organized properly for data mining.

If, instead of real estate, you investigate people, each person would be represented by one row in the data, and all the details about the people would be organized into columns. If you investigate chest x-rays, each chest x-ray would be represented by one row in the data, and all the details about the chest x-rays would be organized into columns. In data analysis terminology, the things you're studying — the things in the rows — are called *cases* or *records*. And the details about them, which are in the columns, are called *variables*. You will also hear the columns called *fields,* especially in the context of databases.

So, data mining requires data organized with a single row for each case and a single column for each variable. Many sources of data are already organized in this way. Statisticians organize data this way by habit. Database professionals may not use this approach for much of their work, but they'll usually understand what you want if you call it a *flat table.*

You'll find subtle variations in data structure. Some types of software use descriptive information in a header before the data, such as certain specialty formats associated with the Orange and Weka data-mining applications. Some complex analytic procedures have additional or slightly varied requirements (these are quite unusual). But the core of the data still has the cases in rows and variables in columns.

Getting Data from There to Here

Your first hands-on step with data is getting it from wherever it is to the place where you need it to be.

The steps you will take to import data for use in data mining can vary a lot from one situation to another. Your own skills, your work style, company policies and procedures, and the specifics of any particular project may affect the way that you go about accessing data. The most important influences include

- ✔ **Data format:** The format the data is in. Examples include relational database, NoSQL database, text file, spreadsheet, XML, or others.
- ✔ **Data organization:** The structure of your data. The data structure may be convenient for data mining (and your particular project) or not.
- ✔ **Software:** Each product has its own procedures for importing data, and variations exist, even within a single product.

Text files

Text formats are common, and you're likely to encounter them often. You'll find several varieties, but some of the most common are *comma-separated value (* `.csv` *), tab-delimited,* and *fixed-column* text. Most public data sources, including government sources and nonprofit agencies, offer data as text files. Many researchers love text files because they are not tied to specific products or platforms, and they are compact (that is, they use minimal space for the data they contain). Here's the news about text files:

- ✔ **The good news:** Every data-mining application can import data from text files.
- ✔ **The bad news:** Every data-mining application has its own way of importing data from text files, and some of them are pretty challenging to use.
- ✔ **Even worse news:** Some data-mining applications can import some kinds of text files but not others.

Consider an example. Figure 12-2 shows data in a text file. The data is in `.csv` comma-separated value format. The first row contains variable names, separated by commas. All the other rows contain the data, one row for each brand of cigarettes. The data includes the brand name, the region where it is sold, tar content, and other variables. These values are separated by commas. This data is well organized for data mining. What's the process for opening this data?

Figure 12-2:
Sample data
in a text file.

Here's how it's done in four example data-mining applications. Review these procedures, and you'll start to understand how these applications look and how they are used.

To open the sample data in KNIME (see Appendix C for information about KNIME and where to get it):

1. **Start KNIME. (See Figure 12-3.)**

2. **Find the CSV Reader in the Node Repository (a menu). It's grouped with other tools for importing data. (See Figure 12-4.)**

3. **Drag the CSV Reader to the work area. (See Figure 12-5.)**

4. **Right-click and select Configure. Browse to find the cigarette data. (See Figure 12-6.)**

5. **Adjust settings. Make sure to select the proper delimiters (commas) and indicate that column headers (variable names) are in the first line of data (See Figure 12-7.)**

6. **Click the Execute button (shown in Figure 12-3) to import the data.**

   The CSV Reader will show a green indicator (see Figure 12-8, bottom right) when the data has been imported.

The Execute button

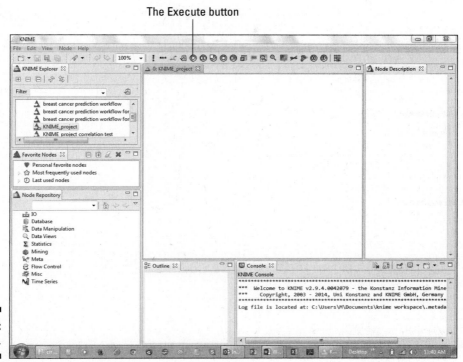

Figure 12-3:
KNIME.

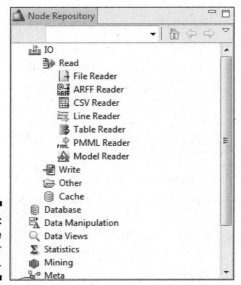

Figure 12-4:
Finding the
CSV Reader
in KNIME.

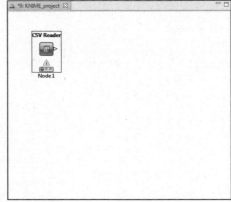

Figure 12-5:
CSV Reader
in the
KNIME work
area.

Figure 12-6:
Browsing to
find the cig-
arette data
in KNIME.

To open the sample data in Orange, follow these steps (see Appendix C for information about Orange and where to get it):

1. **Start Orange Canvas. (See Figure 12-9.)**

2. **Find the File widget. It's in the Data group, the only data import tool. (See Figure 12-10.)**

3. **Click the File widget once to place it on the work area. (See Figure 12-11.)**

4. **Right-click and select Open. Browse to find the cigarette data. (See Figure 12-12.)**

   Oops! The drop-down list of file types doesn't offer an option for the .csv format. You'll have to convert the data to another format before you can open it in this data-mining application.

Figure 12-7: Adjusting import settings in KNIME.

Figure 12-8: KNIME CSV Reader after importing data.

Figure 12-9:
Orange
Canvas.

To open the sample data in RapidMiner, follow these steps (see Appendix C for information about RapidMiner and where to get it):

1. **Start RapidMiner Studio. (See Figure 12-13.)**

2. **Find the Read CSV operator. It's grouped with other tools for importing data. (See Figure 12-14.)**

3. **Drag the Read CSV operator to the work area. (See Figure 12-15.)**

4. **Click the Read CSV operator. Settings for the Read CSV operator will be displayed in the Parameters area (See Figure 12-16.)**

5. **In the Parameters area, click the Import Configuration Wizard button and use the wizard to browse for the cigarette data. (See Figure 12-17.)**

6. **Adjust settings. The wizard gives you cues to help get the settings right. (See Figure 12-18.) Click the Finish button to return to the work area.**

7. **Click the Execute button (shown in Figure 12-13) to import the data.**

   The Read CSV operator will show a round green indicator (see Figure 12-19, lower left) when the data has been imported.

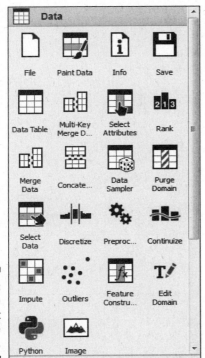

Figure 12-10:
Finding the
File widget
in Orange
Canvas.

Figure 12-11:
Placing the
File widget
on the work
area.

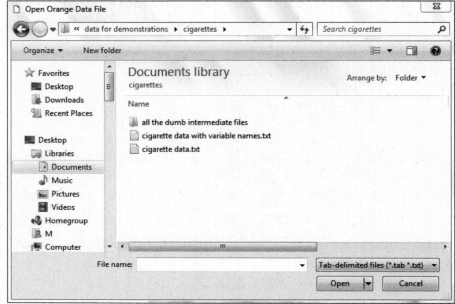

Figure 12-12:
The list of file types in Orange Canvas doesn't include `.csv`.

The Execute button

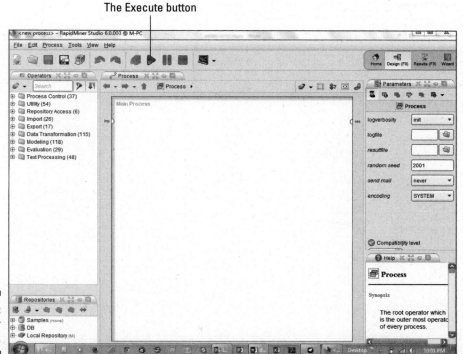

Figure 12-13:
RapidMiner Studio.

Figure 12-14:
Finding the
Read CSV
operator in
RapidMiner
Studio.

Figure 12-15:
Dragging
the Read
CSV opera-
tor to the
RapidMiner
Studio work
area.

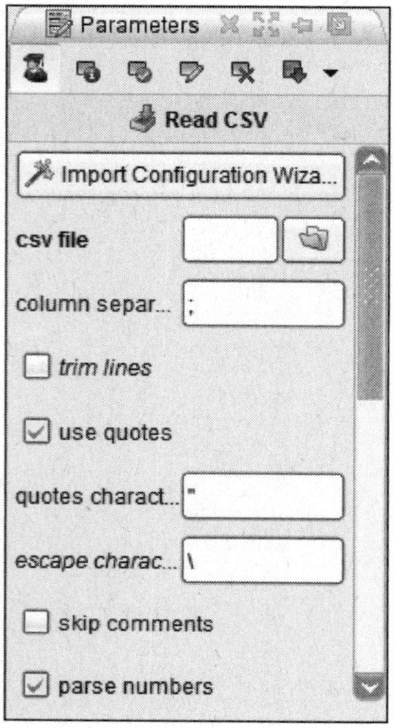

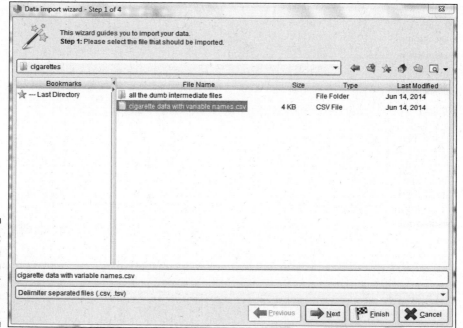

Figure 12-16: Settings for the Read CSV operator.

Figure 12-17: Using the wizard to browse for the cigarette data.

Figure 12-18: Adjusting data import settings with a wizard in RapidMiner Studio.

Data import wizard - Step 2 of 4

This wizard guides you to import your data.
Step 2: Please specify how the file should be parsed and how columns are separated.

File Reading

File Encoding: windows-1252

☐ Trim Lines

☐ Skip Comments   #

Column Separation

◉ Comma ","   ○ Space
○ Semicolon ";"   ○ Tab
○ Regular Expression   \s*|\s*

Escape Character: \

☑ Use Quotes   "

brand	whoregion	country	tar	tarmpcig	nicotine	nicmpcig	co	compcig	filter
HighSociety	AFRO	Nigeria	11.1	0.8	0.5	0.04	9.4	0.6	4.8
Marlboro(US	AFRO	Kenya	14	0.4	1.1	0.09	10.4	0.2	11.1
Marlboro(US	AFRO	Nigeria	12.6	0	0.9	0.13	9.8	0.2	12.3
Sportsman	AFRO	Kenya	13.4	0.4	1	0.13	10.6	0.2	4.4
PeterStuyves	AFRO	SouthAfrica	13	0.2	1.3	0.15	9.6	0.2	4.4
Marlboro(L)	AMRO	Mexico	15.8	1.8	0.89	0.13	13.9	0.3	0.8
Broadway	AMRO	Mexico	14.9	0.7	0.89	0.37	13.4	1.8	0.5

Row, Column	Error	Original value	Message

⬅ Previous   ➡ Next   🏁 Finish   ✖ Cancel

Figure 12-19: Read CSV operator after data import.

Main Process

Read CSV

fil   out

To import the sample data in Weka, follow these steps (see Appendix C for information about Weka and where to get it):

1. **Start Weka KnowledgeFlow. (See Figure 12-20.)**

2. **Find the CSVLoader in the Design toolbar. It's grouped with other tools for importing data. (See Figure 12-21.)**

3. **Click the CSVLoader, and then click in the work area to place the CSVLoader in the work area. (See Figure 12-22.)**

4. **Right-click and select Configure. Browse to find the cigarette data. (See Figure 12-23.)**

5. **Adjust settings. (See Figure 12-24.)**

6. **Click the Run Process button (shown in Figure 12-20) to import the data. The Status area updates (see Figure 12-25) when the data has been imported.**

The Run Process button

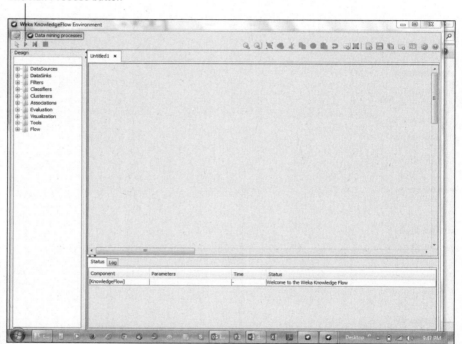

Figure 12-20: Weka Knowledge-Flow.

The look of the applications, the organization of the tools, and the details of setup vary, but the main steps are all quite similar. As long as your application can read the format that you have, the results will be the same.

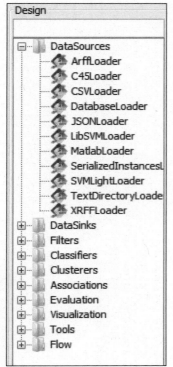

Figure 12-21:
CSVLoader
in the
Design
toolbar.

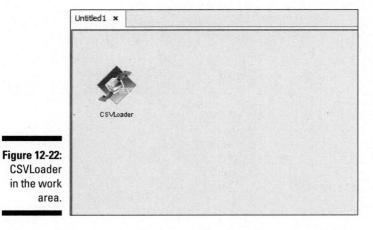

Figure 12-22:
CSVLoader
in the work
area.

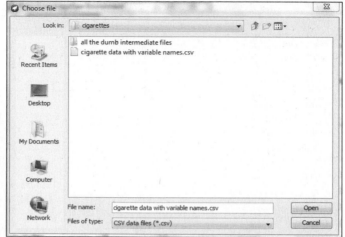

Figure 12-23:
Browsing to find the cigarette data in Weka Knowledge-Flow.

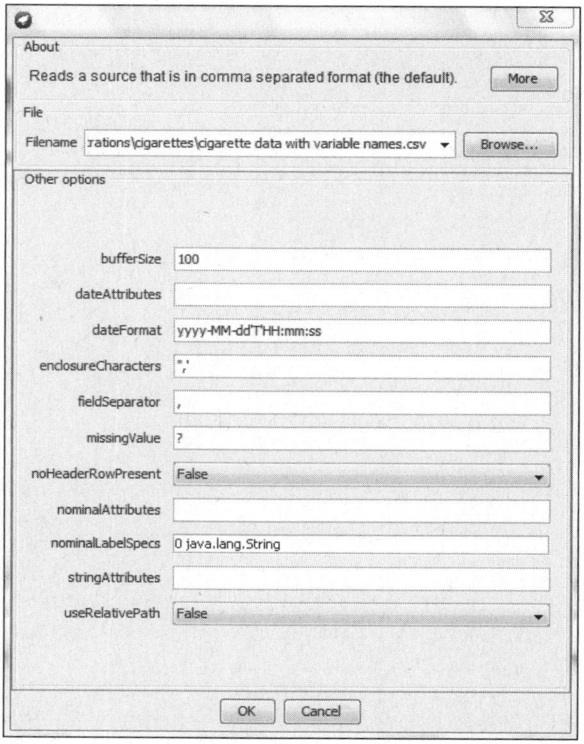

Figure 12-24:
Adjusting data import settings in Weka Knowledge-Flow.

Figure 12-25:
Status
update after
data import.

Status	Log			
Component	Parameters		Time	Status
[KnowledgeFlow]			-	OK.
CSVLoader	-M ? -B 100 -E "," -F ,		-	Finished - 77 insts @ 4812 insts/sec (read speed); 4812 insts/sec (flow through...

Databases

Data collected by large organizations in the course of everyday business is usually stored in databases. But database administrators may not be willing to allow data miners direct access to these data sources, and direct access may not be the best option from your point of view either. Direct access to operational (used for routine business operations) databases can be a bad idea because

- ✔ **Data miners use a lot of data.** You could unintentionally tie up resources and interfere with ordinary business operations.

- ✔ **Legal and other business obligations matter.** You could unintentionally violate a data privacy law or other data management requirement if your data access is not properly controlled.

- ✔ **Operational databases are not organized for data mining.** You could spend a lot of time struggling to get the data you need, and still not be sure of getting it right.

When you need data from an operational database (and you have the appropriate approval to use the data), you should discuss your needs with the administrator responsible for that data. You'll need to explain exactly what data you need, the format you need for data mining, and whether you need the data just once or on an ongoing basis. The best approach for one-time requests is often for the administrator to extract the data for you and deliver it in a text file or other acceptable format.

Ongoing data access is another matter. The administrator may not want to provide data extracts over and over, and giving you direct access to business systems is risky. A common solution is to create an *analytic database*. This is an ordinary relational database that is separate from conventional business systems. Data is routinely (and automatically) transferred from business systems to the analytic database, and data miners can access it at any time.

If you use an analytic database, make sure that it is organized properly to support data mining. Help your database administrator by sketching a diagram like Figure 12-1 to show how the data must be organized. If the database administrator insists that the data can't be stored this way, ask whether it's possible to create a *view* (a stored query that can be queried as if it were a conventional data table) with the organization that you need.

Many data-mining products are able to read data from databases. The steps required vary based on the

- Design of the data-mining application
- Structure of the source database
- Middleware, usually called a *driver* (*ODBC driver, JDBC driver*), special software that mediates between the database and applications software

Documentation for your data-mining application should tell you whether it can read data from a database, and if so, what tool or function to use, and how. The administrator who sets up the analytics database can provide details about accessing the database.

If you're already comfortable working with databases and other applications, you'll find nothing surprising about doing the same things with a data-mining application. If databases are new to you, get a knowledgeable person from your organization to walk you through the process with your own database and data-mining application.

Spreadsheets, XML, and specialty data formats

You may need to use data that's in a spreadsheet, XML (extensible markup language), or any of dozens of less common formats. The key question will always be: Does your data-mining application import data in that format?

As long as your data-mining application has a tool to read the data format you need, the process will be straightforward — just a small variation on the examples you can read in the "Text files" section, earlier in this chapter. You may need to select a different data import tool or change a few settings, but the process will be very similar.

When your data-mining application can't import data in a particular format, try these alternative approaches:

- **Check your data source for other formats.** Many sources offer choices.
- **Convert the data format yourself.** Some conversions are easy, and some are difficult.
- **Use a different data-mining application.** Data import capability is an important factor in your choice of data-mining software, but if you're already committed to a particular product, it may not be practical to change.

Becoming fluent in data mining

The data-mining profession has its own vocabulary.

Traditional data analysts call something that you'd like to predict a *dependent variable,* but a data miner may call that a *target* or an *output.* The traditional data analyst's name for something that might influence the dependent variable is *independent variable,* but a data miner may prefer *predictor, input,* or *attribute.*

The kinds of variables that you are using affect your options for data manipulation and modeling. These terms are used by both traditional data analysts and data miners:

Categorical variable types include

- ✔ **Nominal:** Names or categories with no order (such as Male and Female).

- ✔ **Ordinal:** Ranked or ordered categories such as letter grades or stars in a product review. (Ordinal measures are not meant to be used in mathematical operations, even if they are represented by numbers. However, people violate this rule all the time. Sometimes the results are useful. Often, they're not.)

Continuous variable types include

- ✔ **Interval:** Measures such as time and Fahrenheit temperature, which are appropriate to use in some mathematical operations, but not all, because the

measurements scales have no clear zero value. (0 degrees Fahrenheit is not the absence of all warmth, for example, but it is pretty unpleasant.)

- ✔ **Ratio:** Measures such as weights, lengths, and Kelvin temperature, which can be used in mathematical operations and which have a clear zero value.

The range of terms used within data-mining software is large and varied, perhaps too varied. For example, many data-mining applications use visual programming. That means that functions are represented by little icons that can be moved to a blank space on the screen and connected together to define a data-mining process. In this book, I call those icons *tools,* and some products use that term, too. But others call the same thing a *node, operator,* or some other name. In this book, the blank space is called a work area or *workspace,* but in your data-mining application, it might be called something else, such as a *canvas.* (In the example processes in the "Text files" section, earlier in this chapter, you'll notice the same things called by different names in different products.)

Refer to the glossary in Appendix A for a more extensive list of data-mining terms, and be sure to read the documentation for your data-mining application for product-specific terms.

Surveying Your Data

After you have imported a dataset into your data-mining application, the next step is to review the variables one by one. In your review, you'll examine variables to make sure that you understand what each represents, to find out whether the data is complete, and to assess the quality of the data that you have. The review helps you determine whether your data is adequate to support your data-mining goals.

The data review is part of the data-understanding phase of the CRISP-DM process for data mining. You can find more information about the process in Chapter 4, and you can read about an example data review in Chapter 2.

You will need summaries for each variable of things such as

- ✔ Number of missing cases
- ✔ Minimum and maximum values
- ✔ Averages and standard deviations (measures of variability)
- ✔ Values of categorical variables

Some platforms provide data summaries for a slew of variables in one step. Others will require many steps to get this information. One example of a data summary appears in Chapter 2. Here's another, which picks up from the data import in KNIME shown earlier in this chapter. Figure 12-26 shows the process just after importing data.

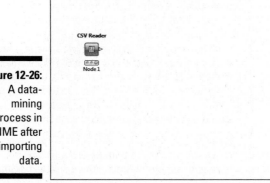

Figure 12-26:
A data-mining process in KNIME after importing data.

To create a data summary using KNIME, first complete the KNIME-related steps in the "Text files" section, earlier in this chapter, and then do the following:

1. **Find the Statistics node in the Node Repository (see Figure 12-27) and drag it to the work area. (See Figure 12-28.)**

2. **Click the small arrow on the right side of the CSVReader, and then click the arrow on the left side of the Statistics node.**

3. **Right-click the Statistics node and choose Execute and Open Views from the menu. (See Figure 12-29.)**

   KNIME will display a summary report (see Figure 12-30). It provides key summary statistics for each continuous variable quickly and easily.

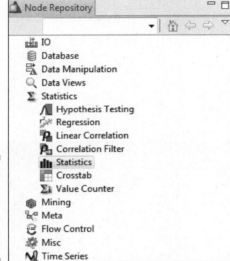

Figure 12-27: Finding the Statistics node in the Node Repository.

Figure 12-28: Adding the Statistics node to the process.

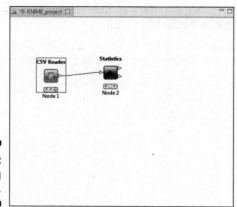

Figure 12-29:
Connecting
two nodes.

Row ID	D tar	D tarmpcig	D nicotine	D nicmpcig	D co	D compcig	D filter	D filter2
Minimum	6.8	0	0	0	5.9	0	0.1	0.1
Maximum	9,915	4.1	1.63	0.67	17.4	2.7	99	99
Mean	270.73	0.969	0.901	0.106	11.505	0.674	14.062	4.042
Std. deviation	1,585.012	0.853	0.23	0.105	2.396	0.605	16.731	15.659
Variance	2,512,261.803	0.728	0.053	0.011	5.741	0.366	279.923	245.207
Overall sum	20,846.2	74.6	69.34	8.18	885.9	51.9	1,082.8	311.2
No. missings	0	0	0	0	0	0	0	0
Median	?	?	?	?	?	?	?	?
Row count	77	77	77	77	77	77	77	77
No. NaNs	0	0	0	0	0	0	0	0
No. +infinities	0	0	0	0	0	0	0	0
No. -infinities	0	0	0	0	0	0	0	0

Numeric columns   Nominal columns

Figure 12-30:
Data sum-
mary dis-
played in
KNIME.

Chapter 13

Dealing in Graphic Detail

. . . .

In This Chapter

▶ Using familiar graphs in familiar ways

▶ Using familiar graphs in unfamiliar ways

▶ Adding new graphs to your bag of tricks

. . . .

*Y*ou may be new to data mining, but you already know some important tools of the trade. Graphs like bar charts, histograms, and scatterplots are important data-mining tools. Data miners use these conventional graphs in conventional ways, and in unconventional ways, too! And now that you're a data miner, you can expand your repertoire with special graphs that help you pack more information on a page (without losing main ideas), spot common patterns, or evaluate predictive models.

This chapter introduces you to the data miner's arsenal of graphs and graphing tools. You'll find that graphs are one of the easiest ways to get started in data mining, especially since data miners often use the sorts of graphs (or variations of those graphs) you've probably already used elsewhere.

Starting Simple

All data miners use graphs, and all data-mining applications offer some graphics capability. Some data-mining applications offer only graphs that you might remember from your elementary school days, like bar charts and scatterplots. That's because these simple graphs are the ones that data miners use most often.

Eyeballing variables with bar charts and histograms

A basic part of the data-understanding phase of the data-mining process (refer to Chapter 5 for much more about this process) is investigating variables one at a time, reviewing their distributions, and checking for obvious data quality issues. Bar charts and histograms are visual summaries that make it easy and quick to understand variable distributions.

The two chart types are very similar. If the variable is categorical, use a bar chart; it will have one bar for each category, and the height of the bar shows the frequency of each category. If the variable is continuous, use a histogram. In the histogram, each bar represents a range of values for the variable.

Your data-mining application may make it very easy to get these charts. They are often included in the output of general-purpose data summary tools, like the example shown in Figure 13-1.

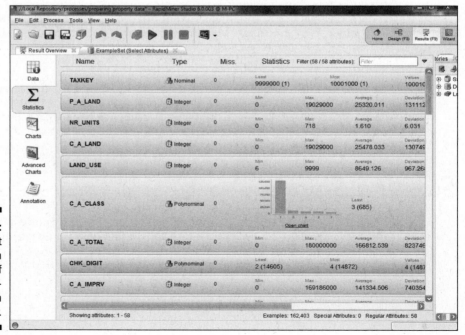

Figure 13-1: Bar chart included in the output of a data summary tool in RapidMiner.

But it isn't always simple to get the chart you want. Look closely at Figure 13-1, and you'll see the phrase *Open chart* beneath the bar chart. Clicking this link opens a chart editor. You'd expect to see a chart that's identical to the one in the data summary open in the editor, right? Figure 13-2 shows the chart editor as it looks when opened this way. Not identical! You'll have to fuss with setup (see Figure 13-3) to get back to the same point.

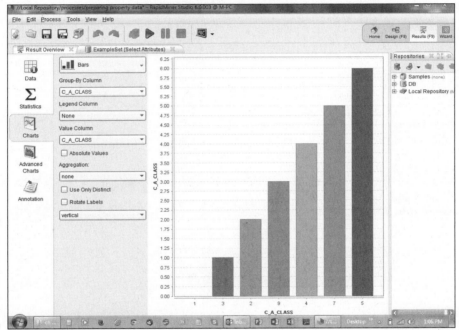

Figure 13-2:
Charts look different when opened in a chart editor!

But this chart editor offers value in other ways. It gives you more options, such as creating more sophisticated chart structure (Figure 13-4 shows an editor that allows complex graph structure) or controlling cosmetic elements like color. Charts editors also provide pathways to export graphs to use in your reports or presentations.

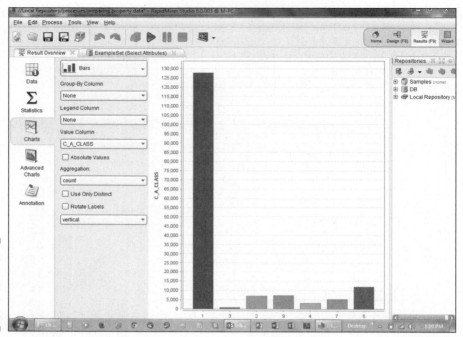

Figure 13-3:
Correcting
the setup to
get a basic
bar chart.

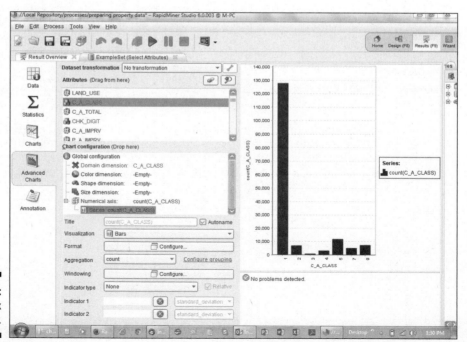

Figure 13-4:
A complex
chart editor.

The complexities of chart setup seen in this section are matters of product design. A data-mining application may make some operations very easy and others remarkably complex, or not possible. No one magic product outshines all others for ease of use, but one may fit your work style better than others. So, before you settle on a product to use, give it a thorough tryout for the kind of work that you need to do.

Relating one variable to another with scatterplots

The first step toward predictive modeling is relating variables to one another. A simple, remarkable tool for that is the scatterplot. It's used to relate one continuous measure to another. Data miners sometimes stretch the rules and use it with categorical variables as well.

The horizontal (x) axis of the plot represents values of one variable; the vertical axis (y) represents a second variable. You may not have a sense of which variable is independent and which is dependent for every pair of variables. If you do, the independent variable should be on the horizontal axis. Each point on the plot represents the coordinates, the pair of values for the two variables within a single case. (These pairs are sometimes called *xy pairs*).

Find your scatterplot tool (Figure 13-5 shows this tool on the menu of Orange; the location for the tool varies by product) and set up a basic scatterplot tool by selecting two variables to use. The example in Figure 13-6 shows an interactive display; the scatterplot appears immediately. In another tool, you might need additional steps to execute and create the chart.

The scatterplot example in Figure 13-6 relates auto mileage to engine horsepower. Low horsepower is associated with high mileage, and the higher the horsepower, the lower the mileage. You can easily see this pattern in the data. You might notice a shape, not linear but somewhat curved. This could provide hints about what model types to try later.

Data-mining applications often have some interactive features in graph displays. For example, Figure 13-7 shows that hovering your mouse over a point reveals the exact values of the two variables for that point. This is easier than trying to read the values from the axes!

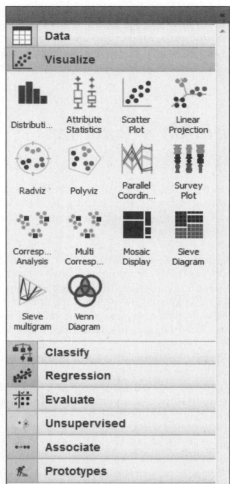

Figure 13-5:
Finding the
scatterplot
tool in
Orange.

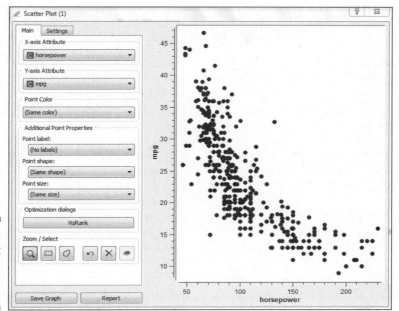

Figure 13-6:
Scatterplot
of auto mile-
age versus
horsepower.

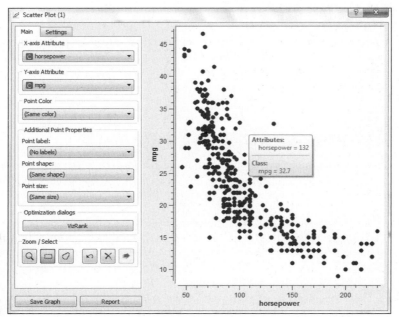

Figure 13-7:
Hovering
reveals
details.

Just say *No* to pie charts

Data miners often use bar charts, histograms, and scatterplots, but you may never meet one who uses pie charts.

What makes a bar chart so different from a pie chart? Both represent relative frequencies of categories. A bar chart is linear, and viewers visually compare the lengths of the bar. A pie chart is not linear. In a pie chart, the relative frequencies are represented by area on the graph surface.

It's hard for people to accurately compare areas. People are pretty good at comparing lengths (one dimension) and not as good at comparing areas (two dimensions). You don't even want to know what happens with volumes (three dimensions) or exponential scales. How do I know this? Research! (Who did the research? Me, I did it. So there!)

What's worse, the pie chart is round. If people can't accurately compare the areas of rectangles (as I know from research), I might suspect that they're even worse at comparing pie slice–shaped areas.

You'll find no glamour in using fussy charts. Avoid nonlinear representations of any kind. Don't use pies, cute shapes, or nonlinear scales. Don't use three-dimensional bar charts. Keep your graphs simple and informative to get good results and support good business decisions.

Building on Basics

Data miners often take advantage of special features to pack more information into simple charts. Labels, overlays, and interactive selection are hallmarks of data-mining applications, special features that allow you to be more productive.

Making scatterplots say more

Figure 13-6 shows a scatterplot that relates auto mileage to engine horsepower. You can see that mileage drops as horsepower increases. That's a beginning step in understanding the factors that determine mileage.

Mileage decreases as horsepower increases, as seen in Figure 13-8 (this is the same scatterplot shown in Figure 13-6, exported as you might to use it in a report or presentation). Mileage increases with time, as you can see in Figure 13-9, a scatterplot of mileage versus model year. It would be helpful to get these two ideas into one graph.

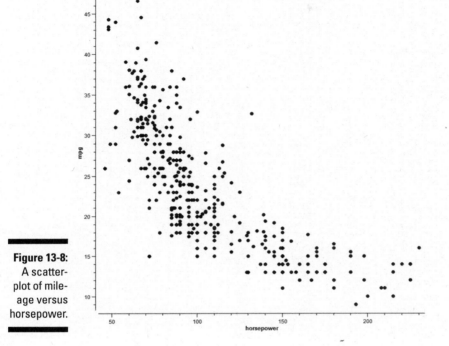

Figure 13-8:
A scatter-
plot of mile-
age versus
horsepower.

Common data-mining approaches for integrating more than two variables in a graph include

- **Labels:** Labels are values of a string or categorical variable that have been superimposed on the scatterplot. Figure 13-10 shows a scatterplot labeled with the model year of the car. (Datasets with many points or long labels can make these charts unreadable, though! The solution is to use only a sample of the data. Setup for this kind of sampling is shown in Figure 13-11.)

- **Overlays:** With overlays, values of a categorical variable define the points' shape or color. Figure 13-12 shows the setup for a scatterplot to overlay model year on the mileage-versus-horsepower scatterplot, and the exported overlay scatterplot appears in Figure 13-13. It may be easier to read color overlays than point shape overlays. The setup is usually much the same.

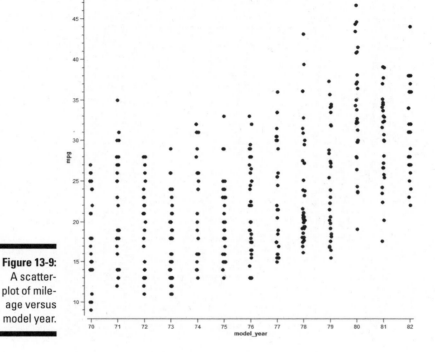

Figure 13-9:
A scatter-
plot of mile-
age versus
model year.

Another thing to keep in mind with scatterplots: You may have multiple points falling on the very same spot! If so, you may not be able to tell a point for one case from a point for 100 cases. The remedy is to check for an option to make multiple instances visible. Look for point size or *jitter* (moves points slightly off their true locations to make all of them visible) options.

Interacting with scatterplots

Interactive scatterplots are great time-savers for data miners.

Say that you see an interesting group of cases in a graph, and you want to further investigate just those cases. If you're looking at just one or two points, you might get the information you want by hovering, as shown in Figure 13-7, but that's not satisfactory when you are interested in more than a couple of points.

Data selection tools in interactive scatterplots give you more power to select data. Figure 13-14 shows the same graph setup, but with a group of points selected by clicking and dragging the mouse around them. This is not just a visual feature. You can export the selected points as a new dataset (see Figure 13-15). This is very handy and fast!

If the points you need don't fit nicely into a rectangular selection, you have other options. Refer to the Zoom/Select area in Figure 13-14. You can see a button with a rectangle for rectangular selection and another with a roundish shape for free-form selection.

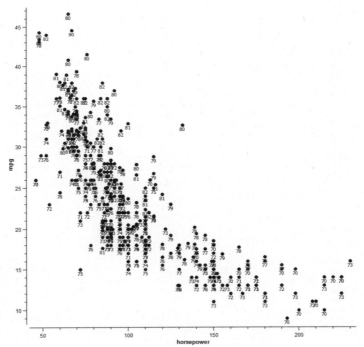

Figure 13-10:
A scat-
terplot with
labels.

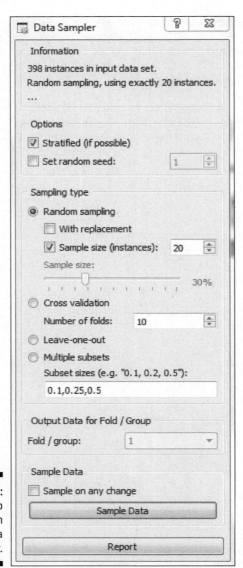

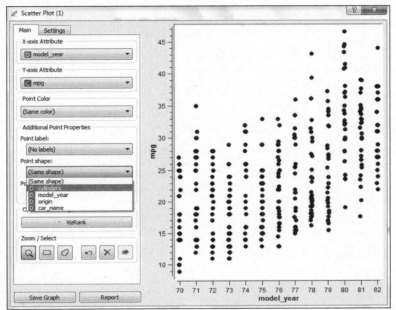

Figure 13-12:
Setting up
an overlay.

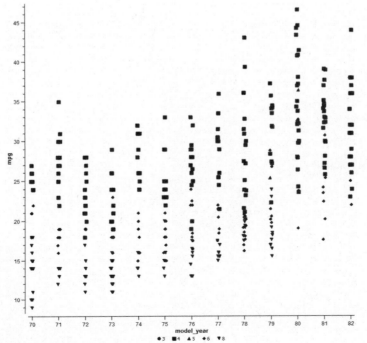

Figure 13-13:
Overlay
scatterplot
using point
shapes.

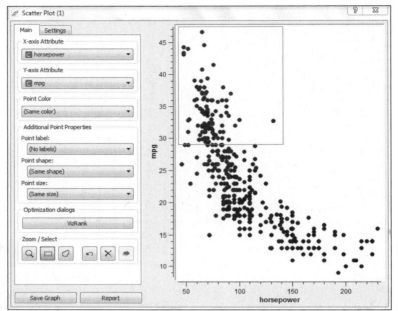

Figure 13-14: Rectangular selection.

	mpg	cylinders	displacement	horsepower	weig
1	30.0	4	79.0	70	2074
2	30.0	4	88.0	76	2065
3	31.0	4	71.0	65	1773
4	35.0	4	72.0	69	1613
5	31.0	4	79.0	67	1950
6	32.0	4	71.0	65	1836
7	31.0	4	76.0	52	1649
8	32.0	4	83.0	61	2003
9	31.0	4	79.0	67	2000
10	33.0	4	91.0	53	1795
11	33.0	4	91.0	53	1795
12	29.5	4	97.0	71	1825
13	32.0	4	85.0	70	1990
14	31.5	4	98.0	68	2045
15	30.0	4	111.0	80	2155
16	36.0	4	79.0	58	1825
17	33.5	4	85.0	70	1945
18	30.5	4	98.0	63	2051
19	33.5	4	98.0	83	2075
20	30.0	4	97.0	67	1985

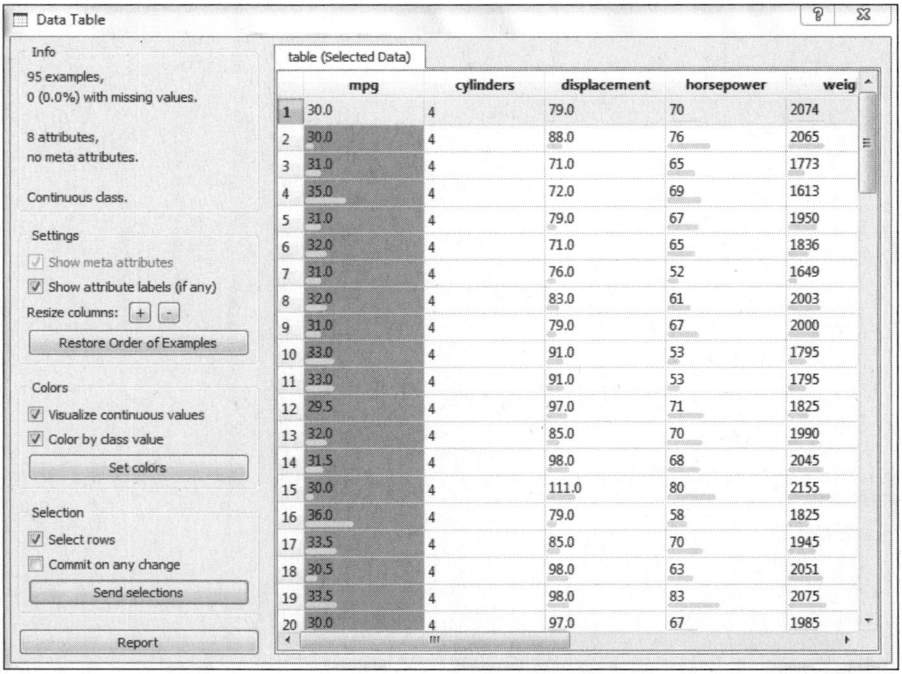

Figure 13-15: Dataset created by selection in a graph.

Here's a free-form selection example using data on the nicotine content of cigarettes sold in different parts of the world. This scatterplot (shown in Figure 13-16) shows nicotine per cigarette for samples from the six United Nations regions. (This is a nontraditional use of a scatterplot, because region is not a continuous variable; it's categorical. Data miners often use traditional tools in nontraditional ways.) The points within a region don't fall in a perfect vertical line. Small shifts (jitter) to the left and right are made for readability and appearance only. A few cigarettes have exceptionally high levels of nicotine, and you want to select those cases.

A drop-down menu (see Figure 13-17) offers selection options. Polygon selection lets you mark a free-form area on the scatterplot. To mark, click on the graph to make a starting point, and then click again and again around the group of points you want until you have made the shape you need. (See Figure 13-18.) A right-click indicates that you have completed the selection; this is visible from the highlight on the graph. (See Figure 13-19.)

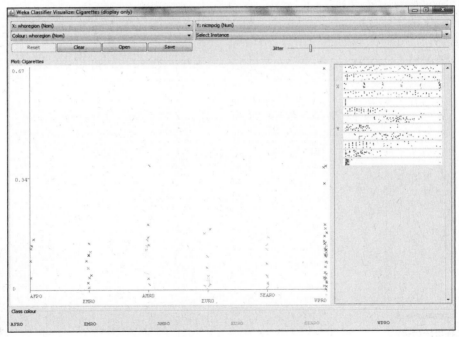

Figure 13-16:
Interactive
scatterplot
in Weka.

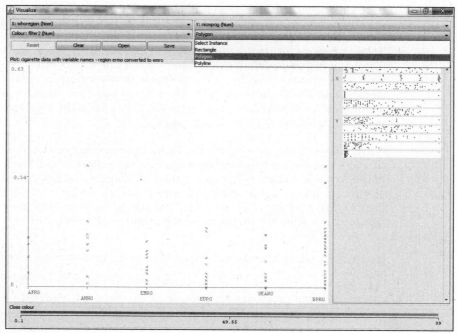

Figure 13-17:
Choosing
polygon
selection.

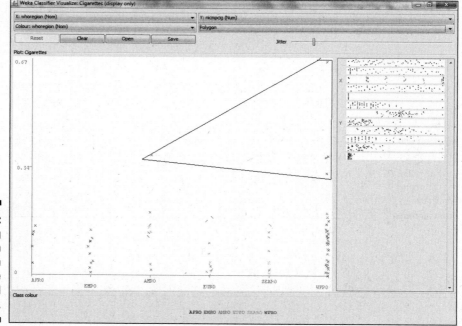

Figure 13-18:
Clicking
points on
the graph
defines the
selected
area.

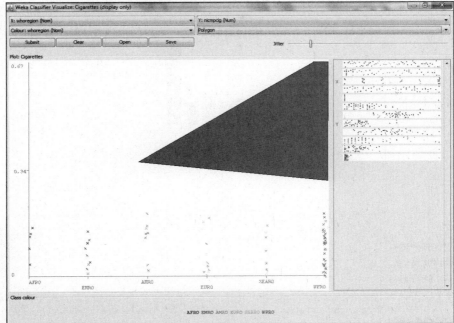

Figure 13-19:
Highlighting
indicates
completed
selection.

Working Fast with Graphs Galore

Data miners work fast. One way to improve your productivity is to take full advantage of tools that let you do several things at once.

It's time-consuming (and boring) to set up a number of graphs separately, one at a time. So use these alternatives whenever you can:

- **Data summaries:** Tools that let you quickly ask for summaries of many variables, and get the summaries all at once. Bar charts and histograms are often included in the output. (Refer to Figure 13-1 for an example.)

- **Chart matrix:** The output is a grid (*matrix*) of small bar charts and histograms, so you can review many data distributions quickly. Figures 13-20 and 13-21 show two examples. They were created with different products but are very similar in function and appearance.

- **Scatterplot matrix:** A grid of small scatterplots. Each small graph shows the relationship for a single pair of variables (usually uses continuous variables). You input a list of variables (see Figure 13-22), and the scatterplot matrix shows you every possible pairing.

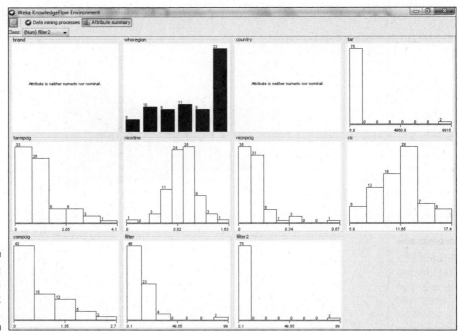

Figure 13-20:
An example
chart matrix
from Weka.

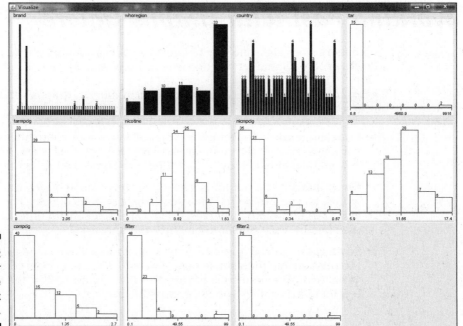

Figure 13-21:
Another
example
chart matrix
from Weka.

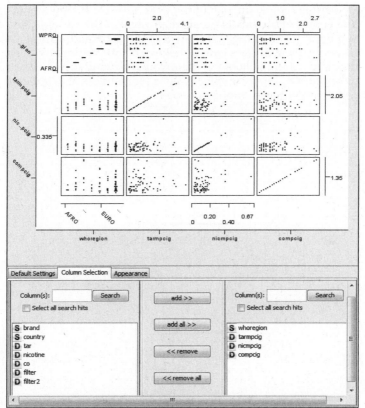

Figure 13-22:
A scatter-plot matrix.

Extending Your Graphics Range

Because data miners lean heavily on basic graphs, some data-mining applications offer little or nothing more. Others provide a wide range of graph options, from the common to the exotic. It's not necessary to use all of these (read what one expert has to say about this in the nearby sidebar "Putting graphics in context: An interview with Laura Kippen"), but you may benefit by selecting and using a few that suit your own needs.

Data miners often use these graphs:

> ✔ **Boxplot (also called *box and whiskers*):** Histograms describe distributions of continuous variables, but have limited value for showing details. A boxplot (see Figure 13-23) is an alternative. The heart of the image is

a box; this represents half of the data, taken in the middle of its range. The center of the box is the median value of the variable, and the lower and upper ends of the box represent the 25th- and 75th-percentile levels, respectively. Whiskers extend below and above the box, representing the range of the bulk of the data. Points beyond the whiskers are taken to be *outliers,* highly atypical values (some plots also indicate *extremes,* which are outliers among outliers).

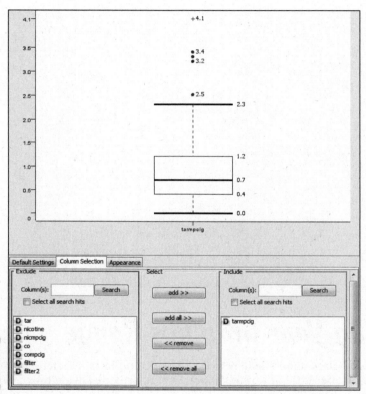

Figure 13-23:
A boxplot.

✔ **Conditional boxplot:** Boxplots for several groups (such as geographic regions) can be placed side by side on a single graph for easy comparison, as shown in Figure 13-24.

✔ **Parallel coordinates:** The plots show values for several variables all together on a single plot, with the values for each case connected by line segments. Common combinations stand out from the rest. For example, look at Figure 13-25, which shows several variables related to cars and fuel consumption. Many cases share certain values, exactly or approximately, forming dark patterns from the many lines following similar paths across the graph. For example, cases for cars with four cylinders, low displacement, high mileage, and late model years form a very dark and conspicuous pattern. (Parallel coordinates plots are hard to read when too many cases are used. If this happens to you, take a random sample of your data, as shown in Figure 13-26, and make a new plot.)

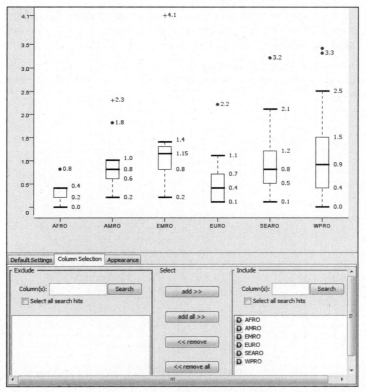

Figure 13-24:
A conditional
boxplot.

✔ **Gains charts (also called cumulative gains):** A gains chart (see Figure 13-27) shows you how much a predictive model improves results over random sampling. Some people are more likely to take action (buy a product, vote for a candidate, break the law . . .) than others. If you know nothing about a group of people, the best you can say is that contacting half of the people will turn up half of those who will take action. But a predictive model can tell you which people are the best prospects, so you can use the model to pick half (or 10 percent or 60 percent, and so on . . .) and get more action. How much more? In the chart in

Figure 13-27, you can see a diagonal line where the *x* and *y* values are always the same; this represents what you'd get by selecting prospects at random. The other line represents the model. The difference in *y* values between the model and the random selection shows how much the model improves your outcome. Read the model line plotted on the chart, and compare it to the line for random sampling.

✔ **Lift charts:** Lift charts are very similar to gains charts. The key difference is that the data is normalized, so that random sampling is always represented as a value of 1 and model results are shown in proportion to random sampling. (Refer to Figure 2-29 in Chapter 2 for an example.)

You may see several different types of charts called lift charts. Some are cumulative, and others are not. Some may even be gains charts (described previously).

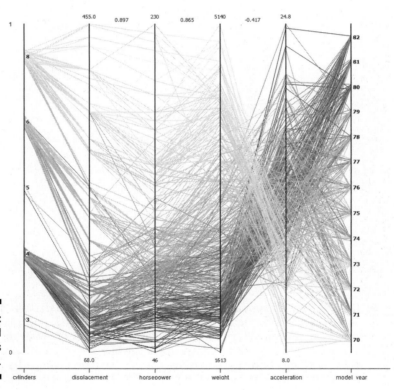

Figure 13-25:
A parallel
coordinates
plot.

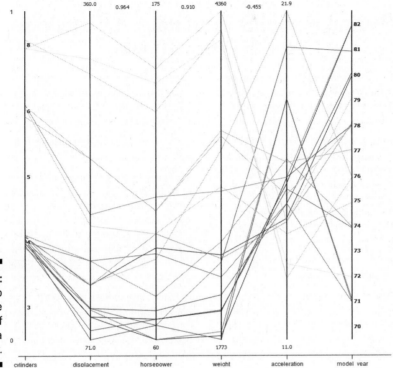

Figure 13-26:
Sampling to
reduce the
number of
cases for a
plot.

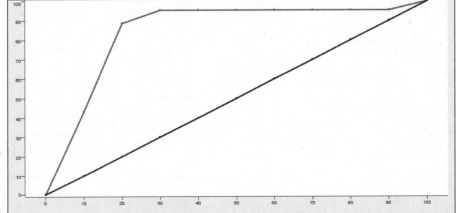

Figure 13-27:
A gains
chart.

Putting graphics in context: An interview with Laura Kippen

Graphs are outstanding tools for communication, and some are lovely to look at, but don't assume that others will immediately see what you see in them.

Laura Kippen integrates graphs with commentary and tables in her reports and live presentations. She's the founder and president of InfoManiacs, a full-service qualitative and quantitative marketing research firm. Laura helps clients make business decisions by using advanced analytics to provide relevant, actionable information.

Q: How important is the final report or live dialogue in the data-mining process?

Kippen: Presentation of information, especially information that was derived utilizing some form of advanced analytics, is critical to the success of a project. Let's face it, if your clients don't get it, they aren't going to be happy.

Q: What role do graphics play in presentation?

Kippen: I don't recall a moment when the chart, graph, or table itself made the light bulb go on. Typically what I have experienced is that a chart or graph elicited a response, but it had more to do with how I highlighted the information and then explained why it was important and not the chart or graph itself.

Q: So, can data miners do without graphs?

Kippen: It's not really my charts that make it all happen; it's all the components of a report that are carefully considered that help clients see the entire story. However, that said, I would never be able to develop and make a compelling story without well-considered graphs, charts, and tables.

Q: Do you find any kinds of graphs that are particularly powerful?

Kippen: Flashy graphics may dazzle but not add information or say anything new. In other words, you can usually make the same point using standard, pedestrian graphs and tables, and clients are likely to respond favorably. At the end of the day, if your report doesn't say anything of value, all the flashy graphics in the world won't save you.

Q: Many data miners feel that they aren't giving clients their money's worth if they don't use fancy graphics. Clearly, you don't buy that. How does your resistance to using glitzy graphics go over with clients?

Kippen: My clients like what I give them and they come back for more.

So, here are the lessons that data miners can learn from Laura:

- Conventional graphs can be effective when used well.

- Eye-catching graphics don't necessarily add new information.

- Graphs may be only part of what makes an informative report for a client — but they're an indispensable part.

Chapter 14

Showing Your Data Who's Boss

· ·

In This Chapter

▶ Picking and choosing data

▶ Recycling variables

▶ Consolidating data

· ·

A beauty expert told a story about a sought-after makeup artist, whose ability to make people look their best attracts a slew of celebrity clients. She explained that, if this makeup artist spent an hour with a client, 50 minutes was devoted to preparation, carefully cleaning the skin, moisturizing, and taking other steps to lay the groundwork for excellent results. As a data miner, you, too, will devote most of your time to preparation. Your effort will be rewarded, because good data preparation lays the groundwork for excellent data-mining results.

Data preparation takes time and patience. Many people spend much more time than necessary to do their data preparation, or get poor results, because they have never had the patience to devote time to mastering data-mining skills. Poor data preparation skills can cause failure to build an effective predictive model (perhaps while your competitor succeeds) and waste hours, even days, of valuable time on each project.

If you want to become an outstanding data miner, make routine investments of your own time and patience to develop your data preparation skills. You'll need two kinds of information:

▸ **Types of data manipulation:** If you don't know what's possible and potentially useful, you won't look for it or know what it is when you see it.

▸ **Capabilities and methods within your tools:** Most data-mining applications offer a wide range of data manipulation techniques, but the steps required vary a lot from product to product.

No book could give you the step-by-step instructions for every data manipulation method in every product; that would take many thousands of pages and require updates nearly every day. But if you understand what's possible, and why each technique is useful, you will know what to look for in any data-mining application.

Attend relevant, face-to-face training for your data-mining application. Don't skimp on training! The money you spend on software and the time you spend using it could be wasted if you don't make the most of what you have. (If you can't attend live training, get self-study books and tutorials for your data-mining application, read them, and do the exercises!) And don't stop there. Review training materials from time to time, and explore documentation and tutorials for fine points to deepen your knowledge.

This chapter introduces a wide range of data manipulation methods that data miners use to prepare data for modeling. It's important that you become familiar with all of these so that you will know what to look for within your data-mining applications, and why.

Rearranging Data

Before you build models or do calculations of any type, you should arrange the data to make your work as easy as possible. You can control data format, display, and the way that data will be treated in your analysis.

Controlling variable order

The order of variables (columns) in a dataset is usually just a matter of how they were arranged in the source file or the database query that was used to import them. That arrangement may not be convenient for you. If you have many variables, it may be hard to spot the ones you want to see. Or perhaps some order makes sense to you, and you'd like the variables arranged that way.

Data-mining applications often allow you to change the order of variables, but instructions rarely show up clearly in the menu or help. These functions are usually buried within tools that serve broader purposes. Look for subtle options like these within data viewers and dialog boxes for other procedures (especially those for data manipulation and data export):

- **Drag and drop:** Tables that display data or *metadata* (such as variable names and formats) may be interactive, allowing you to change variable order by dragging and dropping columns.

- **Up and Down buttons:** Buttons labeled with the words *Up* and *Down,* or arrows pointing up or down, let you move variables up and down within lists to change order. Both types are shown in Figure 14-1.

- **Selection order:** When you select variables from a list (as you would to use only a few of a dataset's variables in a particular procedure), the order in which you select them may persist in subsequent operations.

✔ **Sort gestures:** When viewing variable lists (metadata), you may have sort options that enable you to rearrange variables, perhaps in alphabetical order or by type.

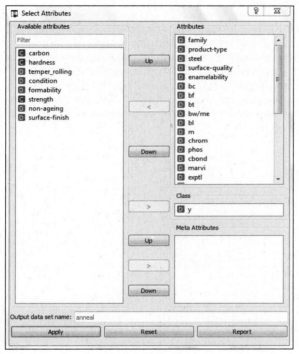

Figure 14-1:
Up and Down buttons let you change variable order.

You may encounter situations where the arrangement of variables is not purely cosmetic. (For example, the Orange data-mining application expects the dependent variable to be the last variable in the dataset.) If you can't find a way to reorder variables within your data-mining application, go back to your source data and change the format with another tool; then reimport the data into your data-mining application.

Formatting data properly

When you see a list of ZIP Codes, you don't try to add and subtract them. You know that they represent places. You understand this because you have lots of experience seeing and recognizing ZIP Codes.

Humans use experience when they interpret the data they see, but computers can't. Your data-mining software will do its best to identify the kind of data in each column, but data types are often ambiguous. So, it might interpret a ZIP Code as an integer or continuous measure. In the end, it's up to you to define the proper format.

Functions for setting data formats and roles (such as denoting the dependent variable for modeling) can be buried within a variety of places in your data-mining application. You might define the formats and role of variables within a data file before you even open a data-mining application (the native data formats for Orange and Weka allow this), as part of the import (see Figure 14-2) or sometime later in the process. You may have tools built for this purpose, like the tools shown in Figures 14-3 and 14-4, or you may define these properties within other procedures.

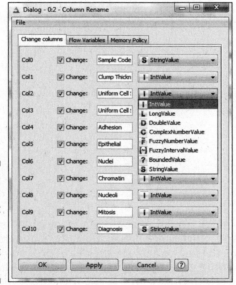

Figure 14-2:
Name and
format
change
within a
data import
tool.

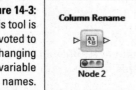

Figure 14-3:
This tool is
devoted to
changing
variable
names.

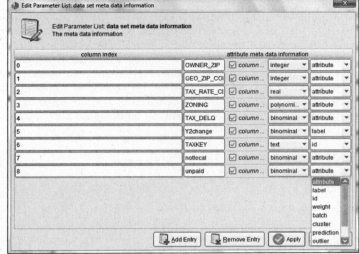

column index		attribute meta data information		
0	OWNER_ZIP	☑ column ...	integer ▾	attribute ▾
1	GEO_ZIP_CO|	☑ column ...	integer ▾	attribute ▾
2	TAX_RATE_C|	☑ column ...	real ▾	attribute ▾
3	ZONING	☑ column ...	polynomi... ▾	attribute ▾
4	TAX_DELQ	☑ column ...	binominal ▾	attribute ▾
5	Y2change	☑ column ...	binominal ▾	label ▾
6	TAXKEY	☑ column ...	text ▾	id ▾
7	notlocal	☑ column ...	binominal ▾	attribute ▾
8	unpaid	☑ column ...	binominal ▾	attribute ▾

attribute
label
id
weight
batch
cluster
prediction
outlier

Add Entry   Remove Entry   Apply

Figure 14-4:
Role options
within
a name
change tool.

Each data-mining application has its own set of variable types and its own limits on how each type can be used. Some of these limits are based in theory. For example, you can only add and subtract numbers, not letters. But others may be just a matter of how the application was designed. So, for example, you may find that a particular modeling tool in one application allows you to predict both categorical and continuous variables, but a similar tool in another application may allow modeling of only one or the other.

Labeling data

You might have a geographic region variable with four possible values: *East, West, North,* and *South.* You could store the information as strings, the full words typed out, or in a shorter code, such as 1 for East, 2 for West, and so on. Using the code reduces data entry time, prevents errors, and reduces the memory requirements for storing the data. But the codes aren't meaningful unless you have documentation, or *labels,* to explain their meaning.

Some data formats enable you to enjoy the advantages of using codes while keeping the information about the meaning of the codes in the same file. These aren't typical in data mining — you're more likely to see them in statistical analysis products — but some data-mining applications can use these labeled data formats. Here's how they work.

Consider Figure 14-5, which shows a dataset open in the PSPP statistical analysis application. (If you'd like to experiment with PSPP, you can find it at www.gnu.org/software/pspp). The data appears to contain only numbers, but these numbers are codes for values of categorical variables. Figure 14-6 shows the same dataset with labels instead of numeric codes. You can switch back and forth between these two display options using the menu, as shown in Figure 14-7. Although the data is stored as numbers, the labels allow you to see what the data means, whether you are looking at it in the data editor, as in Figure 14-6, setting up an analysis, or viewing the results.

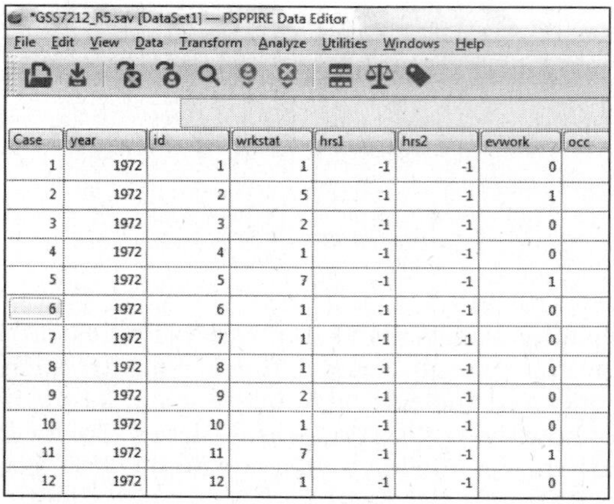

Figure 14-5: Unlabeled data values.

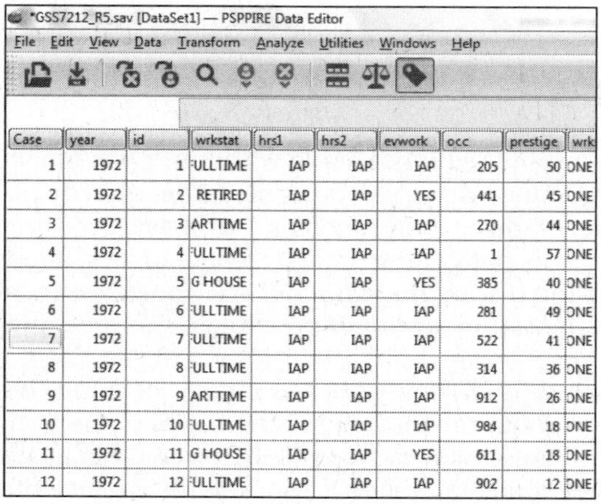

Case	year	id	wrkstat	hrs1	hrs2	evwork	occ
1	1972	1	1	-1	-1	0	
2	1972	2	5	-1	-1	1	
3	1972	3	2	-1	-1	0	
4	1972	4	1	-1	-1	0	
5	1972	5	7	-1	-1	1	
6	1972	6	1	-1	-1	0	
7	1972	7	1	-1	-1	0	
8	1972	8	1	-1	-1	0	
9	1972	9	2	-1	-1	0	
10	1972	10	1	-1	-1	0	
11	1972	11	7	-1	-1	1	
12	1972	12	1	-1	-1	0	

Figure 14-6: The same data values shown as labels.

Case	year	id	wrkstat	hrs1	hrs2	evwork	occ	prestige	wrk
1	1972	1	FULLTIME	IAP	IAP	IAP	205	50	ONE
2	1972	2	RETIRED	IAP	IAP	YES	441	45	ONE
3	1972	3	ARTTIME	IAP	IAP	IAP	270	44	ONE
4	1972	4	FULLTIME	IAP	IAP	IAP	1	57	ONE
5	1972	5	G HOUSE	IAP	IAP	YES	385	40	ONE
6	1972	6	FULLTIME	IAP	IAP	IAP	281	49	ONE
7	1972	7	FULLTIME	IAP	IAP	IAP	522	41	ONE
8	1972	8	FULLTIME	IAP	IAP	IAP	314	36	ONE
9	1972	9	ARTTIME	IAP	IAP	IAP	912	26	ONE
10	1972	10	FULLTIME	IAP	IAP	IAP	984	18	ONE
11	1972	11	G HOUSE	IAP	IAP	YES	611	18	ONE
12	1972	12	FULLTIME	IAP	IAP	IAP	902	12	ONE

Figure 14-7:
Switching
between
display
options.

You may also find other types of data labels in data-mining applications. The native data format for Weka allows you to include comments in a dataset (see Figure 14-8); this gives you a good place to put annotations about the source of the data and other important details. RapidMiner also has an option for annotations; you can use the graphic user interface to enter annotations for individual rows of data (see Figure 14-9).

Figure 14-8:
Weka permits comments within a data file.

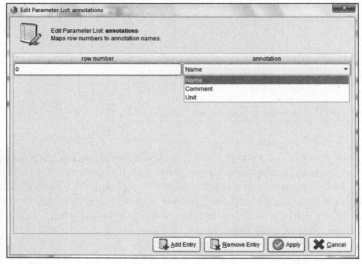

Figure 14-9:
RapidMiner
offers a
place to
enter data
annotations.

Controlling case order

Data miners often sort cases (change the order of rows) to get clearer organization for viewing data or export. Or, you may have a functional reason to sort. For example, some applications require sorting data before merging (joining columns from different data sources).

The steps for sorting vary a lot from one application to another. These are common options that you may find in your data-mining application:

- **Interactive sorting in a data viewer:** Look at the first variable in Figure 14-10, *Clump.* The values change from case to case, with no particular order. One click on the column header (where you see the variable name) sorts the data in ascending order of that variable, as shown in Figure 14-11. A second click re-sorts the cases in descending order (see Figure 14-12). The Restore Order of Examples button returns the data to the original order.

- **Specialized sorting tools:** Data-mining applications often have sorting tools. Look for them in menus for data manipulation or transform. In applications with many tools, you may need to use search to find the right tool; just search for *sort.* Figure 14-13 shows an example; this icon represents the search function in a process. These tools can often handle complex nested sort schemes involving several variables. (See Figure 14-14.)

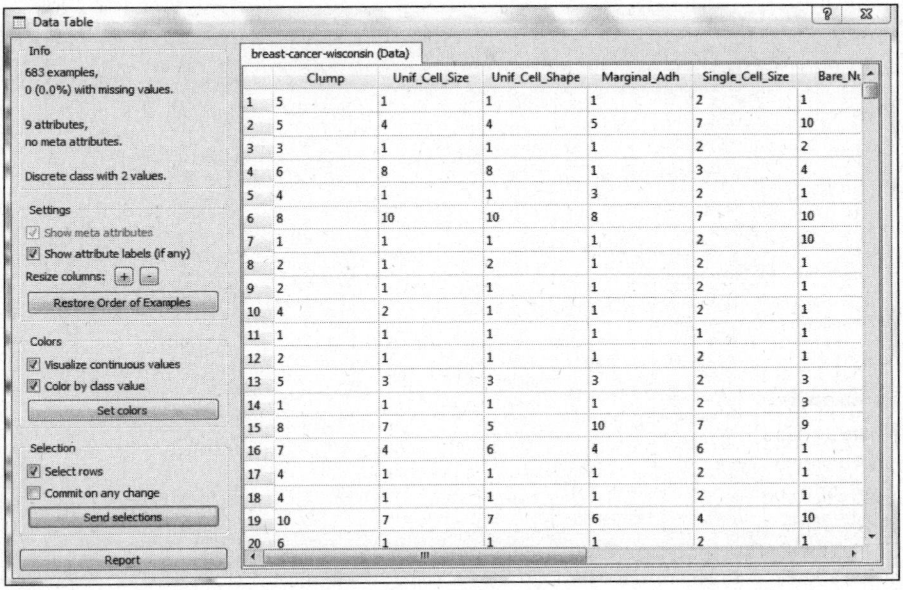

Figure 14-10: Unsorted data.

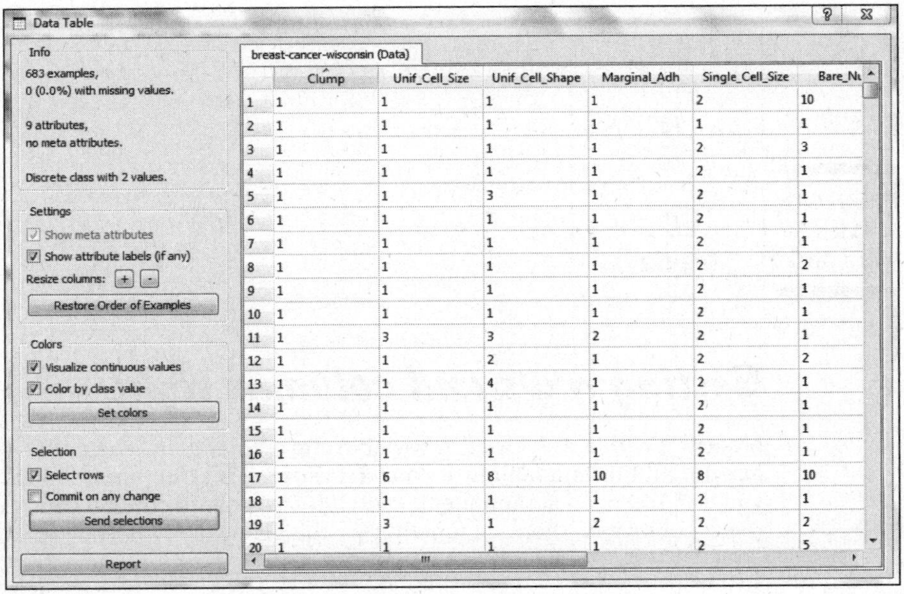

Figure 14-11: Clicking on a column header sorts the cases.

Data Table						

Info
683 examples,
0 (0.0%) with missing values.

9 attributes,
no meta attributes.

Discrete class with 2 values.

Settings
☑ Show meta attributes
☑ Show attribute labels (if any)
Resize columns: [+] [-]
[Restore Order of Examples]

Colors
☑ Visualize continuous values
☑ Color by class value
[Set colors]

Selection
☑ Select rows
☐ Commit on any change
[Send selections]

[Report]

breast-cancer-wisconsin (Data)

	Clump	Unif_Cell_Size	Unif_Cell_Shape	Marginal_Adh	Single_Cell_Size	Bare_Nu
1	9	8	8	9	6	3
2	9	10	10	10	10	5
3	9	10	10	10	10	10
4	9	1	2	6	4	10
5	9	10	10	1	10	8
6	9	8	8	5	6	2
7	9	7	7	5	5	10
8	9	9	10	3	6	10
9	9	5	5	4	4	5
10	9	6	9	2	10	6
11	9	4	5	10	6	10
12	9	10	10	1	10	8
13	9	5	5	2	2	2
14	9	5	8	1	2	3
15	8	7	4	4	5	3
16	8	10	10	10	6	10
17	8	10	10	10	6	10
18	8	10	4	4	8	10
19	8	4	4	1	6	10
20	8	10	10	10	7	5

Figure 14-12:
A second click sorts in descending order.

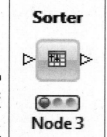

Figure 14-13:
A tool for sorting data.

Getting rows and columns right

A dataset with a row for each variable and a column for each case isn't organized right for data mining. If your data source is structured that way, what can
you do? You need something to switch the rows into columns and columns into
rows. Lucky you, there's a function for that! It's called *transpose* or *flip*.

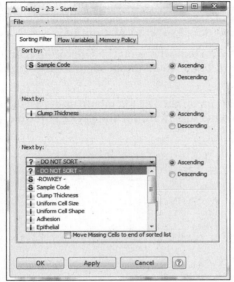

Figure 14-14:
This dialog box enables complex nested sorting.

Putting data where you need it

After you get the data and make changes to suit your needs, you have to put it somewhere. You've already saved data using spreadsheets and other applications, so that knowledge will carry over to data mining, right? Well, not completely.

In most applications, you can save data by finding that option on a menu, like the one shown in Figure 14-15, and using a file browser dialog box to indicate where you want to put a file. But data-mining applications with visual programming interfaces are not organized that way. In your data-mining applications, you will need to find the right tool to save your data. Most data-mining applications have several tools for saving data, and their names vary from product to product, so you may have to hunt a little to find just the tool that you need.

Here's where to look for data export in several data-mining applications. These examples provide clues for finding the data export functions in any data-mining application:

- **KNIME:** Data export tools are found in the Node Repository under IO . . . Write (see Figure 14-16). They are grouped with export tools for models as well as data.

- **Orange:** You only have one tool for saving data in this product, and it is called Save. Find it on the Widget menu under Data in Figure 14-17. The Save dialog box itself (see Figure 14-18) is downright minimalist, but clicking the Browse button (the one with a picture of an open folder) brings up a conventional file browser dialog box (see Figure 14-19). A drop-down menu reveals data export format options.

- ✔ **RapidMiner:** Tools for data export are on the Operators menu, under Export . . . Data in Figure 14-20. You'll find a separate tool for each data format option.

- ✔ **Weka:** Look for data export on the Design menu, under DataSinks (see Figure 14-21), where it wins the award for the geekiest terminology in a data-mining application.

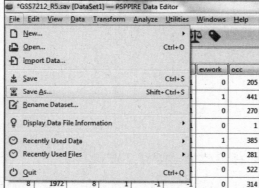

Figure 14-15: Save As option in an application menu.

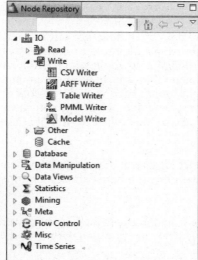

Figure 14-16: Finding data export tools in KNIME.

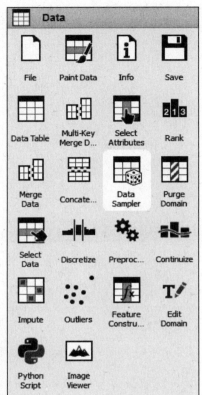

Figure 14-17:
Finding data
export tools
in Orange.

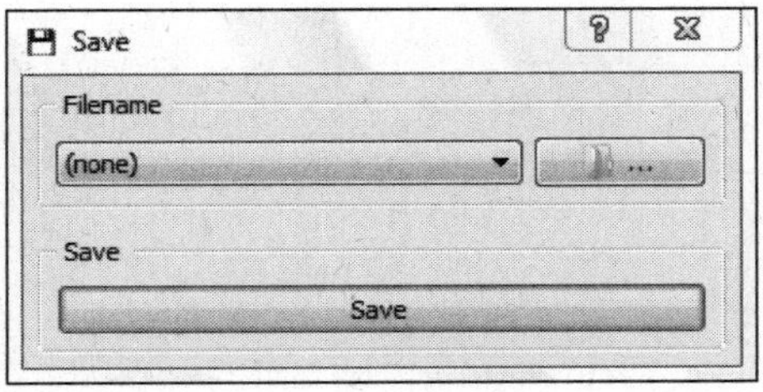

Figure 14-18:
The Save
dialog box in
Orange.

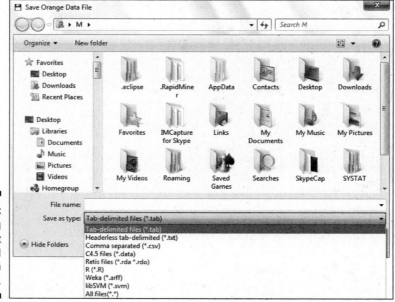

Figure 14-19:
Selecting
file export
type and
location in
Orange.

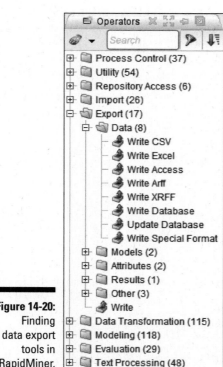

Figure 14-20:
Finding
data export
tools in
RapidMiner.

Figure 14-21:
Finding data
export tools
in Weka.

Sifting Out the Data You Need

Sometimes you'll have more data than you need for a given project. Here's how to pare down to just what you need.

Narrowing the fields

When you have many variables in a dataset, it can be hard to find or see the ones that interest you. And if your datasets are large, and you don't need all the variables, keeping the extras soaks up resources unnecessarily. So, you sometimes need to keep some variables and drop others. Figure 14-22 shows an example in KNIME, where the right tool is called Column Filter. An example setup for this tool is shown in Figure 14-23.

To narrow the fields, look for a variable selection tool in your data-mining application; these are found with other tools for data manipulation. As with other data-mining tools, the names vary from product to product. Look for variations on the words *column, variable,* or *field,* and *selection* or *filtering.*

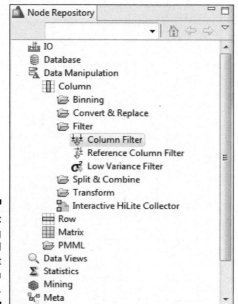

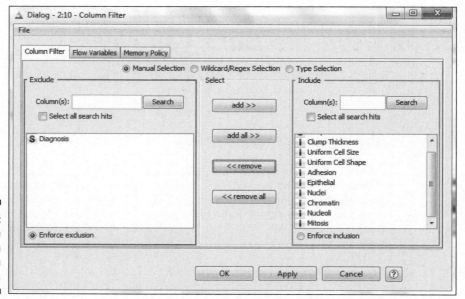

Selecting relevant cases

In Chapter 2, you saw a process for building a very simple predictive model for change of real estate ownership. In that example, cases with incomplete data were filtered out before building the model. Removing incomplete cases is one common example of data selection, or *filtering*.

If that example were carried out in detail to produce a usable model, a lot more data selection would be involved. You'd almost certainly get better results if you considered only one class of property at a time. You'd separate residential properties from industrial, for example. You might compare the behavior of local owners to out-of-towners.

But how would you select only the relevant cases for each segment that interests you? You'd use a data selection tool. See Chapter 2 to see one example, removing incomplete cases.

Figure 14-24 shows a data selection tool in another data-mining application, and Figure 14-25 shows how you'd set up that tool for another kind of selection, this one based on the value of a variable. It's common to use this kind of data selection, and some applications provide all sorts of built-in functions to help you define exactly the cases you want. This one has some exceptional features; it displays summary statistics for the variable and tells you exactly how many cases meet the selection criteria.

Figure 14-24:
Tool for
selecting
cases in
Orange.

Most data-mining applications have tools for selecting just the cases you need. Look in the menus (or search) for *select* or *filter*.

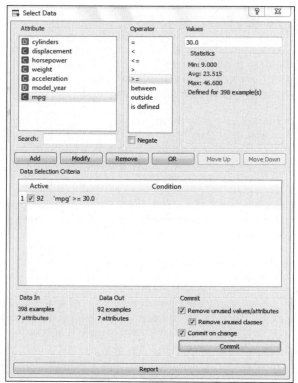

Figure 14-25:
Setting up case selection.

Sampling

A popular notion these days is that more data is better data. This is not a new idea. Data-mining applications have always been developed to work with large quantities of data. Even the name "data mining" suggests large quantities. But often, working with a sample of your data will give you information that is just as useful, make your work easier, and conserve your time and resources.

Sampling plays important roles in data mining. Two of these are described in Chapter 2. First, the data is balanced. That means that the model used equal numbers of cases in each of the groups being compared (in that example, the groups were properties that changed hands and properties that did not), even though one group had many more cases than the other in the original data. Later, the data was split, separated into one subset to use for training a model and another for testing. In Chapter 13, you see how using only a sample of data in a parallel coordinates plot can make it easier to view and interpret. (Scatterplots with thousands of points can be impossibly hard to read!) Perhaps most important of all, sampling just reduces the amount of data, so things run faster.

It's not always obvious where to find sampling tools in data-mining applications. Look for names that are variations on the words *sample* or *split*. Figure 14-26 shows one example, buried three layers into a menu in KNIME. Finding it may be the hardest part. The tool itself (see Figure 14-27) looks similar to others and works much like any other. Setup (see Figure 14-28) may look a little different from application to application, but all of them give you some way to take simple random samples from your data.

Figure 14-26:
Finding the sampling tool in KNIME.

Figure 14-27:
Row sampling tool in KNIME.

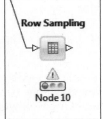

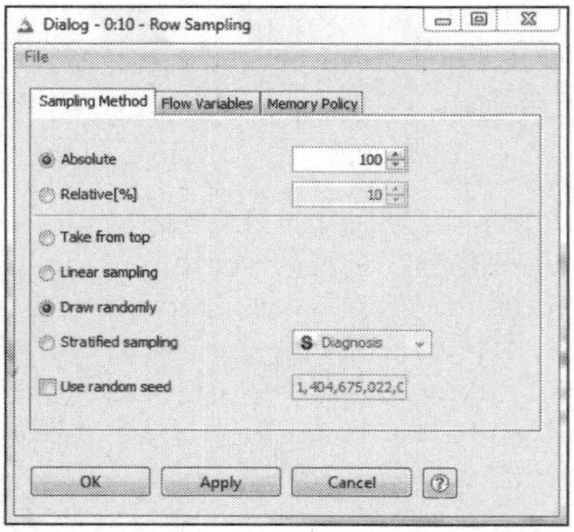

Figure 14-28:
Sampling
dialog box in
KNIME.

Getting the Data Together

When your data is in more than one place, you need ways to put it all together.

Merging

When you join two datasets with different variables, you're *merging* data. Merging is a common operation. You saw an example of merging data in Chapter 2, when a dataset containing general information about real estate parcels was merged with another containing information about which properties changed hands (and which did not). Merging is used frequently in data mining, combining linked data such as

✔ Customer records and marketing campaign data

✔ Before and after test results

✔ Internal and vendor data

To merge datasets, you must have a variable that identifies cases for matching; this is called a *key* or *identifier* variable. And you may have to identify one of the datasets as *primary;* the primary table must have only one case for any value of the key variable.

Some data-mining applications have more than one tool for merging datasets: Figure 14-29 shows the tool for basic merges, and Figure 14-30 shows the tool for setting up more complex merge criteria.

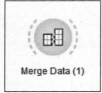

Figure 14-29:
Merge
Data tool in
Orange.

Figure 14-30:
Multi-Key
Merge
Data tool in
Orange.

Appending

If your data sources contain the same variables (more or less; the match does not have to be identical) but different cases, joining them is called *appending* or concatenation. Like merging, this is a common operation. It's used whenever you have new cases for something that you've already been tracking. (Figure 14-31 shows a tool for appending.) The tricky part of finding the right tool is often figuring out what it's called. Look in the menus (or search) for *append, concatenate,* or *merge rows.*

Figure 14-31:
The concat-
enate tool
in Orange
is used for
appending
rows to a
dataset.

Making New Data from Old Data

The following sections deal with using your business knowledge to create relevant new data constructs from existing data.

Deriving new variables

Need to add Variable A plus Variable B to make Variable C? You're *deriving* a new variable.

The calculations that you require to make your new variable might be a lot more complex than just adding two columns together, but that's okay. You can use special functions to help with the process: Standard mathematical functions, statistical functions, string manipulation, and others are all available to you. Refer to Chapter 2 for an example of string manipulation in which you cut ZIP +4 Codes down to the five-character versions.

When you have a continuous variable and need to group the values (such as grouping test scores into percentile ranges, or model scores into deciles), the function you need is *binning*. You may find it in the same tool as other similar functions or in a special tool designed especially for this purpose.

Aggregation

Summarizing data, finding totals, and calculating averages and other descriptive measures are probably not new to you. When you need your summaries in the form of new data, rather than reports, the process is called *aggregation*. Aggregated data can become the basis for additional calculations, merged with other datasets, used in any way that other data is used.

Here's an example of a data aggregation process. A dataset (also used in examples shown in Chapter 2) contains general information about over 160,000 parcels of real estate. This data includes a variety of land uses. What if you'd like to see the average assessed value for the land in each land-use category? Here's how you'd do it.

You'd find the data aggregation tool in your data-mining application. You might use search to find it, as shown in Figure 14-32.

Figure 14-32:
Using search to find the data aggregation tool.

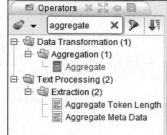

You'd add the tool to a process (see Figure 14-33) and connect it to a source dataset.

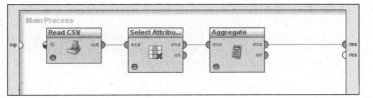

Figure 14-33:
The data aggregation tool within a process.

In the data aggregation tool, you'd choose a grouping variable (see Figure 14-34). In this case, it's the Land Use variable, C_A_CLASS.

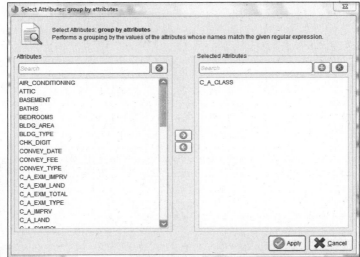

Figure 14-34:
Choosing a grouping variable for aggregation.

Then you'd define the summaries you want (see Figure 14-35). To get average assessed value of the land, you'll select the variable with the assessments to summarize and choose the average function.

When the aggregation is executed, the result is a new dataset (see Figure 14-36), with one row for each type of land use and a new variable for the calculated averages.

Sooner or later, you'll need to aggregate a whole dataset. But when you want to total or average all the data in a dataset, you may run into a problem: What's your grouping variable? The trick is to use a variable with a constant value for the whole dataset. So, create a variable where every value is the same, and then use it as your grouping variable.

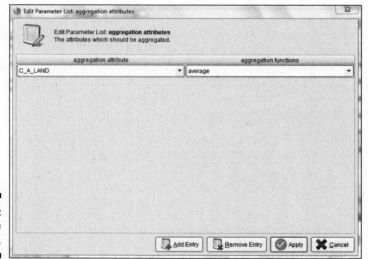

Figure 14-35: Defining the aggregate.

ExampleSet (7 examples, 0 special attributes, 2 regular attributes)		
Row No.	C_A_CLASS	average(C_A_LAND)
1	1	17769.491
2	2	59417.886
3	3	223198.540
4	4	266981.687
5	5	10903.431
6	7	69426.847
7	9	0

Figure 14-36: Aggregated data.

Saving Time

Data preparation takes a lot of time. Your data-mining application may have distinctive time-saving tools already built in and waiting for you, but you won't know it if you don't make a point to see what's there. Make the data-mining process easier and faster by looking for and using special tools for purposes like these:

- **Addressing missing values:** When your data isn't complete, you may need to remove incomplete cases or make intelligent substitutions for blanks. (If the right tool isn't called something obvious, like *missing values,* look for *imputation.*)

- **Weighting:** Need some cases (or fields) to count more than others? Look for weighting.

- **Split file:** Need to do the same actions for each value of a variable? Look for *split file* or *looping* functions.

Chapter 15

Your Exciting Career in Modeling

In This Chapter

▶ Harnessing mathematical models

▶ Investigating decision trees

▶ Exposing the inner workings of neural networks

*N*ow you're really getting to the data-mining goodies. Modeling is the data miner's path to knowing the unknown, or at least making well-informed, valuable guesses about the unknown. Data miners have been known to effectively predict which new customers will go on to become big spenders, which process conditions will lead to serious manufacturing problems, and which insurance claims hint of fraud.

You can be the next data miner to look into the unknown and make exciting discoveries. You won't need psychic powers or a crystal ball, but you'll need a good grasp of data-mining staples like decision trees, neural networks, and clustering.

This chapter introduces you to those staples and helps you on your way to your career in data modeling! This is the part of the job that data miners often love most, because it's here that you'll discover the information that helps drive good business decisions.

Grasping Modeling Concepts

As a data miner, you look for useful patterns in data. Your goal is to discover something that has happened many times in the past, that you can reasonably expect to happen again in the future. You are already doing this informally in your everyday life.

Life is chock full of little patterns. No doubt you have noticed that a gray sky and wind are signs that it is about to rain. That's a pattern. Maybe you've discovered that when your baby gets cranky and runs a fever, he probably has an ear infection. That's a pattern, too. If your boss goes bowling every Tuesday and comes in to work late every Wednesday, well, that's a pattern, too.

Modeling enables you to

- ✔ Discover patterns that are too subtle to identify through informal observation
- ✔ Specify unambiguous descriptions of the patterns you find
- ✔ Apply patterns to make predictions consistently

All your life you have informally used your observations of patterns to predict what will happen in the future or to make educated guesses about facts that you don't know for certain. These predictions drive your actions. When the sky darkens and the wind picks up, you move indoors. When the baby gets cranky and warm, you head for the doctor. On Tuesdays, you check to see whether your boss brought his bowling shoes. If so, you sleep an extra half-hour on Wednesday morning.

As a data miner, you do the same things, but you take advantage of mathematics and computers so that you can make more observations and more predictions. Because you are becoming a data miner, and not a statistician or professor, you won't fuss over theory to do this. The data-mining process may be much more formal than your everyday observations and decisions, but it is still much less formal than classical statistics and academic research.

You walk outdoors at noon. It's dark and windy. You open your umbrella. You've just used a pattern (daytime, dark, windy) to make a prediction (rain) and used that prediction as the basis for a decision (use umbrella). It's significant that you did not feel compelled to identify the mechanisms that cause rain to use the pattern. Though you should look for deeper understanding when you can get it, you may still use patterns that you find useful, even when you don't know why they work.

That's how data miners operate, too.

Any analysis technique that uses data and math to develop well-defined, consistent rules for making predictions is a form of *predictive analytics*. That includes data mining as well as approaches such as classical statistics and operations research. These rules, whether they are very simple and intuitive to understand or vast, incomprehensible networks of equations, are all *models*.

So, at its simplest level, a mathematical model is a prediction-making machine.

In this book, I use the broad term *prediction*. In your work, you may also encounter the term *estimation,* which is often used in the same way, or the term *classification,* which is a prediction for something that is categorical, such as whether a customer will buy or not buy, vote for candidate A or B, or choose the Budget, Standard, or Family plan for mobile phone service.

Cultivating Decision Trees

Decision trees are the most powerful and useful tool in the data miner's tool-kit. You can use them to

- Identify the most effective factors for making predictions
- Discover combinations of factors that define important segments that you might never have spotted otherwise
- Develop simple, meaningful graphics for explaining your findings to managers and clients
- Create rules that are easy to understand and use

You might get by for a long time without any other modeling technique (even the others discussed in this chapter), but no data miner can do without decision trees.

Examining a decision tree

Here's a common prediction challenge: A person applies for a loan. How can the lender determine whether the loan application should be approved? Lenders used to make loan decisions based on personal judgment and intuition, but those days are over. Now they use consistent data-driven rules for deciding which loan applications to approve.

So, how could you determine which factors separate the loan applications that are likely to be repaid from those that are not? You could take records of previous loans, and use the details from the applications as data for analysis. You'd know which loans were repaid in full and which were not, and you'd know a lot about the borrowers, such as the amount and sources of their income, their employment history, and details of their past credit history. You might have information about dozens of factors that have potential as predictors of creditworthiness.

A decision tree derived from that data might end up looking like the example shown in Figure 15-1.

At the top, you can see a summary of all the data used to make the tree. In this example, a total of 100 loans were analyzed — 50 that were repaid and 50 that were not. That might sound odd, because 50 percent unpaid sounds terribly unprofitable. But the data that you use to develop your decision tree doesn't need to have the same proportions of paid and unpaid loans as you have in real life.

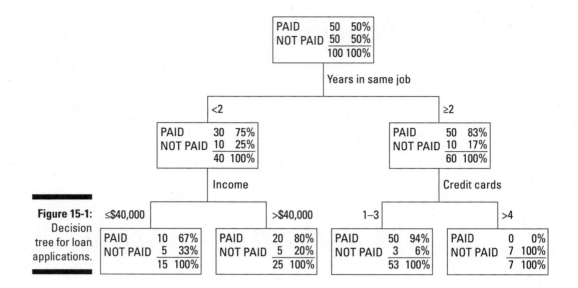

Figure 15-1:
Decision
tree for loan
applications.

The object here is to differentiate the patterns that indicate a loan that won't
be paid from one that will. So, a common data-mining practice is to use equal
numbers of cases in each of the groups that you want to compare. In essence,
you are giving equal weight to the data patterns within in each group.

Next, the tree branches into two subgroups groups based on the length of time
the borrower has remained in one job. Why include this factor and not any
of the others that were available from the loan records? This is the one factor
that has the strongest effect for separating the two groups, as determined by
the mathematical algorithms used to construct the tree. The split refines the
data, defining new groups with greater or lesser frequency of repayment.

The groups may split again and again, and the variables that define second-
level or subsequent splits may not be the same throughout the tree. In this
case, the second split is based on income for one group and number of credit
cards for another. Each split provides a little deeper definition of which loans
are good bets and which not.

Using decision trees to aid communication

It doesn't take a rocket scientist to interpret the decision tree diagram in
Figure 15-1. You see no equations, no mysterious statistics, and nothing complex to interpret. You might not find it pretty, but its simplicity is beautiful!

That's why decision trees are so important for data mining. When you use decision trees for prediction, you won't always know exactly why certain factors are important, but you will surely find out which factors are important and in which combinations. And the tree diagrams provide you with a simple tool that you can present to anyone to help you explain those findings.

You have many variations in the ways that you can build and display decision trees. Although this example has only two-way branches (also called *binary splits*), decision trees with multi-way branching exist. You will have options for the mix of variables that you use and how they are handled. You may embellish the display with tiny bar charts. (Some also offer tiny pie charts, but pie charts are not good choices for data mining. Refer to Chapter 13 for more about pie charts.) Flexibility is also a key to the utility.

You can find many other types of modeling and data analysis techniques, each with its own unique value, but none that make it as easy to present and explain the results of predictive analysis to a wide audience as decision trees.

Constructing a decision tree

I'll walk you through the creation of an example decision tree.

Dr. William H. Wolberg, a physician studying the causes of breast cancer, examined many breast tumors and recorded a number of factors as well as his diagnosis for each of them. What is the potential to use some or all of these factors to automate or aid the process of diagnosis?

In real applications, you should be very familiar with the meaning of the variables in your data, or team with someone who is. Tracking down the explanation that you need can be a lot of work, but it's an absolute necessity for data-mining work. For this practice example, and most practice examples based on publicly shared datasets, a lot of information (even information that isn't private) isn't included with the dataset. In some cases, more information can be found in published research papers that use the data, but that won't always be the case, and not all research papers are easy to obtain or understand.

Understanding the data

Dr. William H. Wolberg, at University of Wisconsin Hospitals, Madison recorded the following attributes for several hundred tumors:

- Clump thickness
- Uniformity of cell size
- Uniformity of cell shape
- Marginal adhesion

✔ Single epithelial cell size

✔ Bare nuclei

✔ Bland chromatin

✔ Normal nucleoli

✔ Mitoses

Each of these was recorded on a scale of 1 to 10. (Unfortunately for us, the documentation does not explain exactly what these attributes are or how the scales are defined.) Also included in the data is the diagnosis, coded 2 for benign and 4 for malignant.

Viewing the workflow

One way to take on this problem is shown in Figure 15-2, which shows a sample process for creating a decision tree for the breast cancer diagnosis data. (This example uses the KNIME data-mining platform.) What's happening in each of these steps?

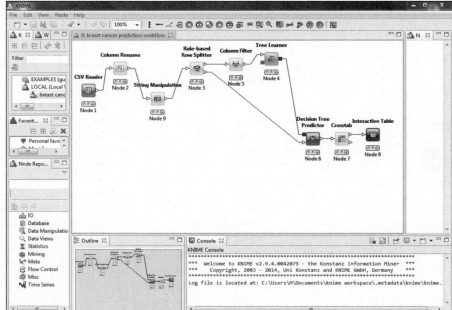

Figure 15-2: Decision tree creation process in KNIME.

✔ **Importing the data:** The data is in a text file in comma-separated variable (`.csv`) format. You can see what the data looks like in Figure 15-3. (Refer to Chapter 12 for more information on importing data.)

✔ **Labeling variables:** No variable labels exist in the data file, so they are typed in by hand, using information from a separate text file that provides variable names and other documentation. See this node before and after labeling in Figures 15-4 and 15-5.

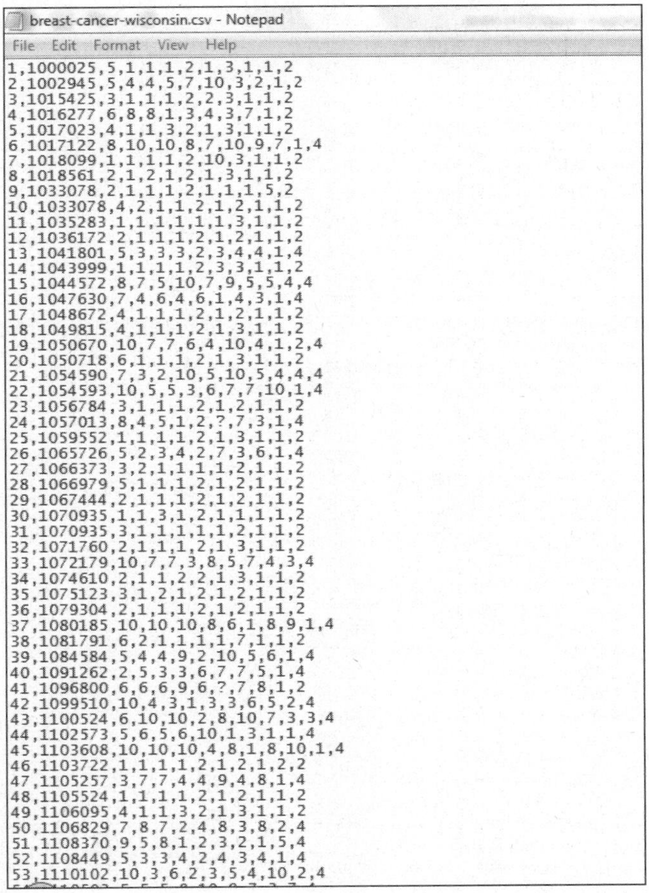

Figure 15-3:
Viewing the
tumor data
in Notepad.

breast-cancer-wisconsin.csv - Notepad

File Edit Format View Help

```
1,1000025,5,1,1,1,2,1,3,1,1,2
2,1002945,5,4,4,5,7,10,3,2,1,2
3,1015425,3,1,1,1,2,2,3,1,1,2
4,1016277,6,8,8,1,3,4,3,7,1,2
5,1017023,4,1,1,3,2,1,3,1,1,2
6,1017122,8,10,10,8,7,10,9,7,1,4
7,1018099,1,1,1,1,2,10,3,1,1,2
8,1018561,2,1,2,1,2,1,3,1,1,2
9,1033078,2,1,1,1,2,1,1,1,5,2
10,1033078,4,2,1,1,2,1,2,1,1,2
11,1035283,1,1,1,1,1,1,3,1,1,2
12,1036172,2,1,1,1,2,1,2,1,1,2
13,1041801,5,3,3,3,2,3,4,4,1,4
14,1043999,1,1,1,1,2,3,3,1,1,2
15,1044572,8,7,5,10,7,9,5,5,4,4
16,1047630,7,4,6,4,6,1,4,3,1,4
17,1048672,4,1,1,1,2,1,2,1,1,2
18,1049815,4,1,1,1,2,1,3,1,1,2
19,1050670,10,7,7,6,4,10,4,1,2,4
20,1050718,6,1,1,1,2,1,3,1,1,2
21,1054590,7,3,2,10,5,10,5,4,4,4
22,1054593,10,5,5,3,6,7,7,10,1,4
23,1056784,3,1,1,1,2,1,2,1,1,2
24,1057013,8,4,5,1,2,?,7,3,1,4
25,1059552,1,1,1,1,2,1,3,1,1,2
26,1065726,5,2,3,4,2,7,3,6,1,4
27,1066373,3,2,1,1,1,1,2,1,1,2
28,1066979,5,1,1,1,2,1,2,1,1,2
29,1067444,2,1,1,1,2,1,2,1,1,2
30,1070935,1,1,3,1,2,1,1,1,1,2
31,1070935,3,1,1,1,1,1,2,1,1,2
32,1071760,2,1,1,1,2,1,3,1,1,2
33,1072179,10,7,7,3,8,5,7,4,3,4
34,1074610,2,1,1,2,2,1,3,1,1,2
35,1075123,3,1,2,1,2,1,2,1,1,2
36,1079304,2,1,1,1,2,1,2,1,1,2
37,1080185,10,10,10,8,6,1,8,9,1,4
38,1081791,6,2,1,1,1,1,7,1,1,2
39,1084584,5,4,4,9,2,10,5,6,1,4
40,1091262,2,5,3,3,6,7,7,5,1,4
41,1096800,6,6,6,9,6,?,7,8,1,2
42,1099510,10,4,3,1,3,3,6,5,2,4
43,1100524,6,10,10,2,8,10,7,3,3,4
44,1102573,5,6,5,6,10,1,3,1,1,4
45,1103608,10,10,10,4,8,1,8,10,1,4
46,1103722,1,1,1,1,2,1,2,1,2,2
47,1105257,3,7,7,4,4,9,4,8,1,4
48,1105524,1,1,1,1,2,1,2,1,1,2
49,1106095,4,1,1,3,2,1,3,1,1,2
50,1106829,7,8,7,2,4,8,3,8,2,4
51,1108370,9,5,8,1,2,3,2,1,5,4
52,1108449,5,3,3,4,2,4,3,4,1,4
53,1110102,10,3,6,2,3,5,4,10,2,4
```

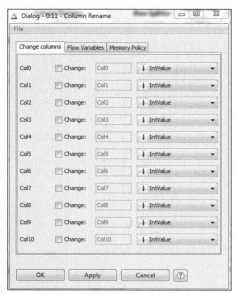

Figure 15-4:
Before
renaming
columns.

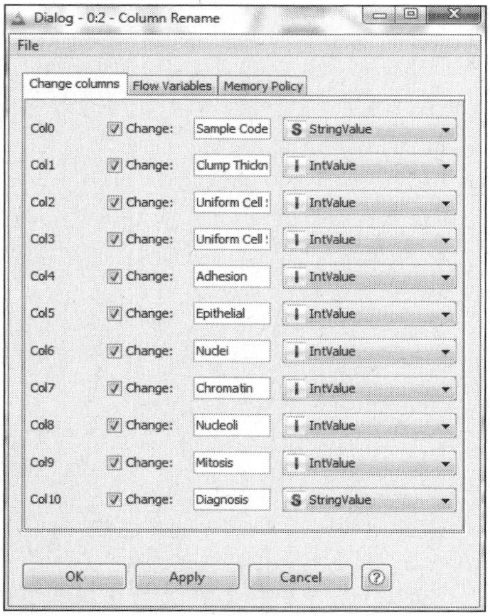

Figure 15-5:
After
renaming
columns.

✔ **Preparing a variable for analysis:** The decision tree tool used in this
example requires a nominal dependent variable. The diagnosis codes
are nominal, but because the codes are 2 and 4, the software thinks

Diagnosis is a number. So, the codes must be converted to strings. Bonus: It's easier to understand the words, anyway. See how this dialog box looks in Figure 15-6 and the instructions for conversion in Figure 15-7.

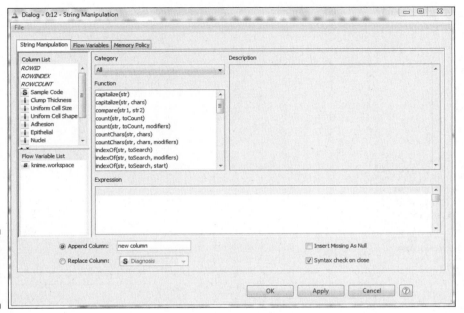

Figure 15-6:
Converting a
number to a
string.

Figure 15-7:
Variable
conversion
instructions.

✔ **Separating cases for learning from cases for testing:** Use some of the data to create the tree, and save some to test how well the prediction algorithm works on fresh data. (This takes thought. Do you have any special considerations about the order of the cases? For example, if your data file had all the cases that were diagnosed benign grouped together at the beginning and those diagnosed malignant at the end, you'd need to take certain steps to ensure that the training and testing data each included both types of cases.) See this node before and after defining the split in Figures 15-8 and 15-9.

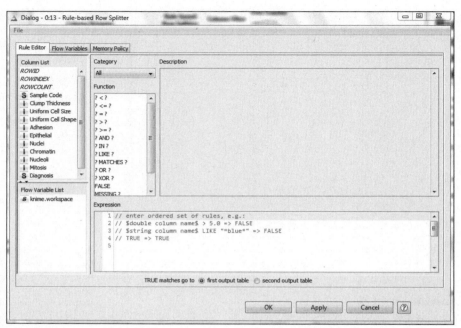

Figure 15-8:
Splitting a
dataset.

Figure 15-9:
Instructions
for splitting
the data.

Expression
```
1 // enter ordered set of rules, e.g.:
2 // $double column name$ > 5.0 => FALSE
3 // $string column name$ LIKE "*blue*" => FALSE
4 // TRUE => TRUE
5 $$ROWINDEX$$ <= 499 => TRUE
```

✔ **Excluding a variable:** One of the variables is a code that shouldn't be used for prediction. See this node before and after excluding that variable in Figures 15-10 and 15-11.

✔ **Creating a tree:** After the data is properly prepared, you can connect a decision tree tool and run it to create a tree and view it. Although most tools offer a number of settings that you can change, you can usually create your first tree without adjusting (or even looking at) any of them. Figure 15-12 shows the tree as it is displayed at first, with just one split. Clicking a plus sign expands that part of the tree. An expanded view is shown in Figure 15-13.

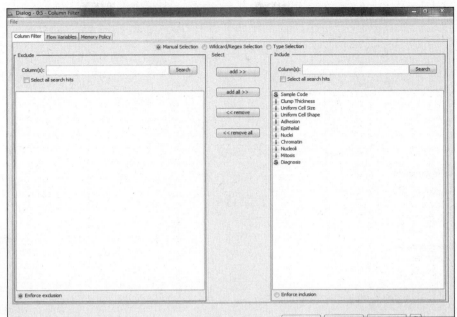

Figure 15-10:
Before
excluding a
variable.

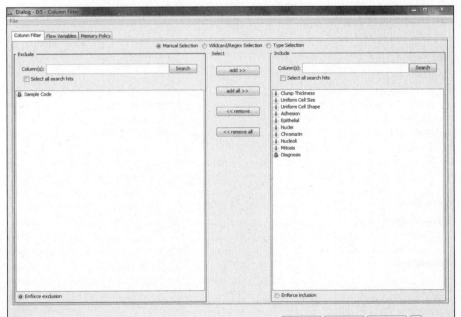

Figure 15-11:
After
excluding a
variable.

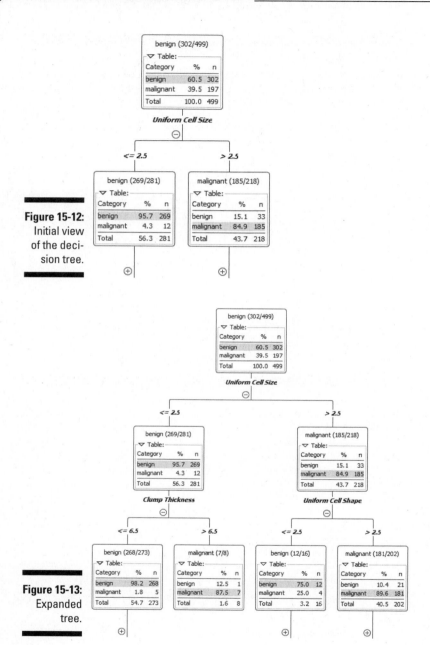

Figure 15-12: Initial view of the decision tree.

Figure 15-13: Expanded tree.

✔ **Making predictions on new data:** The tree looked good, but will the same rules hold up with data that wasn't used to make the tree?

✔ **Comparing predictions to reality:** This is matching the prediction to actual results. See before and after views for setting up the crosstab in Figures 15-14 and 15-15.

✔ **Examining results:** One more step is required to display results. See the results in Figure 15-16.

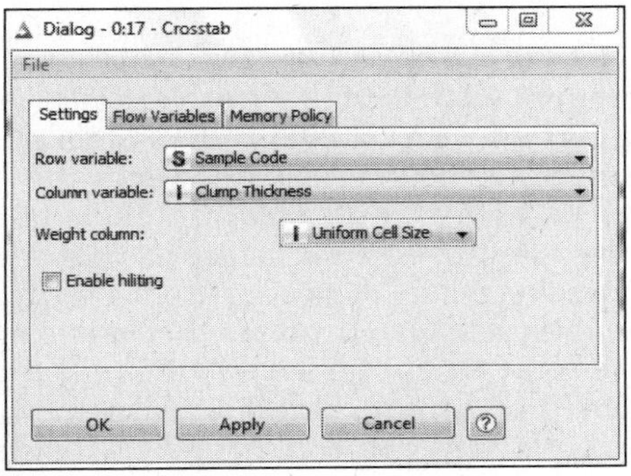

Figure 15-14: Before setting up a crosstab.

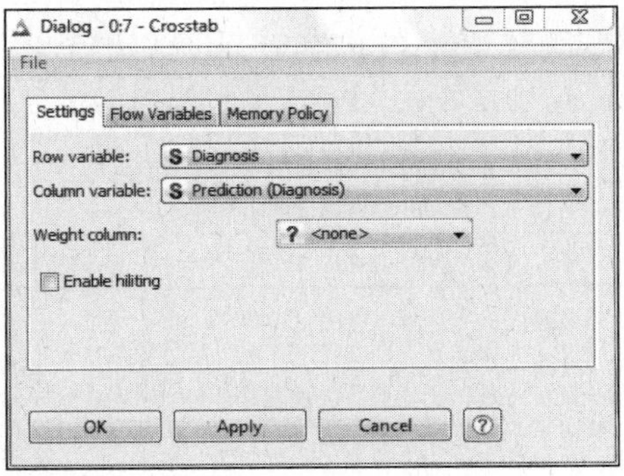

Figure 15-15: After setting up a crosstab.

Figure 15-16: The cross-tab as it is displayed in KNIME.

Row ID	S Diagnosis	S Predicti...	D Freque...	D Expected	D Deviation	D Percent	D Row Pe...	D Colum
Row0	benign	benign	154	122.46	31.54	77	98.718	98.089
Row1	benign	malignant	2	33.54	-31.54	1	1.282	4.651
Row2	malignant	benign	3	34.54	-31.54	1.5	6.818	1.911
Row3	malignant	malignant	41	9.46	31.54	20.5	93.182	95.349

The 3rd Law of Data Mining says that most of the effort in any data-mining project goes into the preparation. Even in this example, which is straightforward compared to most projects, many steps are required before the data is ready to input for modeling. Most of these have to do with adapting the data's format from what you have into what the modeling tool is suited to use.

Examining the tree reveals some useful information. The first branch indicates that Uniformity of Cell Size is the most powerful factor for differentiating benign from malignant tumors, and the best data value for making that split. Expanding the tree reveals more factors, interactions, and again, the right values for the splits.

If the same splitting rules are applied to data that wasn't used to build the tree, will the predictions be correct? The crosstab shows predictions compared to the actual diagnoses for the holdout data. However, the crosstab isn't very easy to read as it is displayed by the software. Table 15-1 shows the same information presented in another way. Each case has both a predicted diagnosis (from the model), and an actual diagnosis (from a doctor). The table shows each of the possible combinations of predicted and actual diagnoses. For example, there were 154 cases that were both predicted benign and actual benign; these were 99 percent of the 156 actual benign cases. The remaining two actual benign cases were incorrectly predicted malignant.

Table 15-1	Another way to present the crosstab		
	Predicted - benign	Predicted - malignant	Total
Actual - benign	154 (99%)	2 (1%)	156 (100%)
Actual - malignant	3 (7%)	41 (93%)	44 (100%)
Total	157	43	200

Each step in the process, represented by its own node, has a label. In this case, the labels are simply the numbers assigned to each node automatically by the data-mining software. But the node numbers don't match the order in which they appear in the process of creating the decision tree. That's common, and it happens just because you may set up a few steps and then find that you have left something out. The nodes are assigned numbers in the order that they are added to the process, not the order in which they operate when it is all complete. It makes no difference to the results; node numbers are just labels. You could change them to any names you like, with no effect on the calculations.

Each node also has a little display with a red, yellow, or green indicator. This will always start as red, shift to yellow when the node has been set up (properly or not), and turn green only when that step has been executed successfully.

Evaluating results

A crosstab comparing predicted diagnoses to actual for holdout data sums up the performance of this decision tree. Of 156 cases that were actually benign, 154 were correctly predicted, or 99 percent. Of 44 cases that were actually malignant, 41 were correctly predicted, or 93 percent.

Using an alternative data mining application often provides alternative paths to get the information you need.

The diagnostic crosstab shown in Table 15-1 was created using a decision-tree model, and two additional tools to obtain the results, as described in the previous section. The results weren't organized in a way that was easy to read. That's why that process may seem a bit complex; it used several tools and several steps just to create a crosstab to evaluate the model results.

Here's another way to get similar information. Instead of undergoing the multistep process shown in the previous section, you could get a crosstab for the model in just one step by using a single tool designed for that purpose. The KNIME Scorer produces a crosstab (shown in Figure 15-17) much like Table 15-1.

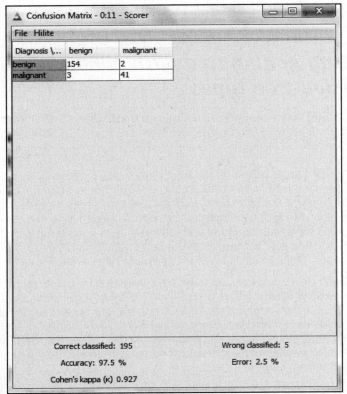

Figure 15-17: The KNIME Scorer crosstab.

If you can get useful results in one step, why would you ever use a longer, more complex process? Each process offers certain advantages. The one-step process was fast and simple, but the longer process provided additional information (row percentages) that is useful for model evaluation. Alternatives like these broaden your options, providing alternative output formats, tailoring results to your intended use, and even letting you get the information you need even when you encounter a bug or other problem with your preferred tool.

Get in the habit of looking for alternative paths like these for your data-mining work. This will help you to master your data-mining application, and gain fine control over your processes and results.

Because so much is at risk in medical diagnosis, it's unlikely that machines will replace doctors for this particular task anytime soon. But other practical ways might exist to use a model like this. For example, automated diagnoses might be used to prioritize cases for review when resources are limited. Doctors and researchers might find that the decision tree provides useful clues to inspire further research, even if they would not use its predictions directly.

Not every application has demands as stringent as potential life-or-death medical decisions. If you got results like these in a model of responses to a direct marketing solicitation, you'd take that model and run with it!

Getting acquainted with common decision tree types

Although you may encounter many names for decision tree algorithms, most are variations on a few major themes. Here are some big names that you should know:

- **CHAID:** This is probably the best known and most widely used type of decision tree. If you took a class in statistics at school, chances are that the first statistical test you learned was the *chi-square test of independence.* CHAID is sometimes described as "chi-square on steroids" because it builds on many tests like the ones you learned in Statistics 101 to construct a diagram of the most important interactions within a dataset. The name is short for *Chi-squared Automatic Interaction Detector.*

- **C&RT:** Here's another decision tree grounded in a technique that may be familiar to you. This one is based on linear regression. C&RT is short for *Classification and Regression Trees,* but the proper name for this kind of analysis is *binary recursive partitioning.* C&RT produces trees with only binary (two-way) splits. (Some experts claim that C&RT is the most *robust* of decision trees. In other words, it produces relatively consistent results from sample to sample.)

✔ **C5.0 (also known as See 5.0):** C5.0 is a proprietary algorithm that most beginning data miners will encounter only in commercial data-mining software (under license from the developer). However, you may find predecessors including C4.5 and ID3 even in free tools, because the details of these algorithms are published.

✔ **QUEST:** A decision tree built for speed. This may be your favorite if you work with really large amounts of data. The name stands for *Quick, Unbiased, Efficient, Statistical Tree*. Like C&RT, QUEST produces trees with only binary (two-way) splits.

All of these decision tree types can be used to predict both categorical or continuous output variables, and all can use a mix of continuous and categorical input variables. But the fact that this is possible doesn't guarantee that the trees in the tools that you use will be so flexible in structure. Some tools are not so flexible! So you'll have to check on what your own tools allow.

Adapting to your tools

The process used to create the tumor diagnosis decision tree was defined, in part, by the particular product that was used to build it, which happened to be KNIME. You could produce the same results with many other data-mining products; it's a matter of finding out what your tools can do and how to use them properly.

Viewed in a different tool, the process may at first seem a lot different. A similar process created in Orange, as shown in Figure 15-18, looks simpler. It does not seem to require all the data preparation steps that were included in the KNIME example.

Although the preparation steps aren't obvious in this example, that doesn't mean that no data preparation is required. It just crops up in different, less obvious places. For example, Orange is designed to work with data in its own specific format, and it so happens that the data required for this process was available in that format. If you had to convert it yourself, you'd find that quite a few steps were involved, and you might spend quite a bit of time on that process. (And this stream doesn't seem to save any holdout data for evaluating the model. Perhaps that's in another file somewhere. More work to come.)

Have a look at the initial tree diagram created by this process in Orange, shown in Figure 15-19. It's rather pretty, but it displays a minimum of information. Again, you'd have to spend time exploring the tool and making adjustments to meet your own needs.

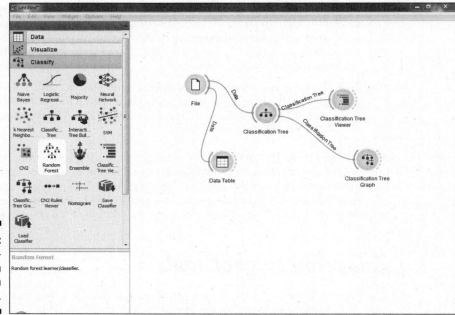

Figure 15-18:
Tree-creation process in Orange.

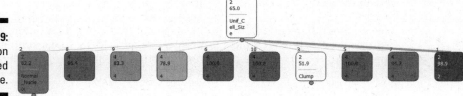

Figure 15-19:
Decision tree created by Orange.

Each product has its own subtle and not-so-subtle variations in capabilities and features, and the best fit for you depends on your particular goals, the kind of data you have, and the interfaces that you are most comfortable using. This can be very personal stuff — one data miner's dream is another's nightmare.

Given enough expertise and time, any results that you could find with data-mining tools could also be found with tools that were not designed for data mining. But the point of data mining is to put analytics into the hands of people who don't have that kind of expertise or that kind of time. So, choose the tool that makes you most comfortable and helps you get the most done in the time you have available.

Data miners need open minds

As you get familiar with the modeling methods used in data mining, you'll find that you like some more than others. Be careful, though, not to let your preferences prevent you from trying a variety of alternatives.

Once, at one of my seminars, I was heckled by two gentlemen who sat together near the front of the audience. The men were apparently big fans of logistic regression, such big fans that they vocally objected to the use of any alternative model. They boldly argued over statistical theory, making claims that simply weren't true. They had come to the seminar because their employers required it, but they were not at all interested in my suggestions regarding the advantages of new modeling techniques.

It's unusual for people to heckle data mining seminars, but it's common that people resist using a variety of modeling techniques in everyday work. What a shame!

Successful data miners don't limit their options when building models. Data mining is based on experimentation, comparing alternatives, and testing results. As you work, make a point of trying alternative model types whenever you can. Comparing alternatives helps you to find the models that work best, and often gives you a better understanding of the patterns within your data.

Keep an open mind and experiment with modeling techniques as they become available to you. Make a point of adding to your knowledge throughout your career, learning more about the software you already have, trying out new features when you get product updates, and exploring new tools and techniques when you can. You'll be a better data miner for your effort, and develop the skill and flexibility needed to provide your clients with the best information you can.

Neural Networks for Prediction

Neural networks are the most mysterious of the data-mining techniques. They can be valuable for prediction and not particularly difficult to use for that purpose, yet produce prediction algorithms so elaborate that they may do little or nothing to promote understanding.

Looking inside a neural network

Neural networks started out as models of the workings of the human brain. Neurons, a type of cell, carry information through our brains and bodies by transmitting electrical signals. It turns out that these mathematical models aren't very good representations of how our brains work, but they have proved quite useful in some other applications.

To understand the structure of a neural network, I'll start with a look at a simple mathematical model and work up one small step at a time. I'll begin with the concept of a straight line and build up to a common type of neural network, a *multilayer perceptron.* (Quick, say that three times fast! Bet you can't. Nobody can.)

A straight line, otherwise known as a *linear model,* takes an input, multiplies it by some value, called a *weight,* and adds another fixed value, called a *constant,* to yield an output. You've probably done something like this in a math class a long time ago. Instead of an equation, think of that as a simple diagram, like the one shown in Figure 15-20, which shows one input connected to one output, with a weight for the connection.

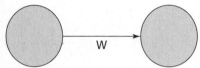

Figure 15-20:
Linear model with one input.

Linear models can also have more than one input. Each one has its own weight. You just multiply each input by its weight, add them up, and add the constant to get an output. This can be represented by the diagram shown in Figure 15-21.

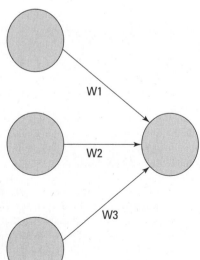

Figure 15-21:
Linear model with multiple inputs.

Remember now that neural networks were invented by brain researchers. These researchers determined that some kinds of problems could not be modeled adequately with conventional linear models. So they dreamed up the idea of a *hidden layer*. The inputs would be used to calculate intermediate values, and those intermediates would be multiplied by weights of their own to produce an output, as shown in Figure 15-22.

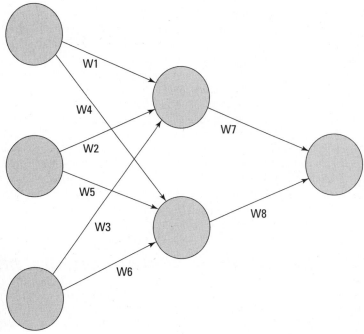

Figure 15-22: A model with a hidden layer.

One more thing: Linear models still only cover a limited range of situations. So, instead of simple lines, the functions are more complex nonlinear forms, hence the squiggles in Figure 15-23.

You can have more than one hidden layer and many, many inputs to a neural network model. If the diagram looks complicated, imagine the elaborate instructions required to carry out the calculations it represents! Some people claim that no equations exist in a neural network. That's not true, but the equations are so complicated that most people don't try to look at them. Even if you did, you would not be able to interpret them as you would with less complex models.

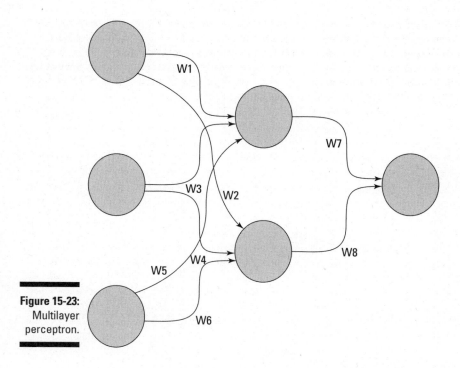

Figure 15-23:
Multilayer
perceptron.

Issues surrounding neural network models

In the previous section, you got an idea of how neural networks work. It's pretty complicated! And the resulting models are not easily understood by intuition. That's why many people describe a neural network as a *black box*.

You can understand that the neural network takes inputs, does calculations, and produces predictions (outputs). But the details of those calculations may be unfathomable. Does it matter? Maybe and maybe not.

If you're using your own money to trade stocks and the neural network works for you, it's no problem if you don't understand everything about the neural network. You only care whether it works.

However, a small change in your situation can make a big difference in whether you are comfortable using neural networks for prediction. Perhaps your job requires trading stocks, not your own, but stocks held by a corporate or trade union retirement fund. In that case, each trade might require a detailed justification. The black box, even if its predictions were consistently accurate, would probably not be satisfactory. (Refer to Chapter 4 for the 8th Law of Data Mining: The value of data-mining results is not determined by the accuracy or stability of predictive models.)

Neural network confessions

Some data miners swear by neural networks. These include some of the most sophisticated practitioners in the field, people with Ph.D.s and deep expertise in machine learning, as well as garden-variety data miners who never worry about the inner workings of the process. They report great success with neural networks for applications as diverse as stock market prediction, character recognition, and network security intrusion.

Others won't touch neural networks. The knowledge that the results are mighty hard to explain is enough to prevent them from even trying these techniques. For those in certain government roles or highly regulated industries where transparency is important, neural networks have little appeal.

You even find those who present rather elaborate theoretical explanations of the limitations of neural networks, but these theoretical limits aren't important for most everyday data mining. What's important is what does or does not work well for you in your own work environment.

Neural networks, down deep, are just groups of equations. It's true that the equations are complex and that a lot of them exist, but the computer shelters you from those details. So, in most cases, the real question is whether a neural network will have good predictive power for your application.

I've used neural networks for nearly two decades. I've taught classes about them. I wrote the first neural network training manual used by one of the largest data-mining vendors. Yet, here's my neural network confession: In my own work, I can't recall a single real client application where a neural network was the most effective model I found.

A modeling technique, any modeling technique, only makes equations to approximate the patterns in your data. If no strong patterns exist, or if their form isn't a good match to the kind of model you use, the results won't have much value. Neural networks are great if certain kinds of patterns exist in your data. If the right patterns aren't there, well, they just aren't there. You'll only know that if you try it. You might get great results, or you might not.

Your clients are not likely to ask you about the specific types of neural networks you use, but it might come in handy to be aware of a few of the biggies. The multilayer perceptron (MLP), described earlier in this chapter, is the most common type. The *Radial Basis Function (RBF)* is a slight modification of the MLP; the modification makes it run faster. You may also encounter a *Bayesian Network.* All these types of neural networks are used for prediction. One common type of neural network, the *Kohonen Network,* is used for clustering, like the methods discussed in the next section.

Clustering

Back when you were a kid, perhaps your favorite toy was Grandma's box of buttons. The buttons were of many different colors and sizes, some had two holes and some had four, and perhaps a few had no holes at all but shanks instead. Some were made of plastic, and others were wood or bone or metal. You had simple round ones and fancy ones with shapes like flowers or jewels. Some may have seemed very exotic. Perhaps a few were broken, but they stayed in the collection anyway.

You could play all afternoon with those buttons, grouping them by color or shape, or more subtle and complex groupings of your own making.

Clustering is just like playing with that box of buttons, only with data instead of the buttons.

Supervised and unsupervised learning

When you think of making predictions, you probably think of predicting some kind of defined outcome. If you are thinking about today's weather, you might want to know whether it will rain — yes or no. A weather forecast is a type of prediction. The models used for weather forecasting are based on historic weather. So the outcome of each day is well defined — it rained or it didn't rain. And you build models to predict that way, comparing days when it rained to identify the differences between the two and predict what will happen in the future.

Situations like that, where the groupings are defined clearly by some known outcome, are applications for *supervised learning*. In supervised learning, you create groupings based on some known result (or value of a variable). The examples given earlier in this chapter, predicting whether a loan would be repaid or a tumor diagnosed as benign or malignant, were both examples of supervised learning.

When you take a mixed batch of buttons and sort them into groups, though, you have no predefined rule about how to form the groups. You examine the buttons, identify interesting features, and sort by whatever similarities you find. Processes like that are called *unsupervised learning*. (Now you know that when you see a child lost in some apparently aimless pursuit, you might be witnessing unsupervised learning.)

Clustering techniques are mathematical processes for unsupervised learning, organizing the cases in your data into similar groups.

Clustering to clarify

Suppose that you took a handful of buttons and sorted them into groups. Perhaps you'd organize them into three batches:

- Small, white buttons with four holes
- Large, dark-colored buttons
- Fancy shapes

What's the use of this? You might use these groupings to decide what to do with the buttons. The first group sounds good for replacing lost shirt buttons. The second might be appropriate for coats. And the third group, the fancy shapes, would be nice for decorative use. Clustering the buttons into groups of similar types can help you to clarify your understanding of what you have, and what to do next.

Using personas

Businesses are often confronted with a big challenge in understanding their customers. Think of your local grocery store. It's open for business with anyone, and its customers have a wide variety of needs and wants. It's hard to plan when you must serve everyone, and very hard for marketers to understand how to communicate with everyone.

Marketers need to understand their target customers to offer appropriate products, tailor messages to customer concerns, and do everything from organizing the store layout to setting prices. When your target customer is everyone, understanding is impossible. The simpler alternative is to use customer *personas,* a few model customer types that, together, represent the bulk of the customer base.

Some people make up these customer personas based on intuition, but it's better to base them on data. Your intuition may be out of date, a poor match for your geography, or just plain wrong.

Getting away from stereotypes

This example might be familiar to you: One persona that gets a lot of attention is the *soccer mom,* often described as a suburban homemaker and mother who drives a minivan and spends much of her time driving her children to activities, such as soccer practice. This persona has been mentioned often for at least a decade. But does that description really resemble the customers of all the businesses who use that persona? One marketer stood up at a large gathering of women, many of them suburban mothers. She asked the soccer moms to raise their hands. Few women raised their hands. Her audience knew about soccer moms and did not identify with that persona; to them, it is a stereotype rather than a realistic representation of their lives.

With the right data, that marketer could discover what's really going on in these women's lives. She might find groups like these:

- ✔ Mothers working full-time outside the home, with young children in daycare
- ✔ Mothers with high-school-age children, who work part-time and want to make a switch to full-time
- ✔ Women without children, who are interested in food and health

Whatever personas you use, it's important that they realistically represent the groups of customers that you serve, and you don't know that unless you have data to prove it. You might create the most detailed of personas, give them names and images, and think of them in everything you do, but it won't mean a thing unless they realistically represent your customers.

Discovering similarities among students

Teachers are often confronted with classrooms full of students with mixed educational backgrounds and needs. A good teacher can do a lot to assess a student's situation during face-to-face interaction, but not every situation provides adequate resources for lots of one-on-one interaction. Even if the time is available, the teaching materials available might not be well suited to each student's needs.

If you studied a diverse group of students and looked at their habits and abilities, perhaps you'd find a few groups with major similarities. It would be more realistic to think that you could adapt teaching materials and methods to three or four major categories than to each of several hundred students, for example.

Researchers at Gazi University collected data on the time that individual students spent on various types of study, and their performance on related tests. Could this data be used to identify and characterize groups of similar students? If so, instructors could get useful information and better help students to succeed.

Looking at a process

One process for clustering data is shown in Figure 15-24. It looks awfully simple, with just two steps: import data and cluster. One reason why so few steps are involved is that the researchers who collected and shared the data did a good job. The variables are the right types (continuous data) for this clustering procedure (*k-means,* the most popular clustering method), and the data is complete; no missing values exist. And each of the two steps required a bit of setup, to do things such as specifying which part of a spreadsheet to import and how many clusters to create.

The data covers 258 students. For each, you have variables for time spent on three types of study (variable names STG, SCG, and STR) and performance on two tests (variable names LPR and PEG). The values in the data are normalized; in other words, they have all been converted to a scale from 0 to 1. Normalization is required to use certain tools, and mathematicians love it, but it isn't very informative for ordinary business users. If you were doing this for a client, you'd want the original data or at least a way to convert the data.

What information is in the results? Figure 15-25 shows that four clusters were created. They are not the same size. The smallest includes only 29 students, while the largest is 104.

A plot, shown in Figure 15-26, reveals the typical characteristics of each group.

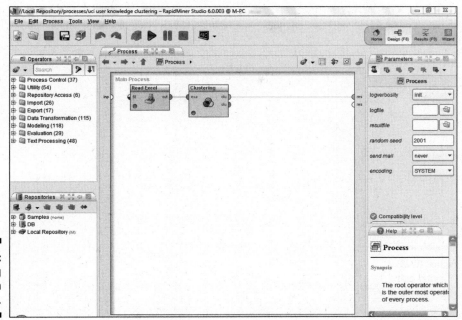

Figure 15-24:
Clustering
process in
RapidMiner.

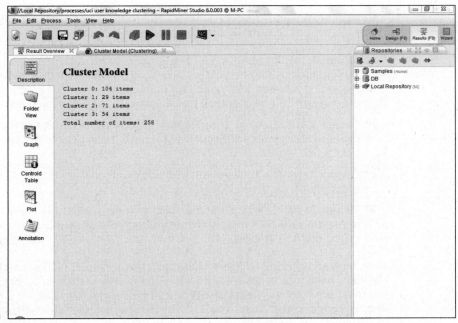

Figure 15-25:
Basic
cluster
information.

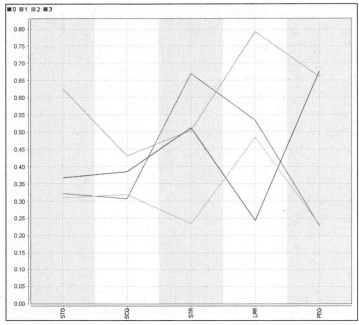

Figure 15-26:
Cluster plot
contrasts
the clusters.

This cluster plot shows test results for the four groups shown in Figure 15-25 (refer to the numbers in the upper-left corner of Figure 15-26):

- ✔ **Group 0,** the largest group, puts a generous amount of time into study, the second highest for each of the three study measures. You'd expect that to pay off in high test scores, and for one test, it does. This group scores highest on the PEG test. But they had the worst performance on the LPR test.

- ✔ **Group 1,** the smallest group, spends a generous amount of time on all types of study and performs well on both tests. (These are the teacher's pets.)

- ✔ **Group 2** studies the least but still does well on one test, LPR. They perform poorly on the PEG test.

- ✔ **Group 3** invests a moderate amount of time in all study areas and scores highest on the STR test. But they are performing worse than any other group on the PEG test.

Now, instead of trying to figure out what's up with each of 258 individuals, the teachers have four groups, each with a distinctive situation. It's likely that the teachers, who are familiar with the students and the content of the tests, would recognize the issues reflected by these clusters. If not, at least they now have the opportunity use this information as a basis for further research. The better they understand what might be behind these group differences, the better they can adapt an educational program to help students do better.

Part V
More Data-Mining Methods

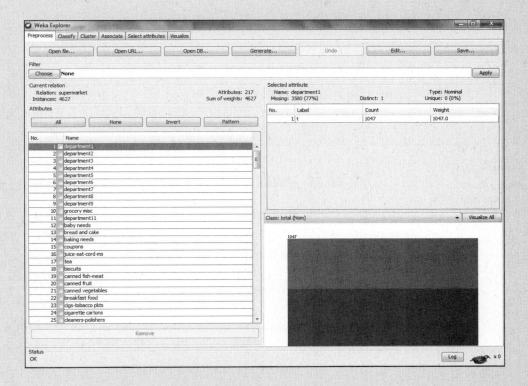

Find out more about the most important data-mining skill at www.dummies.com/ extras/datamining.

In this part . . .

- ✔ Understanding correlation and regression
- ✔ Getting started with segmentation
- ✔ Investigating advanced data-mining challenges — associations, sequences, and text
- ✔ Adding depth and power with sensitivity analysis and meta-modeling

Chapter 16

Data Mining Using Classic Statistical Methods

Data miners are not purists, so no hard dividing line exists between the methods used by data miners and the methods used by traditional analysts. Data miners borrow from traditionalists when it is beneficial and practical to do so. The data miner's toolkit includes some techniques that are familiar even to the strictest of classical statisticians.

Among the old-time favorite techniques of data mining are correlation, linear regression, and logistic regression. This chapter gives you the details on each.

Understanding Correlation

Would you wrap your lips around a car's exhaust pipe and breathe in a lungful of fumes? Of course not! Why not? Because you know that it's not healthy to inhale exhaust fumes (and it would look ridiculous).

You probably also know that it's not healthy to inhale cigarette smoke. Why not? One reason is that cigarette smoke contains carbon monoxide, the same stuff that's in exhaust fumes.

Maybe you know this now, but a few decades ago, people were unaware of the dangers of smoking. In fact, cigarette companies used to advertise their products as healthy. One ad claimed, "More doctors smoke Camels than any other cigarette." Another said, "20,679 physicians say 'Luckies are less irritating.'" Cigarette ads commonly featured images of doctors, scientists, nurses, and even dentists.

So, how did we discover that smoking is unhealthy? It started with correlation.

People noticed that smokers coughed and their throats became irritated. Perhaps they also began to suspect a connection between smoking and certain illnesses. So public health researchers gathered and analyzed data. They related the amount a person smoked to coughing, throat irritation, and the incidence of certain diseases. And the data confirmed that when smoking increased, all those nasty health problems also rose.

When increasing values of one variable go hand in hand with increasing (or decreasing) values of another, that's correlation.

Picturing correlations

Maybe you've noticed: Some smokers cough a lot. Noticing something like that might lead you to wonder: Would data confirm a relationship between the amount a person smokes and the amount that person coughs? To investigate, you'd have to look for a relationship between two continuous variables — the quantity of cigarettes smoked and the frequency of coughing during the day.

How can you tell whether two continuous variables are correlated? One way is to use a simple scatterplot. Put one variable on the x-axis (horizontal) and the other on the y-axis (vertical). If the points resemble a horizontal cloud across the plot, as shown in Figure 16-1, the two variables are not correlated.

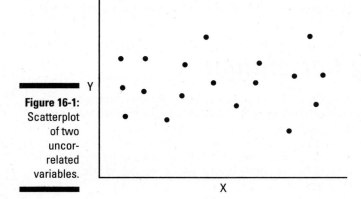

Figure 16-1: Scatterplot of two uncorrelated variables.

Variables are correlated when an increase in one of them is associated with an increase (or decrease) in the other. The complete opposite of uncorrelated variables are perfectly correlated variables, like the pair shown in Figure 16-2. In that case, you see a consistent linear relationship between the two variables, and every point falls on that line without deviation.

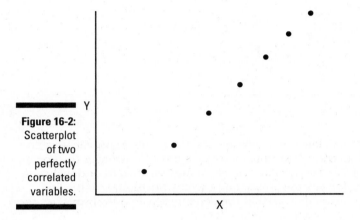

Figure 16-2:
Scatterplot of two perfectly correlated variables.

In real examples, you will certainly encounter pairs of variables that are correlated, but don't expect real-life patterns to look like Figure 16-2. Realistic cases look more like the ones shown in Figure 16-3, which shows a pair of positively correlated variables (when one goes up, so does the other) and Figure 16-4, which shows negatively correlated variables.

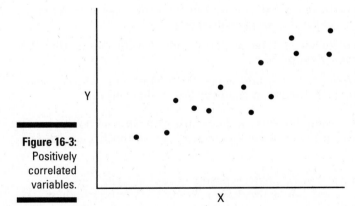

Figure 16-3:
Positively correlated variables.

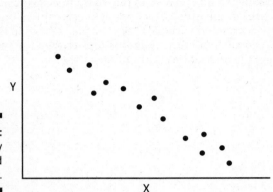

Figure 16-4:
Negatively
correlated
variables.

If the variables are correlated, you will see that the points approximate a line. The closer the points come to forming a straight line, the stronger the correlation. The slope of the line does not matter; it may be upward or downward, steep or shallow, as long as the line is not perfectly horizontal. (If the line were horizontal, that would mean that the dependent variable always has the same value. That's a constant, not a correlation.)

Measuring the strength of a correlation

Correlation is stated as a value (called a *correlation coefficient,* and often abbreviated by the letter *r*) that ranges from –1 to 1, as follows:

- ✓ A correlation coefficient of 0 means that the two variables are uncorrelated (like the variables shown in Figure 16-1).

- ✓ A correlation coefficient of 1 means perfect positive correlation (like the variables shown in Figure 16-2).

- ✓ A correlation coefficient of –1 means perfect negative correlation (meaning that all points fall directly on a downward-sloping line).

So, a correlation coefficient close to 0 implies little or no connection between the variables. The closer the coefficient comes to 1 or –1, the stronger the correlation.

Most data-mining and statistical analysis products can calculate these coefficients for you. Even some calculators have correlation functions built in, which might be handy if you're working with a very small amount of data. The trick is to figure out what the correlation coefficient is called in the product you have. Look for *correlations, correlation coefficient, linear correlation coefficient, Pearson correlation coefficient* (or just plain *Pearson*), or *r.*

Don't confuse *r* with r^2 (*r squared*)! The latter is called the *coefficient of determination,* which I don't discuss in this book.

Drawing lines in the data

When you use correlation functions in data-mining work, you're looking for linear relationships between variables. But if no linear pattern in the data exists (in other words, when the correlation coefficient is near 0 or no linear pattern is visible in the scatterplot), that doesn't necessarily mean that the data has no significant pattern to find. Meaningful patterns don't always follow straight lines.

The scatterplot in Figure 16-5 shows an example of a nonlinear pattern. The graph is curved, with an upswing and a downswing. Variable *y* has a low value when the value of variable *x* is low. As *x* increases, *y* also increases, up to a point. Beyond that point, *y* decreases when *x* increases.

Figure 16-5:
A nonlinear pattern. This pattern can't be detected with linear correlations.

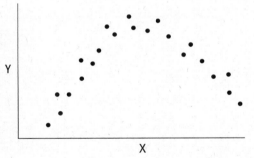

Linear correlations are not the right tool for finding or measuring nonlinear patterns like these. In fact, the correlation coefficient for this pattern would be 0.

If you don't identify an interesting pattern between two variables using correlations, that doesn't mean that you have no pattern to find. It just means that no linear pattern exists.

Giving correlations a try

Generating correlation coefficients from your data is usually just a matter of finding the right tool (in a data-mining product) or menu item (in a conventional statistical analysis product) and selecting all the variables for which you'd like correlations. Correlations only deal with two variables at a time, so when you select more than two variables, your software will calculate correlations for each pair in your list.

The design of a car determines much about how the car performs and how much fuel it consumes. For example, you might expect that the more cylinders a car has, the worse the mileage will be. Correlations can help you to confirm (or refute) such expectations and to quantify those effects.

Figure 16-6 shows a sample workflow (in the KNIME product) for calculating correlations. It has just two steps, one for importing data into the software and one for setting up the correlations.

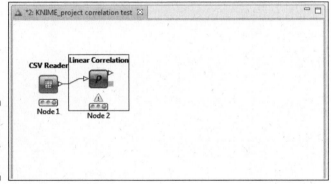

Figure 16-6: Sample workflow for correlations.

The exact number of steps that you require to do any given task may vary from the examples in this book. Data preparation, the design of your data-mining product, and your own specific needs all affect the kinds and number of steps required for your own processes.

You can usually select as many variables as you want all at once when setting up correlations. Figure 16-7 shows a correlation tool setup, including several variables and excluding others. In this example, the variable *mpg* is mileage — miles per gallon of gas. Other factors, such as the number of cylinders and the weight of the car might be expected to have an impact on mileage.

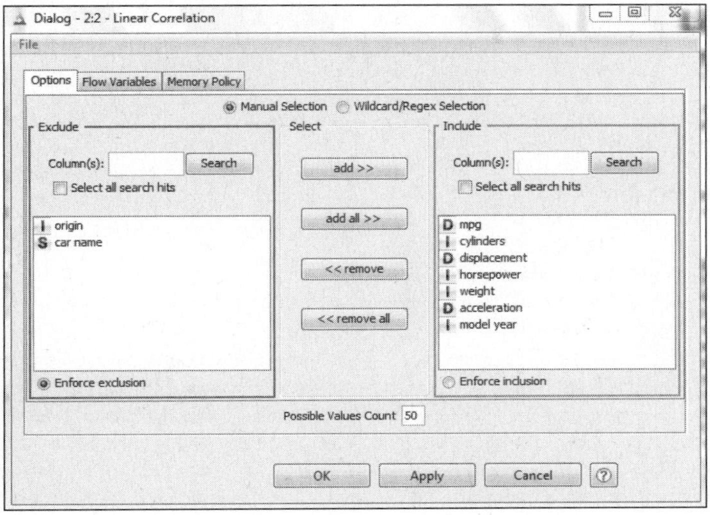

Figure 16-7:
Setting up
correlations.

You will often have a choice of output formats for correlations. A *correlation matrix*, a sort of table that lets you read the correlation coefficient for any pair of variables, is the most common. Figure 16-8 shows the correlation matrix for the example in Figure 16-7. (Refer to the previous section for an explanation of how to interpret correlation coefficients.)

Figure 16-8:
A correlation matrix.

Row ID	mpg	cylinders	displac...	horsep...	weight	acceler...	model y...
mpg	1	-0.775	-0.804	-0.778	-0.832	0.42	0.579
cylinders	-0.775	1	0.951	0.843	0.896	-0.505	-0.349
displacement	-0.804	0.951	1	0.897	0.933	-0.544	-0.37
horsepower	-0.778	0.843	0.897	1	0.865	-0.689	-0.416
weight	-0.832	0.896	0.933	0.865	1	-0.417	-0.307
acceleration	0.42	-0.505	-0.544	-0.689	-0.417	1	0.288
model year	0.579	-0.349	-0.37	-0.416	-0.307	0.288	1

Table "Correlation values" - Rows: 7 | Spec - Columns: 7 | Properties | Flow Variables

One thing you may notice about a correlation matrix: It repeats information. You could find the correlation between mpg and cylinders in the *mpg* row or in the *cylinders* row. What's the point of that? It's just a matter of convenience so that you can examine the correlations in the way that you prefer.

Correlation and causation

Sooner or later, you are bound to hear this said: Correlation does not imply causation.

You may notice that Variable B rises when Variable A rises. Or that Variable C decreases when Variable A increases. Those patterns are correlations. When you hear that correlation does not imply causation, it means that those patterns are not proof that Variable A causes changes in Variables B and C. Correlation occurs in several situations, including

- One variable is the cause and the other is the effect.
- The variables are driven by a shared cause.
- Coincidence.

The idea that correlation does not imply causation is an important concept in all kinds of data analysis. But it's used by some people as an excuse for rejecting all sorts of statistics. You might hear one of them say something like this: "Murder rates rise when ice cream sales rise. Does that means ice cream causes murder?" It's true that murder rates rise in the summer heat, along with ice cream sales, and it's true that this is not proof that ice cream causes murder. But you'll find another side to the matter of correlation and causation.

If one thing does cause another, that will be reflected in the data. If education prevents teen pregnancy, teens who get more education will have fewer pregnancies. If extreme heat causes elderly people to die, a rise in deaths of elderly people will occur during heat waves. If nitrogen in the soil promotes soybean growth, soybean crop yields will be higher in fields with lots of nitrogen in the soil than in fields where the soil is low in nitrogen.

In other words, correlation may not imply causation, but causation implies correlation.

So, if you suspect that Thing 1 causes Thing 2, look for data and find out whether the data supports your theory.

You may have the alternative of getting the correlations in some graphic form. Some products offer a scatterplot matrix, a collection of scatterplots like the ones seen in Figures 16-1 through 16-5, but very small and organized in rows and columns similar to the correlation matrix. Another type of graphic uses color to indicate positive and negative correlations, and intensity to reflect the strength of the correlation.

Output style also varies from product to product. The correlation matrix shown in Figure 16-9 (created with PSPP, a menu-driven statistical analysis tool) includes *significance* measures. These address the question of whether any correlation observed in the data is meaningful or simply an artifact of natural variation in the data points. Significance values close to 0 indicate that the correlation is *significant,* meaning that the evidence suggests it is not merely due to chance variation. (The value N in the matrix is the number of cases used to calculate each correlation coefficient.)

Correlations

		mpg	cylinders	displacement	horsepower	weight	acceleration	model_year
mpg	Pearson Correlation	1.00	-.78	-.80	-.78	-.83	.42	.58
	Sig. (2-tailed)		.00	.00	.00	.00	.00	.00
	N	398	398	398	392	398	398	398
cylinders	Pearson Correlation	-.78	1.00	.95	.84	.90	-.51	-.35
	Sig. (2-tailed)	.00		.00	.00	.00	.00	.00
	N	398	398	398	392	398	398	398
displacement	Pearson Correlation	-.80	.95	1.00	.90	.93	-.54	-.37
	Sig. (2-tailed)	.00	.00		.00	.00	.00	.00
	N	398	398	398	392	398	398	398
horsepower	Pearson Correlation	-.78	.84	.90	1.00	.86	-.69	-.42
	Sig. (2-tailed)	.00	.00	.00		.00	.00	.00
	N	392	392	392	392	392	392	392
weight	Pearson Correlation	-.83	.90	.93	.86	1.00	-.42	-.31
	Sig. (2-tailed)	.00	.00	.00	.00		.00	.00
	N	398	398	398	392	398	398	398
acceleration	Pearson Correlation	.42	-.51	-.54	-.69	-.42	1.00	.29
	Sig. (2-tailed)	.00	.00	.00	.00	.00		.00
	N	398	398	398	392	398	398	398
model_year	Pearson Correlation	.58	-.35	-.37	-.42	-.31	.29	1.00
	Sig. (2-tailed)	.00	.00	.00	.00	.00	.00	
	N	398	398	398	392	398	398	398

Figure 16-9:
The format of a correlation matrix may vary from one product to another.

Understanding Linear Regression

Correlations tell us about linear patterns in data. A correlation coefficient defines a relationship between two continuous variables, telling us whether a linear relationship between them exists and expressing how strong that relationship is.

The next step is to find the equation of the line that relates one variable to another, a process called *linear regression.* Data miners use these equations to predict the value of one variable based on the value of another. Predictions help us to understand how we might control things that we want to control. And when we don't have control, good predictions help us plan.

After we've discovered how to find the line that relates one variable to another, it's a small step up to find linear relationships among groups of more than two variables. This is called *multiple linear regression.*

Working with straight lines

You probably learned a little something about lines in school. A line relates a dependent variable to an independent variable using a simple formula. In school, you probably expressed that relationship as a formula or an equation, but here I'll use words to explain the process.

Call the independent variable *x* and the dependent variable *y*. One way to get the *y* value that corresponds to a given value of *x* is to multiply *x* times a number called a *slope* and then add another number, called a *constant*. The slope determines the steepness of the line, and the constant defines a fixed starting point for the line (the value of *y* when *x* is zero). This is often written as the equation

$$y = mx + b$$

where *m* is the slope, and *b* is the constant, or *y-intercept*.

If you learned about lines in algebra or a basic math class, you may only have encountered examples where every point fit perfectly on the line, as shown in Figure 16-2. In data mining (as in classical statistics), you won't have that kind of perfection. Real-life data doesn't arrange itself in perfect lines, but sometimes a straight line is a useful approximation for a natural pattern in data, as shown in the examples in Figures 16-3 and 16-4.

Confronting too many choices

At school, you may have learned that you can find the formula for a straight line from just two points. This is true, but it isn't much help when you have many data points and they don't form a perfect line. You could choose one pair of points and find a line, but if you chose another pair, you'd get a different line. Nearly as many possible lines exist as points in your data. The question is, which line is best for you to use in making predictions?

Fortunately, you don't need to guess about how to find the best line for your data. A well-defined method exists to do this for you, one that takes advantage of all your data and gives you the one line that fits the data best. This method is called *linear regression*.

Treating each case the same way

Perhaps you run a retail store, and you'd like to have an idea of how much money any new customer is likely to spend in the long term. If you know nothing about the next customer to walk in the door, the best you can do is to assume that this customer's spending will be the same as the average spending level (the *mean*) for all your customers. You know that some customers will spend more and others less, but you will estimate the same, average spending level for everyone.

Imagine tracking the spending behavior of the customers who enter your store. You could give each person who enters the store an identification number, and record the amount that each person spends. A scatterplot of spending versus the identification number might look like the one in Figure 16-10.

No special relationship exists between the identification number and spending, and spending varies from person to person, so the points form a scattered cloud across the graph. If you wanted to predict any individual customer's spending, the best estimate you could make would be to predict that the customer would spend the mean (average) spending amount (calculated by totaling all customer spending and dividing by the number of customers).

You'd make the same prediction for every customer, so the predictions would form a horizontal line across the graph. This horizontal line represents the best prediction you can make with the information you have. It's far from perfect, as the broad scatter of points above and below the line shows.

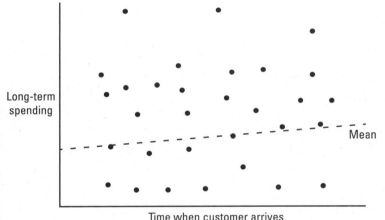

Figure 16-10:
Using the mean to predict customer spending.

Long-term spending

Mean

Time when customer arrives

Treating individuals as individuals

If you knew a little something about the customer, you might be able to make better estimates. What can you know about a brand-new customer? You know what the customer bought and the prices paid. You know whether the customer paid with cash or a credit, debit, or gift card. You know whether the customer used any coupons. If you have a loyalty program, the customer may have joined and given you more information, including an address.

To address your question about how much money new customers are likely to spend in the long term, you'd do well to start by looking at how spending on a customer's first visit relates to long-term spending. (If you have a loyalty program, customer memberships, or accounts, you should have the data necessary to do that.) If you plotted this data with a scatterplot, it might look like Figure 16-11.

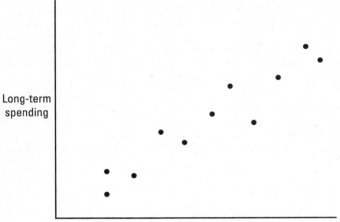

Figure 16-11:
Customer
data reveals
a pattern.

Long-term
spending

Amount spent on first purchase

When you knew nothing about the customers, using the mean may not have looked like a very good way to make predictions, but you had no obvious better option. But when you add relevant information (in this case, first-visit spending), another option can emerge. In this example, the scatterplot shows that the more customers spend on the first visit, the more they tend to spend in the long term as well.

What you need now is a good way to use that information to make better predictions.

If you could draw just the right line through the data, as shown in Figure 16-12, it would resemble the pattern of the data points much more closely than the horizontal line shown in Figure 16-10. That's how linear regression enables you to make better predictions than you could with just an average, by making the line that fits the data most closely.

In this section, *average* refers to a specific kind of average, the *mean*. If you subtract the mean from each real value in the dataset to calculate a deviation and then sum up all the deviations, the sum will equal 0. To take advantage of a predictor variable and make a line that fits the data better than the mean, a little more complexity is necessary. The best-fit line for the data is the one that minimizes the sum of all the squared values of the deviations between each actual value of the dependent variable and the value predicted by the line. Statistical theory provides formulas for those calculations, but you may never need to see them. Your software will take care of that for you.

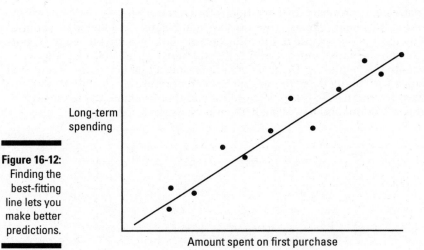

Long-term
spending

Figure 16-12:
Finding the
best-fitting
line lets you
make better
predictions.

Amount spent on first purchase

Finding the best line

Linear regression builds on the concept of correlation to give you a formula that you can use for making predictions and the ability to incorporate several independent (predictor) variables into this formula at once. The steps that you will take to get this formula (perform linear regression) are only a bit more involved than what you've done for correlations.

The linear regression workflow shown in Figure 16-13 looks a lot like the example for correlations shown in Figure 16-6, but here the second step involves a tool for linear regression. Setup, shown in Figure 16-14, is a little different. In linear regression, you must specify one dependent variable — the variable you'd like to predict.

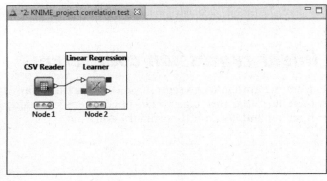

Figure 16-13:
Linear
regression
workflow.

As a data miner, you may do some things that a traditional statistician would never do. The linear regression setup shown in Figure 16-14 includes a couple of statistics no-nos: Several of the independent variables are known to be correlated, and the car's model year isn't a continuous variable; it's a category represented by a number. Being a data miner doesn't eliminate the issues that can come with doing these things, but instead of returning to statistical theory for fixes, you are free to take liberties first and then evaluate the results by testing on holdout and new data. If it works, it works.

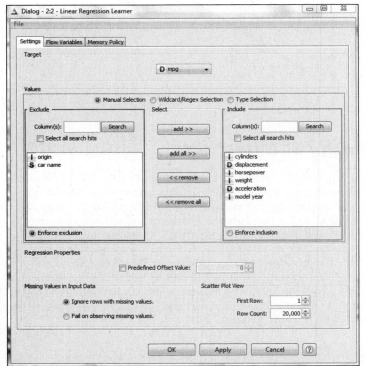

Figure 16-14:
Linear
regression
setup.

Using linear regression coefficients

The formula from the auto mileage regression is shown in Figure 16-15. Maybe that doesn't look like other formulas you've encountered, but after you learn how to read it, you'll find it's a pretty ordinary equation.

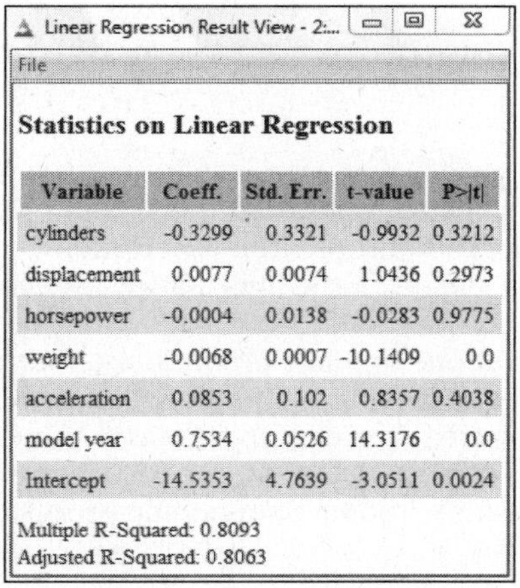

Statistics on Linear Regression

Variable	Coeff.	Std. Err.	t-value	P>|t|
cylinders	-0.3299	0.3321	-0.9932	0.3212
displacement	0.0077	0.0074	1.0436	0.2973
horsepower	-0.0004	0.0138	-0.0283	0.9775
weight	-0.0068	0.0007	-10.1409	0.0
acceleration	0.0853	0.102	0.8357	0.4038
model year	0.7534	0.0526	14.3176	0.0
Intercept	-14.5353	4.7639	-3.0511	0.0024

Multiple R-Squared: 0.8093
Adjusted R-Squared: 0.8063

Figure 16-15: Model results from a linear regression example.

The formula has two parts: regression coefficients (like the slope of the lines you drew in school) for each independent variable, and the intercept (a constant). To make a prediction from a set of values for the independent variables, multiply each variable by its regression coefficient, add up the results for all the variables, and then add the constant (the intercept) to get a predicted value for the dependent variable.

If a car meets this description:

- Cylinders: 4
- Displacement: 156
- Horsepower: 92
- Weight: 2585
- Acceleration: 14.5
- Model year: 82

Its predicted mileage is

(-0.3299×4)
$+ (0.0077 \times 156)$
$+ (-0.0004 \times 92)$
$+ (-0.0068 \times 2585)$
$+ (0.0853 \times 14.5)$

$$+ (0.7534 \times 82)$$

$$+ (-14.5353)$$

$$= 30.75$$

The model estimates that the car's mileage will be 30.75 miles per gallon. Will this be true, all the time, for every car that meets the description above? No, but it's the best estimate you can make based on the information that you have.

You don't have to use hand calculations to make predictions! Your data-mining product can do that for you. (Refer to Chapter 15 for an example of how predictions are made using a decision tree. You can do the same thing for linear regression or any type of predictive model.) Or you can incorporate the formula into another software application. (Some data-mining products will even output the computer code for you.)

Interpreting model statistics

Your linear regression results often include more than just model coefficients. You may have model statistics for each independent variable. The key value to look for will usually be called *p,* or *significance* (or just *Sig*).

Significance can be interpreted this way. The values can range from 0 to 1. Low values (close to 0 and usually not more than 0.05) suggest that the factor is important to the model. Higher values (say, 0.05 or higher) suggest that the factor is not adding value as a predictor.

A result is said to be highly significant when the significance value is low!

You might choose to remove factors that aren't significant from your model and rebuild it. This often yields a simpler but equally effective model.

Applying common sense

From a common sense point of view, the formula for predicting gas mileage derived in the previous section has some problems.

Common sense suggests that any factor that makes a car more powerful or fast, such as the number of cylinders or the displacement, would also cause the car to use more fuel. As any of those factors increases, fuel consumption goes up and mileage goes down. So you'd expect the coefficients of each of those factors to be negative.

But this linear regression model (the formula) isn't consistent with that common-sense expectation. The coefficients for displacement and acceleration are positive.

Recognizing a measurement challenge

Measuring the impact of price in a context that you can't control completely is one of the toughest (and most common) measurement challenges. Here's an example of how it happens, and some alternatives for addressing the problem.

Your business is faced with a question: Should you raise prices? Some managers argue against this, believing that if the prices go up, fewer people will buy, and revenue will drop. They are strict believers in supply-and-demand economics. Others feel that the price of your products is too low, and that customers will still buy them at a higher price. If they're right, raising prices will increase revenue and profits.

You managers have two conflicting ideas:

✔ When prices rise, revenue drops.

✔ When prices rise, revenue also rises.

Because price and revenue are both continuous variables, linear regression is an appropriate analysis technique to use for measuring the effect of price changes on revenue. But it may not be so easy to get data to suit your needs.

If you have a selling environment that you can control, as you would with direct mail sales, you could do a controlled experiment. You'd split a mailing list of customers into several groups, and send each an offer for the same product, using the same copy and the same artwork. You make the offer exactly the same for everybody, with one exception: a different price.

But some selling environments can't be so easily or effectively controlled. If your product is sold in retail stores, you can't offer differing prices to individuals in the same store. Price variations related to special promotions in the stores are probably not a good model for your situation, either, because they always involve more than a price change; advertising and signage in the stores also have an effect. Better alternatives might be to review what happened with past price increases or to investigate store-to-store pricing variations and sales data.

Don't lose faith in your common sense when your results are surprising. Business knowledge is every data miner's foundation, and your knowledge of cars tells you that your model has a problem. (You may have moments in your career when you discover that one of your expectations was simply wrong, but you need a lot of evidence to draw a conclusion like that, not just one surprising model.)

These unexpected results are caused by *multicollinearity,* using independent variables that are correlated with one another. You have several options for dealing with this:

✔ Test your model on new data and in the field, starting on a small scale at first. If it gives you useful results, use it despite its imperfections.

✔ Try using fewer independent variables and see whether you get a model that seems more reasonable.

✔ Find out more about how statisticians address collinearity and use some of those techniques. It's no crime for data miners to borrow methods from other data analysts now and then! (Books that explain multicollinearity and how to address it, in great detail, are available in most university or large public libraries.)

Understanding Logistic Regression

What happens when the thing you want to predict isn't a continuous variable? You will often need to predict that something will, or will not, happen. A customer who visits your website will, or will not, make a purchase. A student will, or will not, pass a test. A tumor will, or will not, be diagnosed as malignant. These are all examples of binary outcomes (a categorical variable with only two possible values). Linear regression isn't appropriate for predicting these.

Decision trees and neural networks, two model types explained in Chapter 15, can each be used for predicting such categorical variables. Still, data miners often turn to a more traditional technique, *logistic regression*.

Looking into logistic regression

Linear regression is based on straight lines, which are familiar to most people. Logistic regression, however, is based on *logit functions,* which are not familiar to most people, and not nearly so simple as a straight line. However, you may know of logits by another name: odds ratios.

Logistic regression gives you a way to predict categories, such as

✔ **Loan:** Repaid or Not repaid

✔ **Tumor:** Benign or Malignant

✔ **Preferred cola:** Coke, Pepsi, or Royal Crown

It works by using a logit function to compute odds (the chance that a given outcome will happen) for each option based on your data. The predicted category is the one which has the most favorable odds.

✔ **The bad news:** Making a prediction with logistic regression involves more steps and more complex calculations than the ones involved with a simpler model such as a linear regression. And, unless you and your audience are both rather familiar with both logarithms and odds, logistic regression results can be challenging to explain.

✔ **The somewhat good news:** Your software does the calculations to make predictions for you (and may even export code that you can integrate into other applications), so you don't have to deal with the complexity of making predictions. But your software won't make explaining the model any easier!

Appreciating the appeal of logistic regression

Logistic regression isn't the easiest model to understand or explain. You always have the option of using a decision-tree model instead (provided that you have an appropriate tool available for doing that). So why would any data miner use logistic regression instead? Some people even prefer logistic regression to all other options. Why?

Logistic regression can be appealing for a number of reasons:

✔ Data miners routinely try every suitable model type for a given application, and sometimes logistic regression happens to be the model type that works best.

✔ Some people are familiar with logistic regression, or at least its name, from workplace exposure or advanced statistics classes (and they trust familiar things).

✔ Some audiences are very familiar with odds ratios and logarithms (perhaps a bunch of engineers who bet on sports), so logistic regression plays to their comfort zone.

✔ Logistic regression creates a single equation for results, and some people prefer that, even if the equation is rather complex.

✔ Logistic regression models tend to be *stable* (not very sensitive to small changes in the data), which is a desirable characteristic and an advantage over some other kinds of models.

Those who love logistic regression the most are usually people who have significant training in classical statistics and a general distrust of data mining.

Looking over a logistic regression example

Figure 16-16 shows the workflow for a logistic regression example. In this example, the object is to predict whether a tumor will be diagnosed as malignant based on factors such as the uniformity of cell size and shape within the tumor. (Refer to Chapter 15 for more information on the data used, the workflow steps, and alternative modeling approaches.)

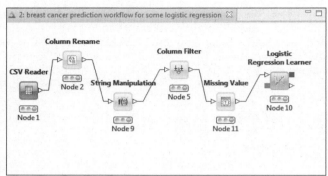

Figure 16-16:
Workflow
for a logistic
regression
example.

This workflow involves several steps that are not included in the correlation or linear regression examples discussed earlier in this chapter. These steps are required for data preparation, such as labeling variables and dealing with missing values in the data. The number of such steps varies with the nature of your data and the design of the tools that you use.

The model coefficients are shown in Figure 16-17. This looks much like the results of the linear regression shown in Figure 16-15, but the meaning isn't quite the same. In this case, the coefficients are elements of a logit function. The calculations required to use input data and these coefficients to predict an outcome are more complex than the hand calculation that was shown earlier in this chapter for linear regression. It could be done by hand, but it's rather a lot of work and easy to make a mistake. Let your tools do it for you! (Refer to the "Cultivating Decision Trees" section of Chapter 15 for a detailed example of making predictions with a model.)

Figure 16-17:
Logistic
regres-
sion model
coefficients.

Logistic Regression Result View - 2:10 - Logistic ...

File

Statistics on Logistic Regression

Logit	Variable	Coeff.	Std. Err.	z-score	P>|z|
benign	Clump Thickness	-0.535	0.142	-3.7672	0.0002
	Uniform Cell Size	0.0063	0.2091	0.03	0.976
	Uniform Cell Shape	-0.3227	0.2306	-1.3994	0.1617
	Adhesion	-0.3306	0.1235	-2.6783	0.0074
	Epithelial	-0.0966	0.1566	-0.6171	0.5372
	Nuclei	-0.383	0.0938	-4.0815	4.47E-5
	Chromatin	-0.4472	0.1714	-2.6093	0.0091
	Nucleoli	-0.213	0.1129	-1.8873	0.0591
	Mitosis	-0.5348	0.3288	-1.6267	0.1038
	Constant	10.1039	1.1749	8.5999	0.0

Log-likelihood = -51.4441
Number of iterations = 10

Chapter 17

Mining Data for Clues

In This Chapter

▶ Finding associations

▶ Using a tabbed graphical user interface

▶ Comprehending association rule metrics

*Y*ou might know the saying, "Where there's smoke, there's fire."

What does it mean? The literal meaning is just what it says. When you see smoke, that's a sign of fire. It's a warning, a clue. You know it doesn't mean that smoke causes fire. And you know it doesn't mean that smoke can't exist without fire. Smoke is a strong indicator of fire, not a cause and not perfect proof.

This smoke-and-fire idea is so significant that people sometimes use the same expression to refer to things that have nothing to do with either one. Often when someone says, "Where there's smoke, there's fire," she means, "This is an important clue."

If you see dark clouds and feel a swift breeze on a summer afternoon, you may suspect that it will rain and choose to carry an umbrella. If you look into a car and notice a baby seat and a diaper bag, you may assume that the owner is a good prospect for your babysitting service, and leave a flyer on the windshield. You look for and use these clues, or associations, in day-to-day life to help you make good decisions. You can do the same with your data.

In this chapter, you discover why associations are important to data miners, how to find them in your data, and how you can take advantage of options that let you tailor association rules to suit your own needs.

Tracking Combinations

In front of the fish counter at a supermarket, you often find a shelf holding bottles of tartar sauce and a basket of lemons. The store has an aisle for condiments and a produce section for fruit, so what are these things doing in the fish department? It's all about the *market basket,* the combination of products bought together in a single purchase.

Store managers know that people often buy fish, tartar sauce, and lemons in combination. Displaying these three products together has benefits for the shopper and the store. The shopper gets the items quickly and easily, eliminating the need to go to three different departments or to track down the tartar sauce among its fellow condiments. The store sells more, because shoppers at the fish counter see and buy items that they like but might have forgotten, or lacked patience to track down elsewhere in the store. Displays like this can increase profits, too, when shoppers buying the fish that's on sale also buy additional items at full price.

If supermarket managers knew about other combinations of products bought together, they could use the same approach to increase revenue and profits throughout the store.

This is where data miners come in. Data miners can find combinations like these by tracking associations in data.

Finding Associations in Data

Many kinds of data hold information about associations. You can find associations in diverse data sources such as the following:

- **Retail:** Products purchased together suggest tactics for increasing revenue.
- **Medicine:** Symptoms and test results occurring in combination suggest specific diagnoses.
- **Social services:** General and economic data reflect common needs for services.

Associations are reflected in data by many cases with identical values for several variables. The association described in the previous section — fish, tartar sauce, and lemons — would show up in a supermarket's sales records as many instances where those three items were included in a single transaction, no matter what other products were, or were not, purchased. The concept is simple, but you'd find it very hard to look at a database with millions of cases and hundreds of variables and spot those combinations.

Structuring association rules

An association rule is a statement like *If Thing A, then Thing B*. So, if we found an association between smoke and fire, the association rule would be *If smoke, then fire*. Here's one example:

```
biscuits=t frozen foods=t fruit=t total=high 788 ==> bread and cake=t 723
```

Here's how this example might read if it were written out in words. *If a purchase includes biscuits, frozen foods, and fruit, then it will also include bread and cake. This was true 723 of 788 times in the data.* The exact notation varies with the data-mining applications you choose, but the idea will always be the same. In this example, `biscuits=t` means that biscuits were purchased (`t` is for true), and `==>` takes the place of the words *If* and *then*. The numbers are counts of how many times each thing happened.

You should also know some concepts that are often used with association rules:

- **Itemsets:** *Itemsets* are groups of things. The group consisting of biscuits, frozen foods, and fruit is an itemset. So is biscuits, frozen foods, fruit, bread, and cake.

- **Consequent:** The *consequent* is the *If* part of an association rule. In the previous example, the consequent is *biscuits, frozen foods, fruit*.

- **Antecedent:** The *antecedent* is the *Then* part of an association rule. In the example, the antecedent is *bread and cake*.

Getting ready

Most of the data-mining process examples in this book use visual programming interfaces. In visual programming, you use icons (little pictures) to represent the steps in your data-mining process. Visual programming is central to data mining, but it's not the only way that data miners work. In this example, I'll use another kind of graphical user interface to derive association rules for purchases in a supermarket.

First open your data-mining application and import the data. The following steps show you how.

1. **Start Weka Explorer. (See Figure 17-1.)**

2. **Click Open File and browse to find the supermarket data. (See Figure 17-2.)**

3. **After the data is imported, you can view data summaries.**

   In Figure 17-3, you see the summary for Department 1. You can see that 1,047 purchases include something from Department 1 and 3,580 cases are missing (indicating that the purchase didn't include anything from that department) in a total of 4,627 cases.

4. **Click the Visualize All button to see visual summaries for all variables in the data. (See Figure 17-4.)**

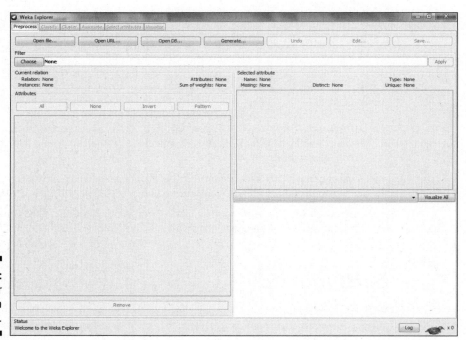

Figure 17-1:
The Explorer interface in Weka.

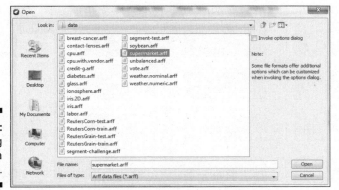

Figure 17-2:
Browsing
for a data
file.

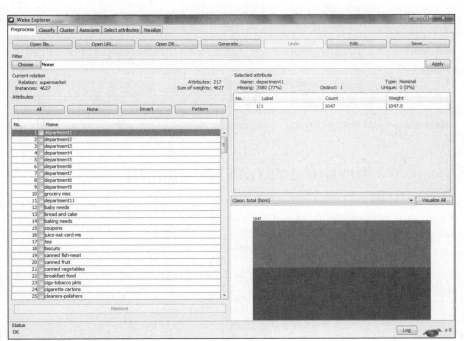

Figure 17-3:
Supermarket
data.

Figure 17-4:
Visual sum-
maries for
all variables.

Shopping for associations

Now you can create association rules. The most popular association rules technique is called *Apriori,* and that's what you'll use here.

To create association rules, follow these steps:

1. **Click the Associate tab. (See Figure 17-5).**

   In the Associator, you'll see that Apriori is the default method and that the name is followed by some cryptic notation. This represents the selected options.

You can select an association rule method. To see the available choices, click the Choose button. (See Figure 17-6.) Data miners most often use the Apriori method; for our purposes here, that's the method you should use as well. If that method is already selected, just close the box without making any changes.

2. **Click the Start button to create rules.**

   Results appear in the Associator output area on the right. (See Figure 17-7.)

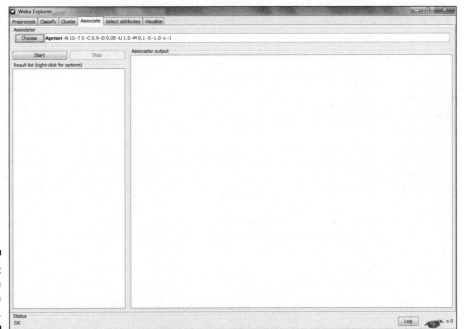

Figure 17-5:
The
Associate
tab.

Figure 17-6:
Association
method
options.

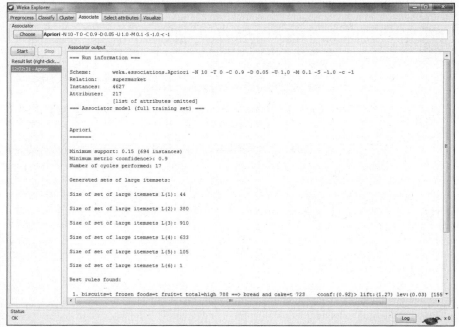

Figure 17-7:
Supermarket
data asso-
ciation
results.

In the results, you'll see a list of rules, beginning with the rule that was used as an example in the "Structuring association rules" section, earlier in this chapter. Here's the list:

```
Best rules found:
 1. biscuits=t frozen foods=t fruit=t total=high 788 ==> bread and cake=t 723
          <conf:(0.92)> lift:(1.27) lev:(0.03) [155] conv:(3.35)
 2. baking needs=t biscuits=t fruit=t total=high 760 ==> bread and cake=t 696
          <conf:(0.92)> lift:(1.27) lev:(0.03) [149] conv:(3.28)
 3. baking needs=t frozen foods=t fruit=t total=high 770 ==> bread and cake=t
          705    <conf:(0.92)> lift:(1.27) lev:(0.03) [150] conv:(3.27)
 4. biscuits=t fruit=t vegetables=t total=high 815 ==> bread and cake=t 746
          <conf:(0.92)> lift:(1.27) lev:(0.03) [159] conv:(3.26)
 5. party snack foods=t fruit=t total=high 854 ==> bread and cake=t 779
          <conf:(0.91)> lift:(1.27) lev:(0.04) [164] conv:(3.15)
 6. biscuits=t frozen foods=t vegetables=t total=high 797 ==> bread and cake=t
          725    <conf:(0.91)> lift:(1.26) lev:(0.03) [151] conv:(3.06)
 7. baking needs=t biscuits=t vegetables=t total=high 772 ==> bread and cake=t
          701    <conf:(0.91)> lift:(1.26) lev:(0.03) [145] conv:(3.01)
 8. biscuits=t fruit=t total=high 954 ==> bread and cake=t 866    <conf:(0.91)>
          lift:(1.26) lev:(0.04) [179] conv:(3)
 9. frozen foods=t fruit=t vegetables=t total=high 834 ==> bread and cake=t 757
          <conf:(0.91)> lift:(1.26) lev:(0.03) [156] conv:(3)
10. frozen foods=t fruit=t total=high 969 ==> bread and cake=t 877
          <conf:(0.91)> lift:(1.26) lev:(0.04) [179] conv:(2.92)
```

I described how to interpret these rules in the "Structuring association rules" section, but what about all the notes after each rule? What does all of that mean? Look at the first rule:

```
1. biscuits=t frozen foods=t fruit=t total=high 788 ==> bread and cake=t 723
        <conf:(0.92)> lift:(1.27) lev:(0.03) [155] conv:(3.35)
```

This is the same rule I showed you earlier in the "Structuring association rules" section, plus some additional information. The rule is ranked number 1, which means that it was the strongest rule based on the metric used for ranking. In this example, rules are ranked based on confidence, a measure of how often the rule turned out to be true in your data. All the text after the rule summarizes several metrics for the rule's performance. You don't need to use every single metric! (But all of them will be explained later in this chapter in the section "Understanding the metrics.")

Refining results

Changing options will change your results. You can usually leave most of these options at their default settings, but two that you may often want to adjust are the metric for ranking rules and the maximum number of rules to generate.

To change these options, follow these steps:

1. **In the Associate area, click anywhere in the white box to open an options editor. (See Figure 17-8.)**

2. **A drop-down menu for metricType lets you select the metric for ranking rules. Open this menu and select Lift. (See Figure 17-9.)**

3. **numRules is the maximum number of rules that you want. Type** 25. **(See Figure 17-10.)**

   You can change this to any number you want, but your data may limit the number of rules you actually get.

4. **Click OK.**

5. **Click the Start button on the Associate tab to create a new set of rules.**

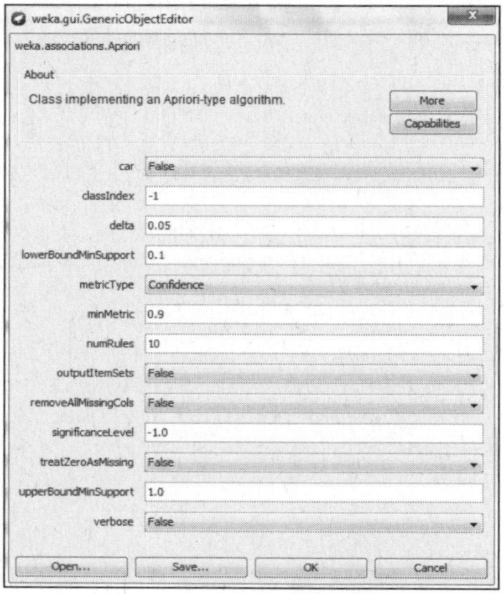

Figure 17-8:
Apriori
settings.

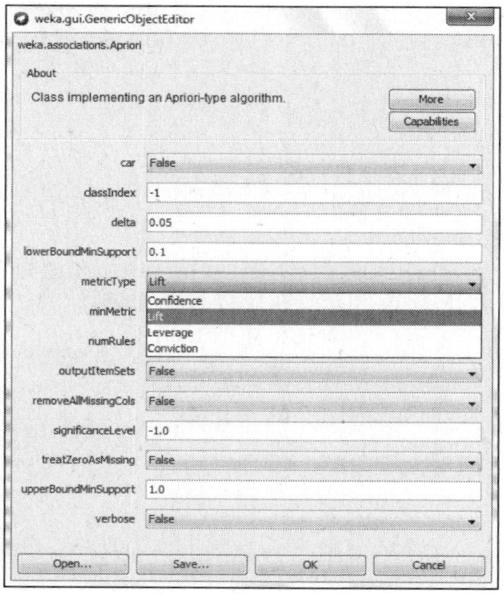

Figure 17-9:
Selecting
the Lift
metric.

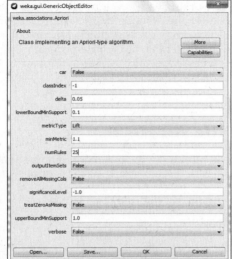

This time you asked for up to 25 rules, and you got all 25. You also changed the metric for ranking rules. Compare the list to the one you got before, and you'll see that the rules are different. Here are your first few rules:

```
Best rules found:
 1. fruit=t 2962 ==> bread and cake=t vegetables=t 1791     conf:(0.6) <
            lift:(1.22)> lev:(0.07) [319] conv:(1.27)
 2. bread and cake=t vegetables=t 2298 ==> fruit=t 1791     conf:(0.78) <
            lift:(1.22)> lev:(0.07) [319] conv:(1.63)
 3. bread and cake=t fruit=t 2325 ==> vegetables=t 1791     conf:(0.77) <
            lift:(1.2)> lev:(0.07) [303] conv:(1.56)
```

These rules are different from the ones with the same ranks in the first example because you changed the metric used to rank the rules, from confidence, a measure of how often the rule is true, to lift, a measure of how much a particular group differs from typical patterns. (Refer to the next section for more on this.)

Clicking the Log button displays a record of what's been done so far in the Weka session. You'll see things like this:

```
Command: weka.associations.Apriori -N 10 -T 0 -C 0.9 -D 0.05 -U 1.0 -M 0.1 -S
            -1.0 -c -1
```

This information is helpful for working with programming interfaces. The string of letters and numbers after the command name represent settings, such as the number of rules to generate or the criteria for ranking rules. This book doesn't go into programming details, but a little programming may come in handy later in your career, especially for automation or fine control over processes.

Understanding the metrics

Some data-mining applications offer a choice of several metrics. These are used in two ways:

- ✓ **Diagnostics:** Assess the quality of the rule.
- ✓ **Ranking:** Put the rules in order.

The most popular association rule metrics are support, confidence, and lift. Here's how they are defined:

- ✓ **Support:** Number of cases, or proportion of cases, that include a particular itemset.
- ✓ **Confidence:** Proportion of cases where the predicted outcome of a rule is correct.
- ✓ **Lift:** Ratio of the frequency of an outcome within a specific itemset to the frequency of the same outcome in the full dataset.

You may also encounter less common metrics, such as these:

- ✓ **Leverage:** Difference between the proportion of occurrences if an itemset in the data and the proportion of occurrences that would be expected if the items (antecedents and consequent) occurred independently.
- ✓ **Conviction:** Similar to lift. Ratio of the expected proportion of cases where the rule would be incorrect if the items were independent to the proportion of cases where the rule is actually incorrect.

Yes, those last two sound a lot more complicated than the others. Perhaps that's why they are used less often. They aren't hard to calculate (the computer does all the work, anyway), but they can be challenging to understand and explain.

Even more metrics are out there, and you may find them appearing in your data-mining applications. Don't overwhelm yourself with metrics! Support, confidence, and lift will take you a long, long way.

Chapter 18

Expanding Your Horizons

You can be a data miner, or you can be an *outstanding* data miner. The difference is just a matter of effort. Invest thought, study, and practice in your new profession, and you'll become a distinguished practitioner.

In this chapter, you find out how to make the most of your tools, widen your analytics range with new techniques, and tackle today's large and complex data sources.

Squeezing More Out of What You Have

The data-mining applications available today, even those that are free of charge, are remarkably powerful and loaded with features and options. You don't need to use all of them (even very experienced data miners rarely, if ever, use every option), but you must become familiar with the major capabilities, and you should never stop investigating and trying new things.

Mastering your data-mining application

Why is data-mining software like unassembled furniture? Nobody likes to read the instructions for either of them.

The first time that you use a data-mining application, it's going to look pretty mysterious. Each product has its own unique work process and features, so even if you've used a similar product before (or two or ten), it may still be challenging to figure out. The examples in this book give you a sense of what to expect, but they won't tell you all the details you'll need to know about the product you choose.

So how can you figure out how to use your software? Training is one solution. Attend face-to-face product training designed for users like you if you can find it and afford it. If you're a data-mining novice, and more of a business expert than a data analysis or programming expert, make sure that the class is meant for you and not college professors! This isn't a big problem if you use commercial data-mining software, but many free tools were made by academics for academics, and you may have trouble finding a class that's right for you.

If you can't attend a class, look for self-study materials. Most vendors have documentation and tutorials bundled with software or available for free download. Some offer full-length books and video tutorials, too. Search online for user groups and training material shared by other users. Video tutorials and other learning materials created by devoted users are available online for each of the products seen in this book.

Fine-tuning your settings

Sometimes your software's default settings are not the right settings. The right settings make the difference between building a model and building a model that's well-suited to your particular business needs. (To see how a couple of small changes to default settings impact the ranking and number of association rules created by the Apriori method, see Chapter 17.)

Every tool in every data-mining application has options. You could work a lifetime and not use all of them, but that doesn't mean that you should never touch any of them. Get familiar with your data-mining tools one by one. When you're comfortable with the basic operation of a tool, take a look at its options. If you're lucky, the documentation will clearly explain each option, what it does, how to use it, and how to interpret results. But you probably won't be that lucky! (That's why we have *For Dummies* books.) So look to books, online advice, and your fellow data miners for better explanations.

Analyzing your analysis

Before you use a model, you look for evidence that it's good. In fact, *evaluation* is one of the six major phases of the CRISP-DM standard data-mining process. (For more about CRISP-DM, see Chapter 5.)

Data miners use many methods to understand and evaluate their models. Testing may be the most important of these, because data miners often disregard modeling rules that statisticians know to be important. Data miners skimp on theory but go big on testing. So, you'll test on new data, test in the field, and monitor performance of your models after deployment, too.

Your modeling tools will offer options for diagnostic metrics, another way to understand and evaluate your model. (See Chapter 17 for descriptions of several metrics used with association rules.)

Your data-mining application may offer you additional methods for understanding and evaluating your models. These offerings vary from product to product. One particularly valuable feature is *sensitivity analysis,* which gives you information about the variables that have the greatest impact on your model's predictions and other details about the elements of the model. You can use this information to

- **Simplify models:** Eliminating variables that have little impact
- **Enrich the information you supply to decision makers:** Variables represent real-life things that decision makers may be able to influence through their actions.

Sensitivity analysis is not available in the free data-mining applications shown in the book, or in any free software that I have found. (Some data miners use an alternative technique called *cross-validation,* but that approach is fairly complicated, and it does not produce the same results.)

Using meta-models (ensemble models)

Here's something data miners do that traditionalists don't do: Data miners use *meta-models.* A meta-model, or *ensemble model,* is what you get when you use two or more modeling techniques together to make one great big predictive model.

You'll find real-life cases of predictive models made by assembling a hundred or more ordinary models. Sometimes the models are chained together — output from one model is used as input for another in sequence — and sometimes the models are used to make consensus predictions based on agreement among several individual models. Meta-models are one of the most distinctive features of data-mining practice.

If you're thinking that this sounds complex, you're right. Meta-models can be extremely complex. (See Chapter 4 for an account model that turned out to be too complex to use, even after the client paid a fortune to get it.)

Should you rush to try meta-modeling? Perhaps not. Not every data miner uses this technique. (I'm not a fan.) But it is a well-known and popular data-mining technique, so you should at least be aware of it.

Widening Your Range

You're comfortable using and explaining a few important data-mining techniques, you know how to use your data-mining application, and you've completed several projects. Congratulations! You're now a successful data miner. Move forward in your data-mining career by exploring new data-mining methods.

Tackling text

Many of the world's growing data resources aren't *data* in the traditional sense (continuous or categorical variables). They're *text,* free-form expressions of human thought. Think of the text sources that you might mine for useful information. These are just a few of many:

- Social media posts
- Technical support requests
- Customer complaints
- Court records
- News reports
- Health records
- Responses to open-ended survey questions
- Email
- SMS messages (texts)
- Résumés

These forms of data won't help you build predictive models, because you can't use them as inputs for modeling — at least, not in their original form. But text analysis methods let you convert text into more conventional forms of data that you can use for modeling.

The most common data-mining uses for text are

- **Sentiment analysis:** Identification of the sentiment expressed in the text. Often, this is just positive/negative or positive/neutral/negative, but sometimes many subtle categories are used. Sentiment analysis is extremely popular, but because sentiment is an elusive thing, results are often unsatisfactory.

- **Classification:** Assigning the text to a category, usually based on its subject matter.

- **Entity extraction:** Finding useful bits within the text, such as names or places.

All of these techniques enable you to create categorical variables describing the subject matter or other characteristics of the text. The new variables can be used for modeling and other data-mining techniques. That's when data mining becomes *text mining*.

Many people reject text mining because the results are less than perfect, but that's foolish. Don't look for perfection. Look for actionable information that you can use to address a specific business problem tied to a measurable revenue or cost-savings opportunity.

To get the most out of text mining, follow these principles:

- **Beware of insights:** Product literature, media reports, and even many conference presentations on text mining focus on getting "insight." The promise of "insight" is so alluring. You start thinking, "I will look deep into my data, and she will reveal her innermost secrets to me, and me alone." Oh, the sex appeal of it. But gaining insight is much too vague a goal.

  It's tempting to believe that you can approach data without a plan and extract pearls of wisdom, but that's unrealistic. Instead, at the beginning of a text-mining project, make the effort to select and quantify a specific business issue to address and determine what information you require to address it.

  A 2014 survey by Altaplana Corporation found that only 42% of the respondents who used text analytics had achieved a positive return on their investment. What makes the difference between those who get positive returns and those who don't? Based on my own long experience in the field, I can tell you that the reason most organizations don't get positive returns on investment is that they never started with a realistic plan for doing so in the first place. (See Chapter 6 for more on planning.)

✔ **Think small:** Use only as much data as justified to address a particular business need. Don't bother buying a Big Data solution to make a pie chart. You want to build a predictive model? Great. In most cases, you don't need to input every single bit of your data into an analytics tool to do that. Use only a sample — you can save a fortune in resources and get results faster.

✔ **Don't get sentimental:** Everybody wants sentiment analysis. At a certain level, that's smart. Knowing how many people are mentioning your product (or any other topic) doesn't mean much if you don't also know something about what they are saying.

But assessing sentiment in text is a tricky business. Humans don't agree with one another consistently when assessing sentiment of text. In fact, even a single person asked to assess the sentiment expressed in a particular bit of text on several occasions will often give different answers. It's hard even to make a presentation on the topic, because the audience invariably gets caught up in picking over the individual cases and debating whether the assessments are acceptable. Where's the actionable insight in that?

Instead of sentiment categories (like positive or negative), look for something better defined and more actionable in your data. Take the example of PayPal's Han-Sheong Lai, who uses text mining to identify customers with intent to close their accounts. Does he look for broad categories of positive and negative sentiment? No. He looks for people saying things like, "I'm going to close my account." You can bet that makes it a lot easier to accurately assess risk and to quantify results.

Detecting sequences

A *sequence* is a pattern of specific things happening in a specific order. Here's an example:

1. Wake up.

2. Take off pajamas.

3. Put on work clothes.

4. Put on shoes.

5. Leave for work.

A sequence is something like an itemset, which is a group of things that happen together. (For more about itemsets, see Chapter 17.) But in an itemset, order doesn't matter. In a sequence, you must know the order of the events.

A shopper enters a department store. He wants to buy black pants. He enters the store and looks around. Where's the men's clothing department? He doesn't see it, so he looks for a directory. He looks in a few wrong places before he finds the directory. He sees that men's clothing is on the other side of the store, so he walks over there to find the black pants. This process goes on and on. Even after he finds the part of the store that sells pants, he must find the kind of pants he wants, in the right color and the right size. Then he'll need to try the pants on in a fitting room, and if they fit, he'll need to pay for them. Many steps are involved in the process, and each time that the shopper finds one of these steps difficult, he might leave without buying his black pants.

Marketers care a lot about sequences like these, because they can have a dramatic effect on sales. You need to know a problem exists before you can correct it. Sequence analysis reveals process problems, and that sets the process of solving the problem in motion. You can also use sequence information to enhance a process. For example, if you identified a pattern of customers entering a store, selecting meat, and going directly to the cashier to pay, you could look for ways of enticing those customers to pick up something more along the way. You might try displaying steak sauce near the meat counter, or popular wines near the cashier.

Sequences are also important in financial modeling, intrusion detection, and genetics research, among other things.

One simple sequence analysis tool is a variation of the parallel coordinates plot. It's a diagram that shows several actions or locations and several steps in a sequence. Each sequence is represented by a series of line segments from point to point. Common sequences stand out when you view the plot. Other sequence analysis methods may not be available in every data-mining application, but you'll see them often in specialty tools for analysis of large datasets, especially those for web data.

Working with time series

A *time series* is a sequence in which the steps take place at defined points in time. Time series analysis is widely used for developing sales and economic forecasting models, and many methods from classical statistics are used for this purpose. Signal analysis, astronomy, and epidemiology are also important applications for time series analysis.

Time series analysis can be tricky. These models are often complex. What's more, the amount and quality of data available for building them is often less than you'd like. Even in the Big Data era, you'll still have moments when you don't have enough data. It's very easy to create a time series model that doesn't make much sense, so before you bet your business on one, get someone on your team who understands the statistics of these models. Data mining is great, but sometimes you still need statisticians.

Taking on Big Data

In the age of electronic computing, collecting data can be easy. So, we collect a lot of it. We collect so much that it's sometimes overwhelming to deal with it.

These are the Three Vs of Big Data (as first stated by Doug Laney in 2001):

- ✔ There's a lot of it (Volume).
- ✔ More is coming in fast (Velocity).
- ✔ It's in many forms (Variety).

Big Data can be difficult, but don't assume that you're up for a huge challenge every time that you hear a data source described as Big Data. Today's mainstream computers and software can handle a heck of a lot of data. If you feel swamped by data, these are your options:

- ✔ **Sampling:** You can often get the information you need with only a small portion of the data you have.

- ✔ **Careful selection of software and hardware:** Choose the technology that suits your situation. Your favorite spreadsheet wasn't designed to manage petabytes of data, and the latest Big Data technologies are serious overkill for a 1-terabyte data source.

- ✔ **Hard work:** No, no, not hard work! Seriously, before you do anything complicated, go back and give some more thought to the other options. But some situations do call for inventive solutions.

Some newer data analysis products are described as *Data Discovery* platforms, which are designed to simplify analysis with massive quantities (petabytes) of data. Do these offer new and different kinds of data analysis that never existed before? No! But Data Discovery platforms may be useful to you. Each of them has its own special user interface designed to reduce the time required to analyze very large quantities of data, and to make the process less complex than usual. Some offer graphic user interfaces; others require programming, but adapt common programming languages (such as SQL) into custom versions that enable users to perform complex data analysis with a few lines of simplified code.

Coming to terms with Big Data

Big Data isn't valuable just because of its quantity. In fact, very large datasets always come with a very large set of headaches. Storage, maintenance, and management of very large datasets are not simple. And just having a lot of data doesn't guarantee a lot of value.

The value of any dataset is determined by the quality of information that you can extract from it. The key to value in Big Data is the detail. In other words, the value of Big Data is in the small stuff.

Every business has a rough idea of how many customers it has, how much they spend in total, and perhaps the average spend per client. But if all you know is the average, what are you going to do — treat every customer as average?

If you could meet each client personally and get to know each person, you wouldn't think of anyone as average. You'd know each person's habits. You'd know that Maria Perez shops for herself each week and buys a gift now and then, while Laura Carter shops for her family of five and Lily Yu does not use your products herself, but often purchases them for her parents. You'd know the times of day when each person prefers to shop, whether each is a relaxed or hurried shopper, and the products that each person prefers.

Because you would know your customers as individuals, you would treat them as individuals. You'd let Maria know that you offer gift wrapping. You'd direct Laura to the economical family-size package of her favorite product. You'd make sure that Lily chose the container that was easy for her parents to open.

Conducting predictive analytics with Big Data

The promise of Big Data is in the details. You want the data to give you the information you'd get if you observed each customer in person. You want to know what each person does. You want to know how each responds to a variety of things — products offered, pricing, presentation, and so on.

You only realize value from data if you do something valuable with it. In a face-to-face customer interaction, you use what you know about the customer to make appropriate suggestions, and the better the suggestions, the more the customer buys, returns, and recommends you to others. The best data gives you useful information. Information creates opportunity. Value enters when you use the information to take meaningful action.

So, what does this tell you about selecting datasets for Big Data applications? Look at the process. First, you need a goal. What do you want to accomplish? Then, you must know your options for action. Can you offer new products or change the selection you offer, or must you work within the bounds of what you have now? Can you develop new ads, new offers?

Now, imagine that you have the same goal, and the same options, in a face-to-face situation. What information would you want? Knowing that, you are ready to look for data sources that meet your needs.

Here's an example. Your brick-and-mortar stores are crowded at peak hours — so crowded that customers often walk away in frustration — while at other times, the stores are nearly empty. You are selling below your potential due to cart abandonment and failure to attract customers throughout the day.

What's your goal? Increase revenue by better distributing activity throughout the day.

You have a marketing budget, authority to send print and email advertisements, and authority to make special offers using coupons and other promotional schemes. You also have some influence over staff scheduling and checkout procedures. This creates options for action.

Now, imagine that you are in the store, observing customers. What useful facts could you observe? Some shoppers habitually shop at off-peak hours. Who are they? Others habitually shop at peak hours. Why? What are they buying? Do certain shoppers vary the times when they come to the store? Who's giving up and walking out? What had those people intended to buy? What can you discover about the reasons for each shopper's behavior? You need to put that information into action.

Perhaps you have found that some of the shoppers who come at busy times are simply not aware of the times when the store is not so busy. An information campaign might work for them. It could be as simple as posting signs in the store or adding that information to your regular circular. Others might be coaxed into shifting their shopping to off-peak times if you made it worth their while, with a discount or special offer. As for the people who already shop during quiet hours, you gain no benefit in offering them incentives for what they are already doing, but maybe you can motivate them to buy more. If you know what they're buying, you might offer a coupon for a product they haven't tried or a deal on a larger quantity of a favorite.

You can't speak to every customer personally. You can't follow everyone around and observe. But you may have access to data that provides you with much of the same information. If you are dealing with many people, and lots of detail, you're talking about Big Data, the kind of Big Data that fuels profitable predictive analytics.

Where can you find detailed information about the behavior of your customers and prospects? Start with the data you already own. Your transaction records are a treasure chest of behavioral data. If you do business online, you'll have weblogs containing revealing details about shopping behavior, including details on the behavior of nonbuyers. Only when you've thoroughly investigated the possibilities of your internal data sources should you look beyond your walls, perhaps to get demographics or information about credit, home ownership, or other factors that might influence behavior. When you have a clear idea of what you want to know, and the limits of your own data, you can shop selectively, and shrewdly, for data that fills in the blanks.

Blending Methods for Best Results

No one data analysis technique is better than all the others, nor is any one class of data analysis (data mining, classical statistics, operations research, and so on) better than all others. You'll get the best understanding of your subject by looking at it in many ways, mixing a variety of data-mining techniques with methods from other disciplines, and refining your understanding with continued investigation over time.

Don't limit your horizons with just what you can do with one data-mining application, one data source, or one person!

- ✔ **Be on the lookout for new tools:** You may have chosen your data-mining application because it's what your employer provides, what you could get free, or what's most familiar. These are all legitimate considerations, but not reasons to be unaware of what's available, old or new. Your needs will change over time, and so will your options.

- ✔ **Find out about the techniques that other data analysts are using:** Data analysts go by many titles, and each uses a different mix of techniques. Find out what your colleagues are doing and why, because you may be able to use the same methods and get valuable new information to address your own business needs.

✔ **Meet and collaborate with others:** You're just one person. A diverse team can apply a wide range of knowledge and skills to your business problem. Play nicely with others, because data mining isn't about you; it's about solving business problems. (You'll understand and become a much better data miner, too!)

Part VI
The Part of Tens

 Get clued in on ten data-mining mistakes at www.dummies.com/extras/ datamining.

In this part . . .

- ✔ Getting involved with the first professional organization for data miners
- ✔ Finding out where you can read more about data mining
- ✔ Having some work-related laughs
- ✔ Getting an inkling about complementary analytics methods

Chapter 19

Ten Great Resources for Data Miners

Fresh information about data mining is made available to you every single day through specialty analytics sites, blogs, professional organizations, and even in the news. Deepen your data-mining knowledge with these resources.

Society of Data Miners

Professional organizations help members to advance their knowledge and careers. Members build networks by meeting peers and more experienced practitioners. They sharpen knowledge through ongoing education. And they protect the profession in a variety of ways, such as establishing meaningful professional certification, establishing ethical standards, and even lobbying on public issues that affect members. The Society of Data Miners (www.socdm.org), founded in 2013, is the first professional organization devoted specifically to data mining.

KDnuggets

KDnuggets (http://kdnuggets.com) is a key data-mining industry news site. Hosted by respected data miner Gregory Piatetsky-Shapiro, KDnuggets provides an active stream of information about data-mining issues, events, jobs, and tools.

It's worth your while to have a peek at KDnuggets on a regular basis. Posts here keep you up to date on hot issues in data mining and related topics. And it's a good starting place for information that may not be utterly new, but is still new to you. Links right on the home page, well-organized by subject, guide you to a wide variety of information resources. Subjects covered include basics like software, classes, and jobs, as well as specialties like competitions, calls for research papers, and even data-mining humor.

All Analytics

All Analytics (www.allanalytics.com) is an industry publication that covers a wide variety of data analysis topics. Sponsored by one of the large software vendors, this site features brief, professionally written and edited posts on data analysis. New articles are posted daily, with thousands more in the archives.

Here are representative posts:

"3 Approaches to Justifying Analytics Results," by Bryan Beverly, a statistician from the U.S. Bureau of Labor Statistics

"Cellphone Tracking: Protection vs. Privacy," by Ariella Brown, writer and social media consultant

"Anatomy of a Data Management Project," by Fabian Pascal, founder, editor, and publisher, Database Debunkings.

The New York Times

When you hear people at a cocktail party arguing over the value or ethics of somebody's data-gathering or analysis practices, chances are that the argument started with something that appeared in *The New York Times*.

The New York Times (www.nytimes.com) often features stories about data analysis, but that's not necessarily what you'll see in the headline. The articles that get people talking about data have titles that describe what people are doing, not how they do it.

Here's an example: In Charles Duhigg's 2012 piece "How Companies Learn Your Secrets," he described one retailer's interest in finding customers expecting the birth of a child, because people often change shopping habits when they have a baby. The article's headline does not scream data analysis, but that's what it was all about, and that article became the talk of the industry, as well as the seed of many an argument, for months after its publication. Look past the titles, and you'll see that *The New York Times* contains fresh information that relates to data analysis most every day.

Forbes

Forbes (www.forbes.com) is a business publication that emphasizes the business dealings and prospects of publicly traded companies and industries. It often features posts on the market for various data-related products and services. Get started with Forbes by checking out the posts of these contributors who focus on data-related topics — Gil Press (Pressed Data), Piyanka Jain (Putting Data to Work), Naomi Robbins (Effective Graphs), and Lisa Arthur (The Marketing Revolution).

SmartData Collective

SmartData Collective (http://smartdatacollective.com) is an analytics industry site that features curated content by analytics professionals. Most articles found here are reposted from lesser-known blogs of independent analytics practitioners and small industry sites, and you find original content as well. New posts appear daily.

Representative posts are as follows:

"What You Need to Know About Cloud Analytics," by Timo Elliott, innovation evangelist at SAP

"What the 'Small Data' Revolution Means for Marketers," by Noah Jessop, cofounder and CEO of CommandIQ

"How Data Will Make Air Travel Safer," by Travis Korte, a research analyst at the Center for Data Innovation

CRISP-DM Process Model

CRISP-DM is the predominant data-mining process and the unofficial industry standard as well as the basis for many of the guidelines described in this book. The CRISP-DM Process Model, a detailed guide from the industry consortium that developed CRISP_DM, explains elements of the process, why and how it was developed, and many step-by-step data-mining details. You can obtain it at ftp://ftp.software.ibm.com/software/analytics/spss/support/Modeler/Documentation/14/UserManual/CRISP-DM.pdf.

Nate Silver

Nobody in the world of data analysis communicates like blogger and statistician Nate Silver. That's why he's the most famous statistician in the world. (He's the only famous statistician in the world, evidence that the rest of us need to work on our communication skills!) Nate's also a master of data analysis, so learn from the best by reading his blog at `www.fivethirtyeight.com`.

Meta's Analytics Articles page

If you loved this book and can't bear to wait for a sequel, you can find out more about data mining and the wonderful world of analytics right now with the articles I've archived at my website at `http://bit.ly/metaarticles`. Example articles are as follows:

Discover secrets of analytics management in "Analytics, Schmanalytics! How to Evaluate an Analyst."

Get shocking behind-the-scenes details on the analytics industry in "Secrets of a Software Vendor."

Develop skills you've only dreamed about in "How I Met Your Model."

And much, much more!

First Internet Gallery of Statistics Jokes

Need a joke for your presentation? Or perhaps you just want a little break. Visit the go-to location for geeky statistics humor: `http://my.ilstu.edu/~gcramsey/Gallery.html`.

Chapter 20

Ten Useful Kinds of Analysis That Complement Data Mining

*T*here's an old saying: "When all you have is a hammer, everything looks like a nail." It's common to become so comfortable with your tools that you feel reluctant to try alternatives. You can become convinced that there's nothing your favorite tool can't do. Beware of this sort of thinking. It puts you at risk. It may prevent you from getting the information you need, to waste your time and money, or to even damage your reputation. You don't have to be an expert in every technique, of course, but a little knowledge about other tools and approaches can prepare you well for new challenges. This chapter introduces you to ten such approaches. Follow up these introductions by exploring the topics on your own.

Business Analysis

Business analysis is the study of business systems and processes with the aim of improving them. Business analysis can help organizations run more efficiently, comply with the law and other standards for good practices, and avoid costly missteps. Business analysts facilitate organizational change by identifying stakeholder needs and evaluating the feasibility of alternative solutions to business problems. Many are experts in information technology and organizational structure.

As a data miner, your first encounter with a business analyst might come when your organization decides to explore data mining. The business analyst might take the lead in identifying how data mining can be applied in your organization, how to integrate data mining with information technology functions, and how to ensure that data mining does not interfere with everyday operations. Later, you might support the business analyst by working with raw data to perform a data analysis relevant to a business problem that's important to the business analyst (most business analysts don't have significant skills in data mining or statistics).

The meaning of the term *business analysis* is slippery. Confusingly, people with job titles like *business analyst*, *systems engineer*, or *systems analyst* may be true business analysts, but they are just as likely to be something else. It's not uncommon for those job titles to have other meanings. The International Institute of Business Analysts (IIBA; www.iiba.org) works to better define the field of business analysis and the role of the business analyst. The organization is a key resource for those who want to become, or hire, a business analyst.

Conjoint Analysis

Shoppers make choices, balancing preferences for particular features with the limitations of the products available and their shopping budget. Think about the other side of that process. If you are a product manager or marketer, to attract customers, you need information about the features they find most appealing and the prices the market will bear.

This is the role of *conjoint analysis*, a technique for obtaining information about consumer preferences. In conjoint analysis, data is collected from individuals asked to evaluate a variety of theoretical product options. These studies can vary from simple (such as the ones that ask respondents merely to rate or rank each option) to complex (such as studies that use special adaptive software that modifies options as the interview progresses).

Conjoint analysis is a specialized technique that calls for interactive data collection and analysis tools built specifically for this purpose. (You won't see it in data-mining applications, because the highly controlled data collection process required for conjoint analysis is quite different from the data-mining convention of using what's on hand. Some general-purpose statistical analysis tools offer conjoint analysis, but only with very limited capabilities.) Interpreting the output of these tools requires some training and practice. This training is worthwhile if you need conjoint analysis frequently, but for occasional needs, it may be better to enlist the help of a conjoint analysis specialist.

Conjoint analysis is a specialty dominated by a relatively limited number of vendors and practitioners. Vendor-neutral classes on conjoint analysis are hard to find. If you'd like to explore the topic more thoroughly, be on the lookout for the occasional workshops offered by marketing and survey research professional organizations or universities.

Design of Experiments

If you're a data miner, when it comes to data, you take what you can get. Your data may be collected in the course of routine business or through another preexisting channel, but that's not always sufficient. Sometimes you need specific kinds of data, or data that fulfills certain conditions, and that's where experiments come in.

For example, say that you're investigating a problem in a manufacturing process. As a data miner, you explore the process data on hand and look for clues to solving the problem. You might identify certain process conditions (temperature, pressure, and so on) or locations in which the problem does or does not crop up. Based on this, you come up with a theory or hypothesis — about the ideal conditions for the process, say, or the need to replace certain equipment. But you'll need more evidence to make your case.

This situation calls for a traditional statistical analysis approach. A planned experiment, one based on rigorous statistical theory, is a good choice for situations like this. The experiment may provide evidence that supports your case, or it may not. Either way, by conducting it, you avoid risk to your company's finances and to your own reputation.

If, like most data miners, you aren't trained in the design of experiments or in strict statistical methods for analysis of the results, this is the time to bring in a statistician. A poor design can easily sink an experiment — by introducing error, for example, or by altering the meaning of the results so drastically that the experiment fails to say anything of consequence about your theory. The American Society for Quality (http://asq.org/index.aspx) is a good source for information on the design of experiments. Many of the members are experts, and the society offers classes and publishes books on this topic.

Marketing Mix Modeling

Because so many advertising options are available — TV, radio, print, online, and more — it's not always easy to figure out which combination of media provides the best value for your needs. With this in mind, marketers use *marketing mix modeling* to gain an understanding of what's working and how best to allocate their spending. Marketing mix modeling uses statistical analysis on sales and marketing data to evaluate different marketing approaches and to optimize a company's advertising choices.

Data-mining applications are not designed for marketing mix modeling. Although some methods (such as linear regression) are common to both subjects, marketing mix modeling often leans on econometric and simulation techniques that aren't typical for data miners. For this reason, marketing mix modeling is usually done using applications designed specifically for that purpose. Although many marketers make use of marketing mix modeling, not so many are skilled at it. They often lean on consultants who are experts in these models. You should consider working with these experts, too, to fill occasional needs, or to train you if you wish to do your own marketing mix modeling.

Consumer packaged goods (CPG) marketers have been using marketing mix modeling for decades, and it is now becoming popular in other industries. Competitive pressure throughout the economy is one reason. Another is U.S. Sarbanes-Oxley legislation, which requires greater controls and reporting for large expenditures by publicly traded companies.

For more information on marketing mix modeling, try the Advertising Research Foundation (`http://thearf.org`) and the Direct Marketing Association (`http://thedma.org`).

Operations Research

Consider that you have 3,000 products in 12 warehouses and 800 orders to deliver those products to customers in 14 states using a mix of your own trucks and any of 22 supplemental delivery services by Thursday. You must find the most cost-effective way to get everything where it needs to go, on time. For a complex problem like that, your best approach is to do *operations research*.

Operations research applies mathematical optimization, simulation, and other methods to identify ways to obtain maximum value from available resources. It's widely used in industries that have complex logistic challenges, such as transportation and the military. It's quite different from data mining because much of the process involves no data and is based entirely on theory.

The Institute for Operations Research and the Management Sciences (`www.informs.org`), better known as *INFORMS,* and the Operational Research Society (`http://theorsociety.com`) are authoritative sources for information on operations research.

Reliability Analysis

Here's a little-known fact: Two completely different categories of analytics exist, each called *reliability analysis*. Here's the story on each of them:

- ✓ **Engineering:** In engineering, reliability analysis is exactly what the name suggests: the study of making products and their parts consistently perform as expected. It draws on mathematical modeling methods such as probabilistic risk analysis, finite element analysis, and simulation to predict how systems will function in a variety of conditions. Reliability analysis is used in manufacturing and other industries to ensure product quality and protect safety. The nuclear power industry is the most aggressive user of reliability analysis (and many of that industry's detailed risk studies are publicly available), but other manufacturers, especially manufacturers of electronics, automobiles, and toys, also use it.

  For good information on engineering reliability analysis, investigate the American Society for Quality Reliability Division (`http://asq.org/reliability`) and the IEEE Reliability Society (`http://rs.ieee.org`).

- ✓ **Psychometrics:** In psychometrics, reliability analysis refers to consistency in a measurement. A measurement is said to be *reliable* if it produces the same result time after time.

  This type of reliability analysis is most often used in the development and evaluation of standardized tests. The standardized tests used as part of the college admissions process, for example, are developed with the aid of reliability analysis. Many exams used for professional certifications also use this process.

  For more about psychometric reliability analysis, touch base with the Psychometric Society (`www.psychometricsociety.org`).

Just when everything seemed clear . . .

A second type of reliability analysis is used in engineering. This second type is related to the testing of measuring instruments, such as calipers and gauges. It refers to the ability of the measuring instrument to produce consistent results.

Statistical Process Control

It's commonly understood that the first step to better quality is to make your processes predictable and consistent. It's a little like learning to cook something new. First you learn to make the recipe properly, and then you make small changes and see whether you can improve it.

Statistical process control formalizes that approach, using statistical measures developed for the purpose and special graphs called *control charts*. It is a longtime staple of manufacturing industries, and is coming into widespread use in healthcare. Although it's also applicable to many service industry applications, it's not often used there.

Although data mining is the product of the computer age, statistical process control originated in the days of paper and pencil computation as a means to identify and eliminate causes of variability in manufacturing processes. (That being said, most people who use statistical process control today rely on software to make their work easier). It has its own distinctive set of charts, metrics, and ways of interpreting these to inform action, not at the executive level, but on the factory floor. Unlike data mining, you can't perform statistical process control with data you've already collected. It requires a controlled, real-time data collection process.

The folks at the American Society for Quality (http://asq.org) are the experts in statistical process control. Many of the members use it every day, many are experts in the field, and pretty much all of them know a lot about it. The society offers classes and publishes books on statistical process control, too.

Social Network Analysis

Question: Which of the following is a social network?

> a) Facebook
>
> b) Pinterest
>
> c) You, your best friend, and all your old school pals

Answer: C

Many people refer to Facebook, Pinterest, and other, similar institutions as *social networks,* but in fact, these are *platforms* — that is, communication tools designed to facilitate interaction among people. The social network is the people! So you, your best friend, and all your old school pals form a social network, a group of people connected by interaction, acquaintances, or other means. *Social network analysis,* then, is the branch of mathematics that aims to understand the behavior of these interconnected groups of people.

For more information on social network analysis, try the LINKS Center for Social Network Analysis (`https://sites.google.com/site/uklinkscenter`).

Structural Equation Modeling

Human behavior is complex, involving many elements, including some that can't be directly measured. Consider the process that establishes a consumer's satisfaction level with a store. Many factors come into play: the consumer's perceived need for the store's product, the customer's attitude toward the store's atmosphere, memories of past experiences in this store and others, the weather, and so on. If you could develop a model of that process, you could understand what factors cause consumers to be satisfied or dissatisfied and see how you might influence them to improve customer satisfaction. That's the role of *structural equation modeling* (sometimes called *path modeling* or *causative modeling*).

Structural equation modeling is well-established in academic social science research, yet few businesses have adopted it. If you have the right application, this is an opportunity to adopt a proven technique and yet be on the cutting edge in your industry. A good source for more information on structural equation modeling is the American Psychological Association (`www.apa.org`).

Refer to Chapter 16 for a discussion of the relationship between causation and correlation.

Web Analytics

Data mining and other techniques designed to explore relationships among variables enable you to discover a wealth of useful information from Internet activity data. Still, this is the fancy stuff. You may have a need for some basic reports that summarize activity at a very simple level, such as tabulations of total downloads for various types of content, graphs of activity by time of day, or maybe a little bit of A/B testing (a test you can use to compare different versions of marketing materials, such as different subject lines in an email, or a red versus blue button on a web page, and find out which works better). This is the common meaning of *web analytics*.

The place to look for information on web analytics is the Digital Analytics Association (`www.digitalanalyticsassociation.org`).

Appendix A

Glossary

- -

analysis: Thoughtful investigation of real-world systems.

analytics: Analysis that involves math. (This term is used very differently by different people, and may refer to anything from simple historical data summaries to highly complex predictive models. Always ask questions!)

association rules: Tools for identifying combinations of items often found together. The most common use of association rules is for market basket analysis.

assumption: Something presumed to be true. Assumptions are the basis of all statistical analysis. (It is important that the analyst choose methods based only on assumptions that are reasonable for the application.)

average: Any measure that describes the middle (more formally, "central tendency" or "location") of a distribution. In analytics, the term "average" usually refers to the mean, but may refer to median or mode.

Bayesian network: A type of neural network. The Bayesian network is based on the fundamentals of probability theory. (See also *neural network.*)

binary: Having exactly two alternative states.

binning: Organizing data into groups. This may be done for ease of analysis, or to protect privacy.

causation: The act of producing an effect or making something happen. The phrase "correlation does not imply causation" means that the fact that two things are observed to happen together is not enough to prove that one caused the other.

Chi-square: A test statistic, probably the most widely used of all statistical hypothesis testing methods. Typically used in combination with cross-tabulation tables.

Chi-squared Automatic Interaction Detector (CHAID): A type of decision tree. CHAID is based on the chi-square statistic and tests of independence between categorical variables.

classification: Techniques for organizing data into groups associated with a particular outcome, such as the likelihood to purchase a product or earn a college degree.

Classification and Regression Tree (C&RT): A type of decision tree. C&RT is based on linear regression methods.

cluster analysis (clustering): Techniques for organizing data into groups of similar cases.

coding: In text analysis, categorization of text based on its meaning. These categorizations can be used in the same ways as any other categorical variable. Historically done manually, automated coding processes are now becoming available.

correlation: Association in the values of two or more variables.

Cross-Industry Standard Process for Data Mining (CRISP-DM): Just what it says, or as the folks from the CRISP-DM project put it, "an industry- and tool-neutral data-mining process model."

crosstabulation (crosstabs): Summarizing interactions of categorical variables in a table.

dashboard: A predefined report for online viewing, usually consisting of simple tables and graphs, with some options for user interaction. Dashboards are usually designed for use by business managers to support the decision-making processes.

data mining: An umbrella term for analytic techniques that facilitate fast pattern discovery and model building, particularly with large datasets.

dataset: A collection of related measurements. In the data-mining context, this usually refers to an organized electronic file or database containing records of routine business activity or other information relevant to a particular data-mining project.

decision tree: A family of classification methods whose results are usually represented in a tree-like graph.

dependent variable: In a model, a variable whose value directly depends on the values of other (independent) variables. The dependent variable is usually the element that data miners try to predict or control. (See also *independent variable.*)

forecasting: Predicting future values of some variable. Forecasting methods are often used for prediction of sales, prices, or other economic measures.

frequency: The number of times a specific value occurs within a dataset.

good places to find bad jokes about data analysis:

```
www.btinternet.com/~se16/hgb/statjoke.htm
www.ahajokes.com/m027.html
http://my.ilstu.edu/~gcramsey/Gallery.html
```

holdout data: Data that was not used in the model-fitting process (neither for training nor testing). Used to evaluate the model's performance after the fitting process is complete.

hypothesis: A presumption or belief. Inferential statistics are grounded in the making and testing of hypotheses. In inferential statistics, a hypothesis is an assertion about the relationship that exists between two measured phenomena.

hypothesis testing: The heart of inferential statistics, involving the evaluation of two hypotheses, known as the "null" and "alternative" hypothesis. The "alternative" hypothesis states that two measured phenomena are in some way related, and the "null" hypothesis is simply the default belief that no such relationship exists. Hypothesis testing analyzes sample data to determine which of the two the data best supports.

independent variable: In a model, variables that can influence the dependent variable. These may or may not be controllable. A sales forecasting model might have a dependent variable of total annual sales (in dollars) and independent variables such as the rate of inflation, advertising expenses, and the number of sales calls made, among other factors.

input: Independent variable.

Kohonen network: A type of neural network. Unlike the other types of neural networks mentioned in this book, Kohonen networks are used for clustering (also called *unsupervised learning*) applications.

linear regression: In statistics, a method of modeling the relationship between dependent and independent variables. Linear regression creates a model by fitting a straight line to the values in a dataset.

logistic regression: Like linear regression, a statistical method of modeling the relationship between dependent and independent variables based on probability. However, in binary logistic regression, the dependent variable (the effect, or outcome) can have only one of two values, as in, say, a baby's sex or the results of an election. (Multinomial logistic regression allows for more than two possible values.) A logistic regression model is formed by fitting data to a logit function. (The dependent variable is a 0 or 1, and the regression curve is shaped something like the letter "s.")

market basket analysis: The identification of product combinations frequently purchased within a single transaction.

market research: The gathering of information about customers and prospective customers.

model: An equation, or set of equations, used to describe the behavior of a system.

multilayer perceptron (MLP): A type of neural network. The MLP is the most common, and arguably the simplest, neural network used for classification.

multivariate: In statistical literature, a model with more than one dependent variable. Also a term used to describe certain tests where more than one independent variable is varied at the same time.

neural network: A family of model types capable of simulating some very complex systems.

node: In some data-mining applications, a function (such as building a particular decision-tree model, creating a scatterplot, or deleting incomplete cases from a dataset, among many other possibilities) represented by a small picture, or *icon*, rather than by menu items or code. In neural networks, an element of the network structure.

operations research (OR): An umbrella term for optimization and other mathematical methods used to support decision making.

outlier: A data value so atypical that including it in an analysis may lead to useless or misleading results. Analysts sometimes choose to exclude these values, or to specifically investigate their effects on model performance.

output: Dependent variable.

overfitting: Occurs when a model accurately describes the data used for training, but which produces errors or makes poor predictions when applied to other data samples.

overtraining: See *overfitting*.

parameter: A value that describes some aspect of the distribution of values in a population. True values of parameters are generally unknown, hence the need for statistics.

population: All the items of the type you want to study. If you study people, for example, the population might be all the people who are living or may be born. If you study bill payments, the population might be all possible bill payments.

prediction: An expectation for a future occurrence.

predictive analytics: Analytic methods used to make predictions. The practice of using mathematical modeling to predict outcomes.

predictor: Independent variable.

profiling: In statistics, the term has the same meaning as "classification."

quick, unbiased, and efficient statistical tree (QUEST): A type of decision tree, QUEST is designed for speedy execution, and is an important consideration for some data miners who work with large datasets.

radial basis function (RBF): A type of neural network. The radial basis function is a variant of the multilayer perceptron, designed to produce results more quickly than the conventional multilayer perceptron.

random sample: A subset of the population for which every member of the population has an equal chance of being selected.

regression: A family of methods for fitting a line or curve to a dataset, used to simplify or make sense of a number of apparently random data points.

report: A collection of data summaries, usually comparisons of sums, averages, and percentages.

response: Dependent variable.

ruleset: A collection of "if . . . then" statements that can be used to make predictions.

sample: A subset of a population. A sample may include all or only a portion of the data that you have available.

segmentation: In marketing, the act of defining any customer group of interest, not necessarily through the use of any analytic methods. In data mining and statistics, segmentation is the same as clustering. However, analysts and others often use this term casually to refer to classification.

sentiment analysis: Text analysis methods used to obtain information about the opinions or attitudes of a speaker or writer (or a population of speakers or writers).

significant: An effect that can be clearly separated, using statistical analysis methods, from natural variation (noise) in the data. (Note that something can be "significant" in this sense and still be utterly unimportant from a practical standpoint.) Data miners don't use this term much, if at all. Statisticians use it all the time.

statistics: The science of inference about populations based on mathematical analysis of sample data.

structural equation modeling: An umbrella term for a variety of methods used to determine whether a model believed to represent a real-world system is actually consistent with the data.

structured data: In statistics and data mining, any type of data whose values have clearly defined meaning, such as numbers and categories.

survey research: Asking people questions and using the responses as data.

testing dataset: A sample of data used at each iteration of the training process to refit a model (but you might also hear this term used to describe holdout data). This term is most often used in the context of fitting a neural network model to data; software fits a model form to a subset of the data (called the *training dataset*, and then assesses the fit of the model to another subset, called the *testing dataset*. This process may be repeated thousands of times, and the final neural network model will be the one that best fits the testing dataset.

text analysis: Analytic methods applied to text.

text mining: Data-mining techniques applied to text. Because these rely on the same underlying analytic approaches as text analysis, text mining is synonymous with text analysis, and the use of the term *mining* is primarily a matter of style and context.

training: In data mining, the process of fitting a model to data. This is an iterative process and may involve thousands of iterations or more.

training dataset: In data mining, a sample of data used at each iteration of the training process to evaluate the model fit.

unstructured data: Text, audio, video, and other types of complex data that won't easily fit into a conventional relational database. Unstructured data isn't as simple as the numbers and short strings that most data analysts use.

validation: The act of testing a model with data that was not used in the model-fitting process.

visual programming: Defining a workflow by manipulating graphic images rather than by typing code or using menus and dialog boxes. Often used for data mining.

visualization: Examining data using graphs. The term is most often used when the graphs are of a new or novel type.

Appendix B

Data-Mining Software Sources

· ·

A data miner is a businessperson who has a feel for numbers, not a programmer, database manager, or statistician. Data mining enables businesspeople to rapidly discover useful patterns in data, build models, and put them into action in everyday business. To do data mining, you need tools to fit the job, tools designed for users like you.

This is not to say that data miners who also happen to be familiar with programming or statistics should not take advantage of those skills. But data-mining tools should be designed primarily for business users.

The examples in this book include images of some data-mining tools. Software used for these examples was selected based on two requirements. It had to have a visual programming interface, to help you become familiar with this key element of the data-mining process, and a free version available, so that you can try out what you see in this book, even if you have no money to spend on software.

Moving Forward

When you take on real projects in your workplace, you'll have your own needs and priorities. Technical support will be a necessity. Specific capabilities for data import or analysis methods may be important to you. Your employer may have requirements for software purchasing that affect your choices. You'll need options beyond the few used in the examples used in this book.

Even if you have no immediate need and no money to spend, it's a good idea to start getting familiar with what's available, because you may not have a lot of time for reflection when your situation changes.

Tools best suited for data mining will offer the following:

- ✔ A graphical user interface that does not require programming
- ✔ Visual programming capability for speed and clarity
- ✔ A broad selection of exploratory graphs and modeling methods

Visual programming interfaces are key for turning businesspeople into data miners, making the data-mining process understandable and rapid. Because they are available in only a few products, be sure to explore those products first.

Discovering What's Available

Not many vendors offer tools with visual programming interfaces similar to the ones recommended here and used in the examples in this book. In fact, only a handful of products are available that meet all three criteria recommended here: a graphical user interface, visual programming, and a generous selection of graphs and modeling methods. Even those may not suit every real-life application that you encounter.

You may not find a single ideal tool to suit your needs. Or you may have a favorite tool that suits you well, but that same tool might not be satisfactory for others on your team who have different priorities and skills. You may love a particular tool, but find that the cost is too high or the support does not meet your needs. So it's valuable to be aware of a variety of tools and vendors.

Software vendors are not so strict in their use of the term *data mining*. So you may encounter a wide variety of vendors that mention data mining in their promotional materials, yet you may find them to be very different from the examples in this book. Hundreds of products now offer some type of data analysis capability, and many new ones enter the market each year. Most of them are very useful tools for some purpose, but few are strong matches for data mining.

Although not all software suppliers offer free products, almost all will allow you to try products free for a limited time (typically 30 days). Use these trials to expand your knowledge and to get a sense of whether paid products are worth the money that you would spend.

Software Suppliers

This appendix lists a handful of key analytics software sources. Each of these plays an important role in the data and analysis landscape, and each offers tools with some analytics capability. All of them are known to some extent as data-mining tools.

Alteryx

About the developer: Alteryx Inc. is a privately held corporation based in the United States.

Key product: Alteryx Designer

Technical support: Available

Free product: Alteryx Project Edition

Website: www.alteryx.com

Alteryx is openly challenging market leaders IBM and SAS with advertising that emphasizes freedom from legacy software. These claims are rather bold, however, because most users of traditional analytics tools, from these vendors and others, have developed code in the proprietary languages of those tools that cannot be automatically converted for use in Alteryx's or any other challenger's tools. Those who have invested heavily in any analytics platform will find transitions to new platforms challenging and costly. A transition to new tools is often worthwhile, but have no illusions: It is never easy!

Alteryx is built on the R platform. For more information about the R platform, see the listing for the R Foundation, later in this appendix.

Angoss

About the developer: Angoss Software Corporation was acquired in 2013 by Peterson Partners, a private equity firm.

Key product: KnowledgeSTUDIO

Technical support: Available

Free products: None

Website: www.angoss.com

Angoss is a niche predictive analytics software provider. It offers a general-purpose analytics platform and several industry-specific products. Angoss has a following in finance, insurance, and certain other industries that take advantage of platforms designed specifically for those applications.

IBM

About the developer: IBM is a publicly held multinational corporation.

Key products: IBM SPSS Modeler, IBM SPSS Statistics

Technical support: Available

Free products: None

Website: www.ibm.com

IBM is among the most influential software vendors; its analytics portfolio is arguably the strongest in the industry. IBM SPSS Modeler is the dominant commercial data-mining tool. Developed under the name *Clementine* in the 1990s, it was the first to offer a serious visual programming interface. The product has evolved over the years, adding client/server options, broader data access capabilities, and web and text mining. IBM SPSS Statistics is a full-featured statistical analysis system. It does not have a visual programming interface, but does offer some capabilities strongly associated with data mining, such as decision trees and neural networks.

KNIME

About the developer: KNIME.com AG is an offshoot of the original KNIME development project of the University of Konstanz (Germany).

Key products: KNIME Desktop, KNIME Professional

Technical support: Available

Free product: KNIME Desktop

Website: www.knime.org

KNIME.com AG is a small software and services firm focused on data mining. It offers a data-mining product with a visual programming interface. A version of KNIME is available free of charge, and the company provides additional features, a server version, technical support, and related services on a paid basis.

KXEN, an SAP Company

About the developer: KXEN was acquired by SAP in September 2013. KXEN continues to offer and develop its predictive analytics products.

Key products: InfiniteInsight Explorer, InfiniteInsight Modeler. (SAP also offers SAP Predictive Analysis.)

Technical support: Available

Free products: None

Website: www.kxen.com

SAP AG is said to be the world's largest business software company, producing products for payroll, accounting, enterprise resource planning, and other business applications. It is also one of the oldest, founded in 1972 to build on technology originated at Xerox and further developed by IBM.

SAP acquired niche predictive analytics vendor KXEN in 2013, perhaps to keep up with competitors such as IBM and Oracle, who have been building their own predictive analytics capabilities.

Megaputer

About the developer: Megaputer is an offshoot of research projects at Moscow State University (Russia), Bauman Technical University (Russia), and Indiana University.

Key product: Megaputer PolyAnalyst

Technical support: Available

Free products: None

Website: www.megaputer.com

Some of the most successful products in the world of data analysis built their user base by cultivating college students as users. As the students migrated to the workplace, they encouraged the use of tools they had used in school, and pushed software vendors to add new features to suit business requirements. SAS and SPSS, the two leaders in statistical analysis, both built their user bases this way.

Megaputer is following the same approach, bundling its PolyAnalyst product with popular textbooks that have now been adopted at hundreds of universities. The strategy seems to be effective, as Megaputer products are now in use at a number of U.S. government agencies and corporations.

Oracle

About the developer: Oracle is a publicly held multinational corporation.

Key product: Oracle Advanced Analytics Option

Technical support: Available

Free products: None

Website: www.oracle.com

Oracle produces one of the world's most widely used commercial relational databases. This isn't the first stop for most novice data miners. But those who have invested in Oracle's enterprise software may find it efficient to use products designed specifically for that environment.

R Foundation

About the developer: R is an open source project developed through voluntary collaboration of individuals around the world.

Key product: R

Technical support: R Foundation does not offer support agreements. R has an active user community with user groups around the world; most users participate informally in these groups for informal support.

Free product: R

Website: www.r-project.org

R Foundation, unlike most of the sources included here, is neither a business nor a university. It's a group of individuals and organizations that cooperate to create a language and environment that meets the needs of its members for statistical computing and graphics. R is very popular in academia, due to its flexibility (anyone with the proper skills may build new features and make them available to others) and free availability.

R is primarily a programming language, so it is not a likely choice for hands-on data mining by business users. However, it does have fans among businesses that have staff with the right skills to use it.

RapidMiner

About the developer: RapidMiner is an offshoot of the YALE development project of the Dortmund University of Technology (Germany).

Key product: RapidMiner Studio

Technical support: Available

Free product: RapidMiner Studio Starter

Website: http://rapidminer.com

RapidMiner is a small software and services firm focused on data mining. It offers a data-mining product with a visual programming interface. A version of this product is available free of charge, and the company provides additional features, a server version, technical support, and related services on a paid basis.

Revolution Analytics

About the developer: Revolution Analytics is a privately held company.

Key product: Revolution R Enterprise

Technical support: Available

Free product: Revolution R Enterprise is available free to academics, students, and other researchers.

Website: `http://revolutionanalytics.com`

Revolution Analytics is a software and services firm that builds on the R platform. The company's key product, Revolution R Enterprise, provides a graphical user interface for R. The product is available in a free version aimed at academia and a commercial version tailored for processing large data volumes in distributed computing environments.

The R platform is described in more detail in the section "R Foundation," earlier in this chapter.

Salford Systems

About the developer: Salford Systems is a privately held company founded in 1983 by Dan Steinberg, who remains as president of the company today.

Key product: Salford Predictive Modeler

Technical support: Available

Free products: None

Website: `www.salford-systems.com`

Salford Systems has a history of thought leadership in data mining. It was one of the first to commercialize machine-learning algorithms. Today, the company offers several machine-learning methods, individually or in a combined tool called Salford Predictive Modeler. The company's tools are known for speed and suitability for real-time applications.

SAS Institute

About the developer: SAS Institute Inc. is a privately held multinational corporation.

Key products: SAS Enterprise Miner, SAS Enterprise Guide, JMP, SAS, SAS/STAT, SAS Visual Analytics

Technical support: Available

Free products: None

Website: www.sas.com

SAS Institute is a major player in the analytics industry, and one of the oldest. SAS Enterprise Miner offers a visual programming interface. Its SAS and SAS/STAT product lines are widely used for data analysis and reporting. SAS products are arguably the earliest statistical analysis products in current use, and most still depend on specialized programming skills and SAS's own proprietary language. JMP, a full-featured data exploration and analysis product, has a graphical user interface and is popular with scientists and manufacturers.

Statsoft

About the developer: Dell, a privately held multinational corporation, acquired Statsoft Inc. in 2014.

Key product: Statistica

Technical support: Available

Free products: None

Website: www.statsoft.com

Dell, a major supplier of personal computers, broke out of the hardware mold in 2014 with its acquisition of Statsoft Inc. Statsoft is the publisher of Statistica, one of the most popular statistical analysis products. Statistica has a graphical user interface and an extensive selection of data analysis capabilities. Like SAS's JMP, Statistica is particularly popular in manufacturing.

Tableau Software

About the developer: Tableau Software is an offshoot of research conducted at Stanford University.

Key product: Tableau

Technical support: Available

Free product: Tableau Public

Website: www.tableausoftware.com

Tableau Software is a niche player, offering several variations of its tool for data visualization. Finance professionals often like Tableau, which has a user interface similar to the one used in spreadsheets for creating pivot tables, but produces much more interesting graphical results.

Teradata

> **About the developer:** Teradata is a publicly held multinational corporation.
>
> **Key products:** Teradata Warehouse Miner, Teradata Aster
>
> **Technical support:** Available
>
> **Free products:** None
>
> **Website:** www.teradata.com

Teradata built its reputation on databases with the largest capacity available and the structure to suit that massive scale. Teradata now offers analytics products integrated with its data warehousing systems and positioned as data-mining and *data discovery* platforms.

Be aware that these offerings are not suitable as hands-on tools for business users. Teradata's data-mining concept involves a team that includes separate business analyst and analytic modeler roles, and its data discovery offering is code based, with a simplified SQL interface. While these approaches are very different from those recommended in this book, they may be the most practical options for some organizations dealing with massive and complex data sources.

University of Ljubljana

> **About the developer:** The Bioinformatics Laboratory of the Faculty of Computer and Information Science, University of Ljubljana, Slovenia, develops Orange in cooperation with an open source community.
>
> **Key product:** Orange
>
> **Technical Support:** University of Ljubljana does not offer support agreements. The Orange user community provides informal support through an online forum.
>
> **Free product:** Orange
>
> **Website:** http://orange.biolab.si

University of Waikato

About the developer: University of Waikato is a New Zealand University.

Key products: Weka, MOA

Technical support: University of Waikato does not offer support agreements. The Weka user community provides informal support through a mailing list and online forum.

Free products: Weka, MOA

Website: www.cs.waikato.ac.nz/ml/weka

University of Waikato faculty members develop tools as part of their work toward advancement of the field of machine learning. These tools are used in teaching, by scientists, and in industry. Weka is its general-purpose data-mining tool that offers a visual programming interface and a wide range of analytics capabilities. MOA is for real-time mining of data streams.

Wolfram

About the developer: Wolfram Research is a privately held multinational corporation.

Key product: Mathematica

Technical support: Available

Free products: None

Website: www.wolfram.com

Although Wolfram Research has been around for decades, the company is probably best known today for the relatively new Wolfram Alpha, introduced in 2009. Wolfram Alpha is a *computational knowledge engine* (also known as an *answer engine*), an advancement in search technology that moves beyond searching for phrases or topics to answering questions that require some computation.

You may enjoy trying Wolfram Alpha at www.wolframalpha.com.

The backbone of Wolfram research offerings is Mathematica, widely used by engineers and scientists for performing complex calculations. Wolfram tools are also popular for financial applications, and the company offers an industry-specific platform for finance. Wolfram also offers a product for modeling designs of physical products and systems.

Appendix C

Major Data Vendors

• •

*Y*our own internal data is often the most relevant data you can get. Government and nonprofit sources offer valuable data free. Use these sources whenever you can! When those sources don't meet your needs, you'll have to turn to commercial data suppliers. But which suppliers? This appendix gives you a number of reputable choices. Read on to know where to look next.

Acxiom

Acxiom (www.acxiom.com) is a major source for consumer marketing data. Acxiom's data sources include publicly available property transaction records, auto warranty and service records, consumer-reported product registrations, surveys, census neighborhood statistics, and retailers. It provides

- ✔ Demographics, such as age and gender
- ✔ Home information, such as whether the consumer owns or rents
- ✔ Motor vehicle information, such as make, model, and insurance renewal
- ✔ Economic data, including income range and credit card use
- ✔ Purchase data, types of products purchased, and frequency
- ✔ Interests and indicators of interest, such as sports, arts and crafts, pet ownership, and other such categories

Acxiom also offers marketing platforms and provides value-added services such as propensity scores for spending and other consumer behavior.

Corelogic

Corelogic (www.corelogic.com) is a source for property and financial information. Its offerings are aimed primarily at lenders, insurers, and landlords.

Because so much property information is available directly from government sources, you may wonder why anyone would prefer to pay a commercial data vendor for property records. Here's why: Corelogic draws its data from 10,000 government and proprietary sources. That's a lot of work! Even if the data you need comes from only a few sources, it may still be easier and less costly to get it from a commercial provider that specializes in what you need. Some examples of Corelogic's offerings include

- Floodplain determinations
- Skip tracing (locating debtors who have moved without paying debts)
- Risk scores for prospective renters

Datalogix

Datalogix (www.datalogix.com) provides sales data for consumer packaged goods (CPG), a category that covers thousands of consumable products in categories such as

- Food and beverages
- Clothing and shoes
- Tobacco
- Cleaning products
- Pet care items
- Cosmetics
- . . . and many others

This type of data is used primarily by marketers promoting CPG brands.

Have you ever wondered why chain retailers use those large, fancy cash registers? These elaborate devices do much more than just add prices together. They also record the details of each transaction, and this information is used not only by the retailer but also by data vendors that sell information to CPG marketers and others. Datalogix obtains sales data from a large network that includes more than 50 retail chains and covers more than 7,000 product brands.

Datalogix offers *online audience,* a concept similar to direct marketing mailing lists. For example, if your company makes protective covers for sports cars, you might work with Datalogix to place your message in online channels viewed by sports car owners and enthusiasts.

A Datalogix service that may be of particular interest to data miners is *list enhancement*. If, say, your in-house list of customer behavior information lacks some important elements, such as demographics, you may be able to purchase this additional information from Datalogix.

DataSift

DataSift (www.datasift.com) provides social media activity data. If you'd like to know how often a topic is being mentioned in social media, who's talking, and what they're saying, you can get this data through DataSift.

Many people are under the impression that it is unnecessary to use vendors for social media data, because many social media applications offer access to content via application programming interfaces (APIs). Be careful! Every API has terms of service, and those terms may restrict use in ways that you do not expect, or limit the amount of information you can extract. Also, data vendors may be your only source for historical data from social media sources.

DataSift offers data from more than 20 sources, ranging from the well-known Twitter, Facebook public posts, YouTube, and Bitly to rising voices Sina Weibo, Intense Debate, and Yammer. It is one of only two sources for complete Twitter data.

eBureau

eBureau (www.ebureau.com) is primarily a provider of scoring services for

- Fraud detection
- Credit risk
- Collections
- Consumer lead quality evaluation

The information provided by eBureau is much like the sort that you'd get from credit scores, except that eBureau's information covers a wider variety of applications than just credit. For example, eBureau offers a lead quality scoring service. You could use this service in connection with a lead source to identify the most valuable leads, and purchase only those, avoiding the expense of purchasing leads unlikely to lead to sales.

Equifax

Equifax (www.equifax.com) is one of the three major credit-reporting agencies. It provides information about consumer credit activity and credit scores. It also provides consumer demographics, credit information about businesses, supplier information, and platforms for the management of collections and other business activities.

Experian

Experian (www.experian.com) is best known as one of the three major credit-reporting agencies. It provides consumer and business credit data and credit scoring. Experian also offers many types of consumer data, including

- ✔ Brand preference and psychographic measures for many population segments, including kids and teens; lesbians, gays, bigenders, and transgenders; and Hispanic groups
- ✔ Media behavior, brand preference, and attitudes by location down to the zip code level
- ✔ Consumer online, mobile, and other media behavior

Much of this data is developed through surveys and is not available through other sources.

Gnip

Like DataSift, Gnip (www.gnip.com) provides social media data. It supplies posts and other data from many social media sources, and offers the same advantages over collecting this data through the social media site APIs.

Gnip was the first data vendor to provide complete Twitter data. It now supplies data for 25 social media sources, including popular sites such as Twitter, Tumblr, and Foursquare, as well as less-famous sites like Stocktwits, Estimize, and Sitrion. Gnip also offers certain value-added services for social media data, including *language detection* (identifying the language of the text) and *URL expansion* (restoring the original long URL in place of a shortened version).

ID Analytics

ID Analytics (www.idanalytics.com) focuses on identity fraud risk, providing an identity score to help businesses assess the risk of identity fraud in business transactions. These scores are calculated based on a combination of personally identifiable information (such as date of birth, phone number, and social security number) and device history (computer, smartphone, and so on) to assess the risk of identity fraud.

Intelius

Intelius (www.intelius.com) focuses on information about people and identity, including

- ✔ Verification, such as reverse phone verification and email lookup
- ✔ Information, such as people search and social net search
- ✔ Protection, such as cell phone caller ID and criminal check
- ✔ Marriage, divorce, and death records
- ✔ Business services, such as employment and tenant screening

IRI

IRI (www.iriworldwide.com) provides data on consumer shopping and attitudes, with information of considerable depth for CPG marketers, including unique survey data not available elsewhere. Offerings include

- ✔ Consumer panel data for information about consumer shopping and buying habits, attitudes, and demographics
- ✔ Online health and wellness surveys that provide data to support brand marketing
- ✔ Point-of-sale data for more than 12,500 retail stores

Nielsen

Nielsen (www.nielsen.com) is most famous as the company that creates television ratings. Nielsen tracks television viewing, it's true, but it also tracks audience data for a number of other media platforms, including online, mobile, radio, and social media.

This is not survey data; Nielsen directly measures actual audience behavior. The data is typically used by advertisers to plan their media purchases. After the 2012 U.S. elections, Obama for America's analytics team revealed some of their methods, including a story about how the campaign was able to use television viewing behavior data (often called *set top* data because of the recording device that sits on top of the television) to purchase ad time that reached its desired audience at a lower cost than the challenger Romney's campaign.

Nielsen also provides data about consumer buying behavior, obtained through point-of-sale records in stores and online, and data about shopping behavior and attitudes obtained from panel data from over 250,000 households across 25 countries.

PeekYou

Data miners who want to use information about individuals from online sources often find it challenging to match data sources together. Many names are not unique, and many people use more than one name online.

PeekYou (www.peekyou.com) provides information about web links and how they relate to people. PeekYou uses data from social media, news sites, and other sources, along with its own technology, to create a score to assess the likelihood that individual web pages are associated with particular people — people who may be the creators or the subjects of the page. If you have URLs and want to know who made them, or who the information is about, this is the source to investigate.

You can see what PeekYou has in its index about you. Here's what happened when I tried it. I entered my first and last name, and got a list of several people with that name, with a bit of information about each. I clicked on the right Meta Brown in the list, and got a profile (see Figure C-1) complete with a photo, social media accounts, a past employer, and a brief biography. And it was all a match to me! That may sound simple, but there are others with the same first and last name, and I get calls meant for others by that name all the time.

Figure C-1:
A sample profile from PeekYou.

Rapleaf

Rapleaf (www.rapleaf.com) provides information about individuals based on their email addresses. Rapleaf provides several types of information, including

✔ Demographics, such as age, gender, and zip code

✔ Interests, such as health and wellness, arts and crafts, and business

✔ Purchase behavior for many categories, including charitable donations

Recorded Future

Recorded Future (www.recordedfuture.com) provides real-time threat intelligence information. It collects information from nearly half a million online sources in seven languages. The scope of this data covers a wide variety of threats as diverse as malware attacks, geopolitical instability, and events that pose a threat to corporations or executives.

TransUnion

TransUnion (www.transunion.com) is one of the three primary credit-reporting agencies. It provides credit information about both consumers and businesses. TransUnion's offerings also include criminal records, bankruptcies, demographics, and other data useful for risk management and fraud prevention in a number of industries, including insurance, financial services, and healthcare.

Appendix D

Sources and Citations

● ●

Data Sources

Chapter 2. A Day in Your Life as a Data Miner

Property ownership data

The property ownership datasets used in this chapter were provided by Matt Schumwinger of Big Lake Data (see his profile in Chapter 2) for this case study. These datasets are not publicly available.

Similar data is available for download from the City of Milwaukee, Wisconsin at `http://city.milwaukee.gov/DownloadTabularData3496.htm`.

Chapter 12. Getting Familiar with Your Data

Property ownership data: see Chapter 2.

Cigarette data

This data was collected for research described in "Determination of tar, nicotine, and carbon monoxide yields in the mainstream smoke of selected international cigarettes," *Tobacco Control* 2004;13:45-51 doi:10.1136/tc.2003.003673, A M Calafat, G M Polzin, J Saylor, P Richter, D L Ashley, C H Watson. (Full text here: `http://tobaccocontrol.bmj.com/content/13/1/45.full`.)

The data is available through the journal *Tobacco Control* at `http://tobaccocontrol.bmj.com/content/suppl/2004/02/27/13.1.45.DC1/13145table_1.pdf`.

Chapter 13. Dealing in Graphic Detail

Property ownership data: see Chapter 2.

Auto mileage data

This data was collected for research described in Quinlan, R. (1993). Combining Instance-Based and Model-Based Learning. In Proceedings on the Tenth International Conference of Machine Learning, 236-243, University of Massachusetts, Amherst. Morgan Kaufmann.

This data was obtained from the UCI Machine Learning Repository.

Bache, K. & Lichman, M. (2013). UCI Machine Learning Repository [`http://archive.ics.uci.edu/ml`]. Irvine, CA: University of California, School of Information and Computer Science.

The data is available for download at `https://archive.ics.uci.edu/ml/datasets/Auto+MPG`.

Breast tumor diagnosis data

This data was collected for research described in W.N. Street, W.H. Wolberg, and O.L. Mangasarian. Nuclear feature extraction for breast tumor diagnosis. IS&T/SPIE 1993 International Symposium on Electronic Imaging: *Science and Technology,* volume 1905, pages 861-870, San Jose, CA, 1993.

This data was obtained from the UCI Machine Learning Repository.

Bache, K. & Lichman, M. (2013). UCI Machine Learning Repository [`http://archive.ics.uci.edu/ml`]. Irvine, CA: University of California, School of Information and Computer Science.

The data is available for download at `https://archive.ics.uci.edu/ml/datasets/Breast+Cancer+Wisconsin+%28Diagnostic%29`.

Cigarette data: see Chapter 12.

Chapter 14. Showing Your Data Who's Boss

Annealing data

This is a sample dataset from the Orange data-mining application.

Breast tumor diagnosis data: see Chapter 13.

Property ownership data: see Chapter 2.

General Social Survey

This data was collected for the General Social Survey, a long-term program for social research administered by the National Opinion Research Center.

This data was obtained from the National Opinion Research Center.

Smith, Tom W.; Marsden, Peter V.; Michael Hout; Jibum Kim. General Social Surveys, 1972-2012. [machine-readable data file]. Principal Investigator, Tom W. Smith; Co-Principal Investigators, Peter V. Marsden and Michael Hout, NORC ed. Chicago: National Opinion Research Center, producer, 2005; Storrs, CT: The Roper Center for Public Opinion Research, University of Connecticut, distributor. 1 data file (57,061 logical records) and 1 codebook (3,422 pp).

This data is available for download at `www3.norc.org/GSS+Website/ Download`.

Cigarette data: see Chapter 12.

Auto mileage data: see Chapter 13.

Chapter 15. Your Exciting Career in Modeling

Breast tumor diagnosis data: see Chapter 13.

User knowledge data

This data was collected for research described in H. T. Kahraman, Sagiroglu, S., Colak, I., Developing intuitive knowledge classifier and modeling of users' domain dependent data in web, Knowledge Based Systems, vol. 37, pp. 283-295, 2013.

This data was obtained from the UCI Machine Learning Repository.

Bache, K. & Lichman, M. (2013). UCI Machine Learning Repository [`http:// archive.ics.uci.edu/ml`]. Irvine, CA: University of California, School of Information and Computer Science.

The data is available for download at `https://archive.ics.uci.edu/ ml/datasets/User+Knowledge+Modeling`.

Chapter 16. Data Mining Using Classic Statistical Methods

Auto mileage data: see Chapter 13

Breast tumor diagnosis data: see Chapter 13.

Chapter 17. Mining Data for Clues

Supermarket data

This is a sample dataset from the Weka data-mining application.

Other Sources

This book includes excerpts or adaptations from these sources. All are used by permission.

The Nine Laws of Data Mining, © 2010 Tom Khabaza. Full text at www.khabaza.com.

More information about Khabaza's Nine Laws is available in T. Khabaza (2014). From Data Mining to Cognition: The first intelligence amplifier. In: J. Wyatt, D. Petters, and D. Hogg (Eds.) "From Animals to Robots and Back: reflections on hard problems in the study of cognition." Cognitive Systems Monographs, Springer: London.

Be a Text Analytics Heretic, © 2013 Meta S. Brown

Big Data: Are 3 Vs Sufficient?, © 2014 Meta S. Brown

Gut-Feel Isn't Good Enough, © 2012 Meta S. Brown

How I Met Your Model, © 2013 Meta S. Brown

Selecting Big Data Sources for Predictive Analytics, © 2013 Meta S. Brown

Talk Analytics with Executives: 4 Things You Must Understand, © 2010 Meta S. Brown

Unpublished glossary of analytics terms, © 2009-2014 Meta S. Brown

Index

• *U* •

• V •

About the Author

Meta S. Brown helps technical professionals communicate with everybody else. She's the creator of the *Storytelling for Data Analysts* and *Storytelling for Tech* workshops.

Dedication

For Marty, who never gives me a hard time about work. Ever.

Author's Acknowledgments

A number of experts shared their experience and time to contribute to this book. Each of them is named somewhere in the pages that follow.

The researchers who share data make books like this possible. Sources are cited within the book.

Wiley editors Christopher Morris, Leah Michael, John Edwards, and Kyle Looper are models of professionalism. I wonder if they know how exceptional that is.

Tom Khabaza, technical editor and the world's best data-mining mentor, is a fountain of knowledge and a real mensch.

Laaren Brown and Lenny Hort — authors, editors, and much more — provided excellent advice galore.

Publisher's Acknowledgments

Acquisitions Editor: Kyle Looper

Senior Project Editor: Christopher Morris

Copy Editor: John Edwards

Technical Editor: Thomas Khabaza

Editorial Assistant: Claire Johnson

Sr. Editorial Assistant: Cherie Case

Project Coordinator: Patrick Redmond

Cover Image: ©iStock.com/Media Mates Oy

Apple & Mac

iPad For Dummies,
5th Edition
978-1-118-72306-7

iPhone For Dummies,
7th Edition
978-1-118-69083-3

Macs All-in-One
For Dummies, 4th Edition
978-1-118-82210-4

OS X Mavericks
For Dummies
978-1-118-69188-5

Blogging & Social Media

Facebook For Dummies,
5th Edition
978-1-118-63312-0

Social Media Engagement
For Dummies
978-1-118-53019-1

WordPress For Dummies,
6th Edition
978-1-118-79161-5

Business

Stock Investing
For Dummies, 4th Edition
978-1-118-37678-2

Investing For Dummies,
6th Edition
978-0-470-90545-6

Personal Finance
For Dummies, 7th Edition
978-1-118-11785-9

QuickBooks 2014
For Dummies
978-1-118-72005-9

Small Business Marketing
Kit For Dummies,
3rd Edition
978-1-118-31183-7

Careers

Job Interviews
For Dummies, 4th Edition
978-1-118-11290-8

Job Searching with Social
Media For Dummies,
2nd Edition
978-1-118-67856-5

Personal Branding
For Dummies
978-1-118-11792-7

Resumes For Dummies,
6th Edition
978-0-470-87361-8

Starting an Etsy Business
For Dummies, 2nd Edition
978-1-118-59024-9

Diet & Nutrition

Belly Fat Diet For Dummies
978-1-118-34585-6

Mediterranean Diet
For Dummies
978-1-118-71525-3

Nutrition For Dummies,
5th Edition
978-0-470-93231-5

Digital Photography

Digital SLR Photography
All-in-One For Dummies,
2nd Edition
978-1-118-59082-9

Digital SLR Video &
Filmmaking For Dummies
978-1-118-36598-4

Photoshop Elements 12
For Dummies
978-1-118-72714-0

Gardening

Herb Gardening
For Dummies, 2nd Edition
978-0-470-61778-6

Gardening with Free-Range
Chickens For Dummies
978-1-118-54754-0

Health

Boosting Your Immunity
For Dummies
978-1-118-40200-9

Diabetes For Dummies,
4th Edition
978-1-118-29447-5

Living Paleo For Dummies
978-1-118-29405-5

Big Data

Big Data For Dummies
978-1-118-50422-2

Data Visualization
For Dummies
978-1-118-50289-1

Hadoop For Dummies
978-1-118-60755-8

Language &
Foreign Language

500 Spanish Verbs
For Dummies
978-1-118-02382-2

English Grammar
For Dummies, 2nd Edition
978-0-470-54664-2

French All-in-One
For Dummies
978-1-118-22815-9

German Essentials
For Dummies
978-1-118-18422-6

Italian For Dummies,
2nd Edition
978-1-118-00465-4

ᵉ Available in print and e-book formats.

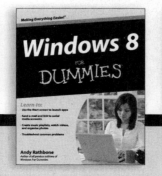

Available wherever books are sold. **For more information or to order direct visit www.dummies.com**

Math & Science

Algebra I For Dummies,
2nd Edition
978-0-470-55964-2

Anatomy and Physiology
For Dummies, 2nd Edition
978-0-470-92326-9

Astronomy For Dummies,
3rd Edition
978-1-118-37697-3

Biology For Dummies,
2nd Edition
978-0-470-59875-7

Chemistry For Dummies,
2nd Edition
978-1-118-00730-3

1001 Algebra II Practice
Problems For Dummies
978-1-118-44662-1

Microsoft Office

Excel 2013 For Dummies
978-1-118-51012-4

Office 2013 All-in-One
For Dummies
978-1-118-51636-2

PowerPoint 2013
For Dummies
978-1-118-50253-2

Word 2013 For Dummies
978-1-118-49123-2

Music

Blues Harmonica
For Dummies
978-1-118-25269-7

Guitar For Dummies,
3rd Edition
978-1-118-11554-1

iPod & iTunes
For Dummies, 10th Edition
978-1-118-50864-0

Programming

Beginning Programming
with C For Dummies
978-1-118-73763-7

Excel VBA Programming
For Dummies, 3rd Edition
978-1-118-49037-2

Java For Dummies,
6th Edition
978-1-118-40780-6

Religion & Inspiration

The Bible For Dummies
978-0-7645-5296-0

Buddhism For Dummies,
2nd Edition
978-1-118-02379-2

Catholicism For Dummies,
2nd Edition
978-1-118-07778-8

Self-Help & Relationships

Beating Sugar Addiction
For Dummies
978-1-118-54645-1

Meditation For Dummies,
3rd Edition
978-1-118-29144-3

Seniors

Laptops For Seniors
For Dummies, 3rd Edition
978-1-118-71105-7

Computers For Seniors
For Dummies, 3rd Edition
978-1-118-11553-4

iPad For Seniors
For Dummies, 6th Edition
978-1-118-72826-0

Social Security
For Dummies
978-1-118-20573-0

Smartphones & Tablets

Android Phones
For Dummies, 2nd Edition
978-1-118-72030-1

Nexus Tablets
For Dummies
978-1-118-77243-0

Samsung Galaxy S 4
For Dummies
978-1-118-64222-1

Samsung Galaxy Tabs
For Dummies
978-1-118-77294-2

Test Prep

ACT For Dummies,
5th Edition
978-1-118-01259-8

ASVAB For Dummies,
3rd Edition
978-0-470-63760-9

GRE For Dummies,
7th Edition
978-0-470-88921-3

Officer Candidate Tests
For Dummies
978-0-470-59876-4

Physician's Assistant Exam
For Dummies
978-1-118-11556-5

Series 7 Exam For Dummies
978-0-470-09932-2

Windows 8

Windows 8.1 All-in-One
For Dummies
978-1-118-82087-2

Windows 8.1 For Dummies
978-1-118-82121-3

Windows 8.1 For Dummies,
Book + DVD Bundle
978-1-118-82107-7

   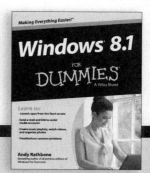

e Available in print and e-book formats.

Available wherever books are sold. **For more information or to order direct visit www.dummies.com**

Take Dummies with you everywhere you go!

Whether you are excited about e-books, want more from the web, must have your mobile apps, or are swept up in social media, Dummies makes everything easier.

Visit Us

bit.ly/JE0O

Like Us

on.fb.me/1f1ThNu

Follow Us

bit.ly/ZDytkR

Watch Us

bit.ly/gbOQHn

Join Us

linkd.in/1gurkMm

Pin Us

bit.ly/16caOLd

Circle Us

bit.ly/1aQTuDQ

Shop Us

bit.ly/4dEp9

Leverage the Power

For Dummies is the global leader in the reference category and one of the most trusted and highly regarded brands in the world. No longer just focused on books, customers now have access to the For Dummies content they need in the format they want. Let us help you develop a solution that will fit your brand and help you connect with your customers.

Advertising & Sponsorships

Connect with an engaged audience on a powerful multimedia site, and position your message alongside expert how-to content.

Targeted ads • Video • Email marketing • Microsites • Sweepstakes sponsorship

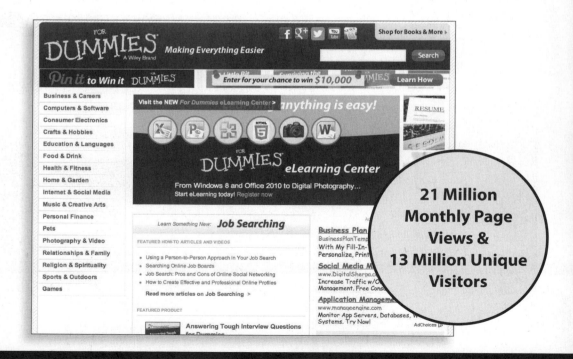

Custom Publishing

Reach a global audience in any language by creating a solution that will differentiate you from competitors, amplify your message, and encourage customers to make a buying decision.

Apps • Books • eBooks • Video • Audio • Webinars

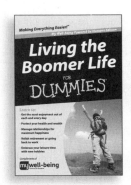

Brand Licensing & Content

Leverage the strength of the world's most popular reference brand to reach new audiences and channels of distribution.

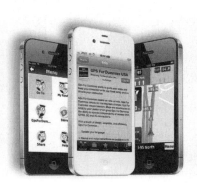

For more information, visit www.Dummies.com/biz

Dummies products make life easier!

- DIY
- Consumer Electronics
- Crafts

- Software
- Cookware
- Hobbies

- Videos
- Music
- Games
- and More!

For more information, go to **Dummies.com** and search the store by category.

FOR DUMMIES

A Wiley Brand